Building the Brewers

Building the Brewers

*Bud Selig and the
Return of Major League
Baseball to Milwaukee*

CHRIS ZANTOW

McFarland & Company, Inc., Publishers
Jefferson, North Carolina

This book has undergone peer review.

ISBN (print) 978-1-4766-7263-2
ISBN (ebook) 978-1-4766-3720-4

Library of Congress and British Library
cataloguing data are available

© 2020 Chris Zantow. All rights reserved

No part of this book may be reproduced or transmitted in any form or by any means, electronic or mechanical, including photocopying or recording, or by any information storage and retrieval system, without permission in writing from the publisher.

Front cover: owner Bud Selig; view of a Brewers game in Milwaukee County Stadium (Wisconsin Historical Society, WHS-50427)

Printed in the United States of America

*McFarland & Company, Inc., Publishers
Box 611, Jefferson, North Carolina 28640
www.mcfarlandpub.com*

In loving memory of my father, Don Zantow, who took me to my first Milwaukee Brewers game in 1978. By doing so, he unwittingly started me on a lifelong obsession with the Brew Crew. Thanks to Dad, I spent my 14th birthday at Game 3 of the 1982 ALCS.

The following pages are also in memory of my good friend, Jeanne Olinger. She grew up with the Milwaukee Braves, sobbed when they left town, and eventually embraced the Brewers as her favorite team. If Bob Uecker ever had a #1 fan, it was Jeanne.

I'm grateful that Dad and Jeanne supported me in writing this book before they passed away.

Table of Contents

Acknowledgments viii

Preface 1

Introduction 4

ONE • The Borchert Field Brewers   9

TWO • Borchert Field to Bushville   25

THREE • You're All We've Got Now   41

FOUR • A Team That Didn't Exist   57

FIVE • The Pilots Take Flight   74

SIX • The Pilots Crash Land   90

SEVEN • One Million or Bust   107

EIGHT • A Fun Place for Fans   124

NINE • Prospects and All-Stars   141

TEN • Saturday Night Massacre   157

Epilogue 174

Chapter Notes 183

Bibliography 198

Index 207

Acknowledgments

This book would not have seen the light of day without the contributions and support of many special people. They were all instrumental in the successful completion of this project. From helping with research, to proofreading and providing encouragement, I am eternally thankful for all their efforts. I would like to express my deepest gratitude to:

My wife, Sarah, for being my biggest supporter, first draft editor, and best friend.

My mother, Mary. She has been my #1 writing fan since I was a little kid—through my years on the high school newspaper and the long hiatus that followed until my recent writing revival.

Both sides of my amazing family. I couldn't ask for better people to support me on this journey.

The incredible team at McFarland & Company for exceptional guidance throughout the entire publication process.

All the candid beta test readers and fact checkers of my manuscript. I appreciate the extra sets of eyes looking over my work before publication.

My wonderful co-workers at American Girl for inspiring me with their creativity and passion each day.

Jim Ksicinski, Rick Napholz, and Pat McBride for providing excellent behind-the-scenes information on what it was like to work for a new baseball franchise. All three offered unique perspectives that helped shape this book. I also need to thank Jim for giving good advice on writing this book from an angle that would help it get published.

Pitchers Lew Krausse, Dave Baldwin, Bob Humphreys, John Morris, Bruce Brubaker, Bob Meyer, Ray Peters, and Ken Sanders, infielder Ted Kubiak, catcher Phil Roof, manager Dave Bristol, and pitching coach Wes Stock for answering my interview questions. Your insights on the franchise move, the city of Milwaukee, living situations, friendships, and support from new Brewers fans allowed me to paint a better picture of how the team adapted to the Midwest—and to one another.

The National Baseball Hall of Fame, Lester Public Library, University of Washington Libraries, and Bob Busser for photographs.

Everyone that has followed my writing process on Facebook, Instagram, Twitter, and my blog. You all have been incredibly supportive, and I'm very thankful for your positive comments.

My deepest apologies to anyone I may have missed. I assure you this was not intentional.

Preface

This might be the only time a routine meniscus surgery led to someone writing a baseball book. In February 2015, I spent a couple of weeks with my right leg up on the couch, recovering from surgery. As a lifelong baseball fan and history buff, I found it an opportune time to get caught up on a stack of baseball books and movies.

One documentary I watched was *The Seattle Pilots: Short Flight into History*. In my opinion, it's an excellent assemblage of archival footage and recent interviews that uncover the story of baseball's "one-year franchise." The film begins to wrap up in bankruptcy court with Bud Selig buying the Pilots and moving the team to Milwaukee.

After watching the documentary, I found myself being bothered by the lack of long-form media about Selig's numerous attempts to acquire a franchise or talk the league into allowing expansion into Milwaukee. I also had a difficult time locating anything that told the story of the Brewers' early days. Most books and videos about the team are either collections of short stories or simply hone in on what many view as the golden era of the franchise (1978–1982). Others are outdated or are out of print.

With the 50th anniversary of Brewers baseball approaching, I decided that a proper telling of the franchise origins and early days of building a fan base was long overdue. I started research by building a timeline of key events and interviewing players, coaches, and team employees who were with the team in 1969–1970. These people were wonderfully giving with their memories and gave me great understanding of happenings behind the scenes and in the public eye.

I supplemented the interviews with compelling historical quotes and information gathered through internet research and archival publications. I felt it important to draw from as many sources as possible to get several different perspectives into the story. While the bulk of my first year working on the initial manuscript involved documentation of interviews, facts, quotes, and data, my historical research continued right up until the end of the three-year writing process.

A golden opportunity from a historian's standpoint came my way in 2016, when I was offered head administrator privileges for the Seattle Pilots' Facebook page. I embraced the role by assembling a daily historical post and celebrating the team in a myriad of compelling ways. This gave me what I felt was a unique perspective when it came time to work on the Seattle sections in the manuscript.

As I started working, it appeared that I had a pretty narrow scope for the book. After finding so many parallels between Seattle and Milwaukee in terms of baseball history, I decided this history was important backstory and a place to start things. I also found importance in sharing Selig's childhood experiences with baseball at Borchert Field in Milwaukee and later as a Braves fan-turned minority owner. I gained a lot of insight into how exposure to baseball at a young age shaped Selig's determination to bring baseball back to Milwaukee, where it could be enjoyed for years to come.

The story of the Brewers' existence has roots in the successes and failures of the Braves and Pilots. Therefore, I believe it is key to tell the stories of the rise and fall of both franchises. From there, this book takes the reader chronologically through the four years Milwaukee did not have a major league baseball team, through courtroom battles and pleas to baseball team owners for a new franchise. It continues into the early years of a young franchise searching for an identity and struggling to stay afloat.

One problem that came up during writing involved widening the scope of the original manuscript. Besides sharing the backstory, for a time I mistakenly thought I needed to move forward through a year-by-year synopsis of the entire franchise history. The original manuscript draft took a turn from meticulous details into high-level summary in the latter quarter, which I felt should be rewritten.

Therefore, while the focus is on the fight to bring a franchise back to Milwaukee, the book concludes in the early years just as the team turns the corner into a legitimate pennant contender. My sincere thanks to Gary Mitchem, Senior Acquisitions Editor at McFarland, for feedback and helping me navigate the rewriting process. His guidance was immeasurable as I assessed what I really wanted to see as a finished product, which brought me full circle to the story I felt hadn't yet been written as I recovered from meniscus surgery.

You'll find no shortage of intriguing characters in these pages— including players, managers, baseball executives, team mascots, and government officials. This is a serious story, but it also has many humorous moments and classic one-liners. It was written not just for avid fans, but also for readers interested in learning more about the backstory of the major league Milwaukee Brewers and the team's place in Wisconsin's and baseball's history.

I hope you enjoy reading this book as much as I have enjoyed researching and writing it!

Introduction

This is the story of the return of major league baseball to Milwaukee after a four-year absence and the very early days of the new Brewers franchise. When the Braves left for Atlanta, it left such a huge void in the city that a civic group led by a young auto dealer named Allan H. "Bud" Selig stepped in and took charge. Selig finally triumphed with his purchase of the Seattle Pilots in bankruptcy court and their subsequent move to Milwaukee. But his success took years of broken deals, missed opportunities, and opposition from baseball's hierarchy.

Yet this isn't just an account of Selig's group overcoming adversity against stacked odds. Milwaukee had 90 years of uninterrupted professional baseball until the Braves packed their bags after the 1965 season. Baseball had become as much a part of Milwaukee's culture as beer and cream city bricks. To properly illustrate the loss of professional baseball, it's important to look back at the colorful history of the sport in Milwaukee.

The city of Milwaukee, Wisconsin, can be traced back to around 1818 and three "founding fathers" who settled in the area between that year and 1834—Solomon Juneau, George Walker, and Byron Kilbourn. Three separate towns grew and were named for each settler, but ultimately this led to bitterness and separatism. Kilbourntown and Juneautown began fighting over a bridge that split the two areas in 1845, but their anger originally stemmed from Byron Kilbourn trying to isolate Juneautown to create a dependence on his town. Kilbourn's residents tore apart some of the bridge during what became known as the Milwaukee Bridge War. No fatalities were reported during the war, but numerous inhabitants were injured.

The war resulted in a plan by local trustees to build three new bridges and draft a city charter. Milwaukee officially was formed on January 31, 1846. Solomon Juneau was elected as the first mayor, as German immi-

Introduction 5

grants flocked to the expanding area. Many fled from Germany during the Revolution of 1848, knowing the land was cheap and mostly unsettled in Wisconsin, which had just been admitted as the 30th state in America.

Milwaukee was becoming known as the "Cream City" due to the color of the bricks from the Menomonee River Valley that were used in construction. One might think the nickname would have been derived from the creamy foam on the top of a cold beer, given the long history of brewing in the city bordering Lake Michigan. Early breweries with names such as New Bavaria and Lake Brewery led to bigger names like Schlitz, Pabst, Blatz, and Miller.

More than 40 brewers operated in Milwaukee from the 1840s to the present day. And while the beer brewers and the rich German heritage remained, the buildings with Cream City brick lost their color by the early 1900s. The brick production declined, yet many of the buildings have now been restored to the original look.

Like Milwaukee and those early brewers, baseball was also in its infancy, with the New York Knickerbockers becoming a team in 1845, the first to play with modern rules. It was only a matter of time before baseball arrived in Milwaukee, and this happened when the West Ends joined the Independent League as an amateur team in 1876.

The American Association's minor league Brewers had the longest run in town, sticking around for five successful decades before giving way to the Braves. Milwaukeeans also saw one-off teams like the women's professional Chicks ballclub and the Negro Leagues' Bears well before major league baseball arrived in the form of the Braves.

The Braves' move from Boston to Milwaukee in 1953 happened abruptly, but that didn't matter to local baseball fans. They were more than ready to support a big league franchise, and attendance exploded in brand-new County Stadium. The team responded by winning more than they lost year after year, all the way through their tenure in Milwaukee. If you had to pick just one team in the 1950s that mirrored its fan base, the Braves would surely be a top choice. They played hard and had a quiet demeanor like that of Milwaukee's working class. The city naturally went crazy when the Braves brought home a World Series title in 1957.

Selig was part of the Braves fan base, with his love of baseball originating at Borchert Field and Brewers games attended with his mother. As Selig's childhood went on, he found he was a better baseball fan than player, so he focused his attention on rooting for the Braves. He later turned from fan into a minority owner, but what should have been a happy time turned sour not too long afterward.

Many sports franchises experience fan apathy. It can be difficult to understand when this happens shortly after championship years. Unfortunately, despite turning in a winning record each season, the Braves saw attendance drop in the 1960s. This downward trend paved the way toward new ownership taking the bold step of announcing relocation hundreds of miles to the south.

As was often the case during the early era of baseball franchise relocations, there happened to be more to the story of the Braves' move lurking below the surface. Milwaukee fans were given the lion's share of the blame for the loss of the franchise, turning many from the sport they previously loved and supported. Anger, frustration, and bitterness lingered in the city whenever the Braves were mentioned.

Selig began working with other high-profile Milwaukee businessmen toward either keeping the Braves in town or acquiring a new franchise either via expansion or purchase. It wasn't an easy road for Selig's ownership group, as they fought a battle on two fronts—reviving support in Milwaukee for a baseball franchise and convincing baseball executives that the city and ownership group were worthy of having a team.

The ensuing years were filled with missed opportunities, dead ends, and heartbreak. Every time it seemed like a team was within reach, something would thwart their efforts. Handshake deals on franchise sales fell through, and expansion teams were awarded elsewhere, while the Milwaukee Brewers Baseball Club, Inc. existed on paper only and in the minds of Selig and his partners.

The ownership group spent as much time going back to the drawing board and regrouping as they spent moving forward. Gains were made with baseball executives with well-attended Chicago White Sox games at Milwaukee County Stadium, but time was running out on the possibility of landing an expansion team.

When all hope seemed lost and expansion might never happen again, a flicker of opportunity came from the west in the form of the floundering Seattle Pilots. Seattle had similarities to Milwaukee, starting with a population of hard-working, industrious people who enjoyed baseball as a source of recreation and entertainment. After decades of backing minor league baseball, the city was rewarded in 1969 with the Seattle Pilots as a major league expansion franchise.

Yet the biggest parallel between the cities by far would be the loss of Seattle's franchise to another city–Milwaukee. Baseball fans in Seattle were as angry as the ones in Milwaukee when the Braves moved, and rightfully so. The Pilots never really had a chance to survive in Seattle due to

Introduction

several factors, with poor attendance and mismanagement at the top of the list.

As quickly as the Braves moved to Milwaukee, the Pilots moved even faster. The team had just a week to relocate operations and numerous details to work out before the 1970 season opener. Building a fan base and an identity for the new team would take a lot more time, as would assembling a competitive team.

In the early days of the Brewers franchise, identity came through making peace with the past, such as having the Braves back for an exhibition game and later signing Hank Aaron to play out his final years back in Milwaukee. Creating a new mascot named Bernie Brewer to live on the Milwaukee County Stadium scoreboard in the summer of 1970 was a less conventional, yet effective, way to build identity.

The team itself went through a long tear-down and rebuilding period as general managers and managers came and went. Selig's contingent trekked around the state of Wisconsin each winter and spoke to anyone who would listen about the process of stockpiling the weak minor league system that came with the purchase of the Seattle Pilots.

Baseball fans came out to watch the team, tentatively at first, as the on-field product went through countless changes. The ownership group fought for increased fan support and a profit, which allowed them to pay star players such as George "Boomer" Scott. Attracting a million fans to County Stadium was critical in providing the finances to keep the team afloat.

As the Brewers worked hard on and off the field to stay viable, other teams threatened relocation. Selig put himself on the inside of many conversations on the state of the sport and franchise stability, first as an owner and later as a committee member studying finances, interleague play, expansion, and the designated hitter rule.

The Brewers were backpedaling in the standings in 1977 as Seattle again landed an expansion team. Having grown weary of losing, Selig shook up the front office and coaching staff, leading to the hiring of general manager Harry Dalton and manager George Bamberger.

Eventually the team took hold, both on the field and in the hearts of fans. Players, coaches, and front office executives have come and gone over the years, and new generations of fans now attend games in a different stadium. After 50 years, the team remains in Milwaukee, clearly woven into the fabric of the local community and the state of Wisconsin. You are about to read how the Brewers became Milwaukee's team and continued building upon the rich baseball traditions of the past.

One

The Borchert Field Brewers

Two babies were born in 1934 who would grow up to have a huge influence on baseball for decades to come. Robert George "Bob" Uecker was brought into the world first, on January 26, and Allan Huber "Bud" Selig was born six months later on July 30. While Uecker has often joked that he was born on his parents' oleo run to Chicago, both he and Selig were actually born in Milwaukee.

Uecker and Selig were children of immigrants. Uecker's parents were Swiss and came to Wisconsin in the 1920s. Selig was brought up in a Jewish family. His father had emigrated from Romania, and his mother was from the Ukraine.

Gus Uecker was able to support his wife and three children through the Great Depression by working on cars. He made up to $4 a day with his mechanical skills. Selig's parents had more of a white-collar background. His mother, Marie, attended college at Wisconsin State Teachers College, which later became UW-Milwaukee. She wound up teaching third and fourth graders in Milwaukee while Bud's father, Benjamin, worked as an automobile dealer. Benjamin had a knack for selling cars and peddled Chevrolets and Fords at three locations.

Their family lives may have been different and they didn't know one another, yet Selig and Uecker both found themselves frequenting Borchert Field during their youth. In a way, they both grew up at the ballpark. Marie Selig enjoyed museums, opera, and the symphony—but she *loved* baseball and passed that love of the game onto her son. Bud and his only sibling (a brother named Jerry) attended games at Borchert Field with their mother. It was the beginning of a life in baseball for Bud, but Jerry didn't get involved in the business of the game, other than a stint as a beer vendor at Borchert.

As Selig and Uecker hung around Borchert Field, they became aware of not just Milwaukee Brewers history, but the city's long love affair with the sport of baseball. Milwaukee was incorporated as a city in 1846, just a few months before the first "officially recorded" baseball game between the New York Nine and the New York Knickerbockers. It would take exactly thirty years for professional baseball to arrive in Milwaukee, and except for three gaps (1879–1883, 1893, and 1966–1969) baseball would remain a deeply-rooted part of the local culture. As the city's population exploded over the next few decades, the mix of immigrants and working classes supported local sports—but they loved baseball in particular.

The West Ends were Milwaukee's first professional baseball team that played in 1876 and 1877. Some enterprising residents in the neighborhood near the West End Grounds built bleachers on their roofs and charged five and ten cents a game. Eventually a canvas screen was built that blocked the view and put them out of business.

The next Milwaukee team was the Grays, who played at Eclipse Park, also known as Milwaukee Base-Ball Grounds. The Grays were the first Milwaukee team to play in the three-year-old National League, and although they won their home opener, they spent the majority of the 1878 season in last place. After the season, the Grays were removed from the league and were sold to pay a bankruptcy judgment of $125.61.

Milwaukee went without a major or minor league team from 1879 through 1883. The minor league Milwaukees (also known as Grays) entered the Northwestern League in 1884 with a brand-new park, the Wright Street Grounds. The vacant land on Milwaukee's north side cost the club $11,592. When the park opened, it had a capacity of 5,300, but within a few years this number was too low in the minds of local baseball officials.

The minor league Milwaukees lasted until late in the 1884 season, when the Union Association gave the city a major league franchise. The new team used the same name and played 12 games before the season ended, all at home. It was the end of the line for the Milwaukees, as the UA folded in January 1885.

Major league baseball returned to the Wright Street Grounds in 1885. The eventual National League champion Chicago White Stockings played two September games at the park. Over 2,000 fans attended each game, and the hope amongst locals was that Milwaukee would receive a new major league franchise. This didn't happen, and minor league games continued at the Wright Street Grounds through 1887.

The Northwestern League was revived prior to the 1886 season, and

One. The Borchert Field Brewers

Milwaukee again had a team, this time called Cream City or simply the Creams. After the league again disbanded following the 1887 season, the owners of Wright Street Grounds raised the rent. The new Milwaukee Brewers club that would be joining the Western League in 1888 decided to build their own park with increased capacity. The Wright Street Grounds attracted local baseball leagues for another year before falling into a state of disrepair.

A vacant lot covering a full city block on Milwaukee's north side was purchased for $25,000. Athletic Park's construction costs totaled $40,000, but the city had a venue with a grandstand, bleachers, and standing room only areas that could potentially hold 10,000 fans. The downside of the park was that it was further from downtown, but it was on a large piece of land and could be reached by streetcar.

Harry Quin was the team and ballpark owner, and he announced a big parade and music when the park opened. Quin didn't consider that the opener was scheduled on a Sunday, which met with a lot of resistance from those not wanting baseball and a party to be held on the Sabbath. Quin backed down and moved the parade to the following Tuesday. An estimated 6,000–8,000 fans saw the first game at Athletic Park, but it was hard to get an accurate total because many fans had a hard time just getting through the gates.

Athletic Park remained mainly a minor league facility though 1894, save for a brief stint in the American Association in 1891. When the run of professional baseball ended at Athletic Park, local games were played on the site and the National Guard held drills there.

The Brewers rejoined the Western League, and investors came together to fund the team—chiefly a lawyer named Matthew Killilea who was elected president of the franchise—and later his brother Henry became the majority owner of the team. The Brewers moved into the Lloyd Street Grounds the following year and remained there until 1901 before returning to Athletic Park.

Ban Johnson was the president of the Western League and would remain a league president for 35 years—guiding teams and owners into the new century as the American League. Johnson had previously been a reporter for the *Cincinnati Commercial Gazette* and was no fan of what he considered the rowdy behavior of the atmosphere of the National League. Johnson's good friend, Charles Comiskey, former player and manager of the Cincinnati Reds, pushed him to take over the WL. Johnson empowered umpires to take care of the rough on-field play, and in turn he doled out fines and suspensions for foul language. His goal was to have a family-friendly league that made good profits. He was successful on both fronts.

The Killileas hired a manager for the Brewers named Cornelius McGillicuddy. Better known as Connie Mack, he was given a $3,000 a year salary plus 25 percent of the team. Mack led the Brewers to a second-place finish in 1900, the best the team would do in the Western League. Mack left the Brewers after that season and became well-known for his 50-year stint managing the Philadelphia Athletics. Mack was elected to baseball's Hall of Fame in 1937, despite not having retired from the sport.

The National League went through an upheaval when the 1899 season concluded. They decided to drop four teams—Louisville, Washington, Baltimore and Cleveland. Johnson saw an opportunity to move teams into the vacated cities. Milwaukee's Republican House hosted Johnson, Charles Comiskey, and others in a meeting that culminated with the organization of the American League. The AL was still considered a minor league due to a National Agreement that was signed way back in 1883. The agreement was drawn up for the NL and old American Association to cooperate peacefully and stage a championship series.

The new American League played the 1900 season before declaring their membership in the National Agreement over and promoting themselves as a major league. It didn't take long for AL team owners to lure players to new clubs, as the NL didn't have a salary cap. This proved to be problematic only for the Baltimore Orioles, as they had issues managing money due to overpaid players. The O's were forced to close up shop and move to New York, where they became the Yankees. But despite this hiccup, with star players and rising attendance, the new league could no longer be ignored.

It was in Milwaukee that the next Baltimore Orioles franchise was born, under the Brewers name. Johnson's intention all along was to move the Milwaukee team to St. Louis, but he needed to find someone willing to operate the franchise in the new city. St. Louis was booming and had the fourth-largest population of all U.S. cities at the turn of the century.

Robert Lee Hedges was on Johnson's short list of potential owners, as he had an extensive business background. Hedges bought the Brewers and moved them to St. Louis, where they became the Browns for the 1902 season. They remained in St. Louis until 1953, when the franchise moved to Baltimore and became the modern-day Orioles. The Brewers' change of location was the last major league franchise move for nearly 50 years—and one that played prominently in Milwaukee baseball history because the next franchise move also involved Milwaukee.

Baseball continued in Milwaukee after the Brewers left town, first with the short-lived Creams at the Lloyd Street Grounds. But it was the next team that would stick around until 1952, until the arrival of the major league Braves—the Milwaukee Brewers Class AA team in the minor league American Association. The Brewers were residents of Athletic Park, as the field had been rebuilt by owner Harry Quin. The new version of the park didn't open to as many fans as it did back in 1888, but those in attendance loved the grounds.

The early years of the Brewers were marked by a rise in popularity, mainly because they were the only minor league team in town, and even coming in second or third place was exciting. Covered grandstands were constructed along first and third base to replace the bleachers by 1910. Other positive, fan-friendly changes included a runway to connect the grandstand and a new set of bleachers in left-center field. A scoreboard and a locker room were also built.

It took until 1913 before the Brewers captured the American Association pennant, and they came back to win it again in 1914. Milwaukeeans flocked to the park in droves—crowds occasionally could hit standing room only capacity and were guesstimated in the 18,000 range. On the flipside, the Milwaukee Creams of the Wisconsin-Illinois League also played games at Athletic Park in 1913, but the team moved to Fond du Lac in late June due to poor attendance.

Charles F. Moll, a prominent Milwaukee businessman and previous president of the league, organized the team. Local newspapers called the team the "Mollys" in reference to their owner, but also used nicknames such as the "Schnitts" and "Assistant Brewers." Besides having multiple monikers, the team went down in history for having four players who went on to the majors, most notably Oscar "Happy" Felsch.

Felsch, a child of German immigrants, paid his dues playing in the Milwaukee sandlots while working as a shingler. Baseball gave him an opportunity to escape the working-class neighborhood on Milwaukee's north side. Felsch turned heads with multiple-homer games in the Deadball Era. The American Association Brewers called him up from the Molls in 1913 and he continued his impressive hitting.

By the following August a bidding war broke out for Felsch, and the Chicago White Sox won out, paying $12,000 and sending three players to the Brewers. The arrival of Felsch in Chicago in 1915, along with other new players such as "Shoeless" Joe Jackson, turned the team around. The team went on to win the 1917 World Series as Felsch put up numbers that compared to Tris Speaker and Ty Cobb.

As quickly as Felsch ascended the baseball ranks to stardom, everything crashed due to his role in the 1919 Chicago Black Sox scandal, which led to a lifetime ban from baseball. The "Pride of Teutonia Avenue" returned home to become a grocer and outlaw ballplayer in south-Central Wisconsin. Years later, his accounts of the scandal became the main source material for Eliot Asinof's book, *Eight Men Out*.

While Felsch continued battling baseball and White Sox owner Charles Comiskey in court, another baseball team set up residence in Athletic Park. The Milwaukee Bears were a Negro Leagues club put together in 1923 after two teams dropped out of the league, but poor management and lackluster attendance put a quick end to the franchise. They never gained a true foothold in Milwaukee and played the majority of their games on the road, finishing at the bottom of the standings. The Bears were gone for good after the season, while the Brewers remained through the Roaring Twenties and beyond, bringing joy to legions of fans such as Bud Selig and Bob Uecker.

By the time the Negro Leagues' Milwaukee Bears played their lone season, a local man named Otto Borchert had become a minority owner of the Brewers. Borchert was an athlete in his youth and had a love of baseball and boxing. His background had been in sales, and he wound up selling options on electric light companies for huge commissions. As of 1919, he owned part of the Cream City Athletic Club, where he held and promoted numerous boxing shows.

Little by little, Borchert bought out the other investors in the Brewers and held the team as his own in 1926. Along the way he rehired Harry Clark as manager—the leader of the 1913–1914 pennant-winning Brewers clubs. The move was good for public relations only as the Brewers struggled this time around under Clark.

Borchert was known around Milwaukee as quite a character and fit in well during the Roaring Twenties with his cane, cigars, and countless derby hats. The Brewers were popular with the fans. Otto Borchert was not. He loved to pander to newspaper writers and photographers and didn't seem to care what the fans thought of him. Borchert enjoyed walking from the scoreboard to the infield at home games, even though this usually brought out the worst from those in attendance. He said that it was their privilege to boo since they paid to get into the park.

Borchert never let the public see his true generous nature, and he told reporters to keep his good deeds quiet.[1] He willingly gave players raises and contributed to causes he deemed worthy, yet most people were unaware of these positive points until after his death, when insiders spoke

One. The Borchert Field Brewers

up. Borchert often let underprivileged children into Brewers games for free. He got a lot of enjoyment from having kids at the ballpark.

One thing Borchert wasn't fond of was having his games broadcast on the radio. Well, at first anyway. He swore that radio somehow was a huge conspiracy to keep paying customers away from his ballpark.[2] In early June 1926, Borchert found out that station WHAD was planning to broadcast a Brewers game. It would be the first radio transmission of a baseball game in the city's history. WHAD was jointly owned by the *Milwaukee Journal* newspaper and Marquette University.

Coincidentally, the Brewers were in the middle of a winning streak—and that made Borchert even angrier. He blasted that if the ball game were broadcast, there wouldn't be anyone there to see it. Borchert called it a crazy move and said radio would ruin him.[3]

It turned out that Borchert was wrong. WHAD broadcast its first game on a Wednesday, and a good-sized crowd still came out to the park. This was even after the *Journal* ran a two-column story announcing the broadcast. Borchert scratched his head over the paid attendance the following Sunday. Over 15,000 fans came out despite the game being broadcast on the radio—and they kept coming throughout an eventual 21-game winning streak. It turned out that radio wasn't the enemy. Rather, radio broadcasts stimulated attendance. A *Journal* writer named Sam Levy did the announcing, joined by Larry Teich the following year. The Brewers' radio broadcasts continued until a break in 1943, when World War II programming dominated radio schedules.

Borchert's early years with the Brewers also coincided with professional football being played at Athletic Park. The NFL's Milwaukee Badgers (1922–1926) and Green Bay Packers (1933) held home games at the park. The Badgers had a hard time drawing even half the fans that local semi-professional and factory teams attracted. The Packers were easily more popular among state football fans. Financial issues due to the lack of attendance, along with a $500 fine for using four high school players in a 1925 game, caused the team to disband.

The Packers played the Badgers each season as a visitor at Athletic Park, and returned on October 1, 1933, to host their first home game. The team achieved their goal of bringing in additional revenue when 12,467 fans attended the game. East Stadium games in Green Bay brought in anywhere from 4,000–10,000 fans per game that season. The game ended up being a one-time visit, as the Packers played at Wisconsin State Fair Park in 1934.

While football stars Curly Lambeau and George Halas appeared at

Borchert, baseball fans were graced with visits from future National Baseball Hall of Famers such as Babe Ruth, Ty Cobb, Satchel Paige, and Dizzy Dean. Another future HOFer came from a local Polish neighborhood and played for the Brewers in 1922–1923. Al Simmons, known as the "Duke of Mitchell Street," went on to play two decades in the majors and became a powerful hitter and a respected fielder.

Simmons spent many years playing for Connie Mack's Philadelphia Athletics and won two World Series titles with the team. By the time he retired after the 1944 season, he had amassed 2,927 hits and a career .334 batting average. Simmons became a coach under Mack and later joined Cleveland's staff in 1950. He returned to Milwaukee in 1951 due to health issues and passed away in 1956, just four days after his 54th birthday. The National Baseball Hall of Fame inducted Simmons in 1953 after he received 75.4 percent of the vote.

As often as players such as Ruth and Simmons were photographed, it was claimed that Otto Borchert was the most photographed sports figure of the era. His office, at the very least, seemed to prove this assertion. Borchert had endless photos of himself hung on the walls, all autographed with "Otto Borchert, Pres."

Borchert's Milwaukee Brewers would remain the only baseball team in town until the latter part of World War II, but he would not live to see that new team. Borchert passed away suddenly at the age of 52 in 1927, in an incident very much in the public eye. On April 27, a dinner was held in his honor at the Milwaukee Elks Club. The Brewers' home opener was scheduled for the following day, and spirits were high. Borchert gave the principal address that night with 700 excited attendees looking on. He had nothing but praise for his team and manager, Jack Lelivelt, who had no written contract.[4]

Borchert was ten minutes into his speech when he suffered a massive heart attack. At first, he collapsed into his chair and then recovered enough to be taken to a separate room. He died just a few minutes later. Shock rippled through those in attendance at the Elks Club as well as the audience listening to his speech on the radio.

Borchert's final words were about his earlier years as a traveling salesman. He said, "In all that time I always made it a point to be loyal to my employers—and give them the best I had."[5]

After his death, several insiders who knew the "true Otto Borchert" came out to sing his praises both as a person and as someone who shaped baseball in Milwaukee. T. J. Hickey, president of the American Association, said that Borchert was a good sportsman, and he had yet to find another club president who would attend the games and root like the fellow who paid his admission at the gate.[6]

Milwaukee Brewers baseball continued with Otto's widow Idabel at the helm, and former owner Henry Killilea came back to help her out. The flag was flown at half-staff on Opening Day in Otto Borchert's memory, and over 15,000 were in attendance to see their Brewers claim an 8–3 victory.

The following year, Killilea bought the club for a huge sum (in 1928 money)–$280,000. It was the most anyone had paid for an American Association team, yet it was an understandable move given that the Brewers were an attendance goldmine.

Killilea decided to recognize Otto Borchert's imprint on Milwaukee baseball by changing the name of Athletic Park to Borchert Field (nicknamed "Borchert's Orchard"). The field had a unique charm that stemmed from an odd shape, with short foul lines of 268 feet to left and right field. Huge power alleys were prevalent because the center field fence was 400 feet away from home plate.

Mrs. Borchert remained on board as owner of the park, using $90,000 profit from the sale of the team to buy the site from Timme Realty. Killilea and Mrs. Borchert worked out a 25-year lease to keep the team in Borchert Field.

Killilea went to great lengths to get a contending team assembled, and the Brewers finished third in 1928 with a 90–78 record. He appeared to be the right man to run the team, and the transition of ownership from Borchert had been seamless. But Killilea had been battling health issues and didn't last long in the top job. He had a heart attack followed by a stroke and passed away in early 1929.

As the Roaring Twenties wrapped up and the stock market crashed, the Milwaukee Brewers again were in a state of transition. Killilea willed the team to his daughter, Florence. Technically she wasn't sole owner, as her father had sold half the team to Phil Ball before he passed away. Ball owned the St. Louis Browns.

Florence Killilea wanted to give ownership a fair shot, and possibly not just because she felt it would hurt and disappoint her father—the Brewers reportedly had a $100,000 profit the previous year. She stated, "Maybe I'll flop, but I'm interested in making a go of it. It's a new prospect that fascinates me."[7]

The club started to lose more games and more money in the early 1930s. Florence Killilea married a surgeon and promoted Louis Nahin to club president, taking a secondary role as vice president. She eventually sold her half of the club to Phil Ball, leaving him as sole owner. Even though she had reservations about running a club in a male-dominated sport from the start, Florence later stated that it was loads of fun, and men were most respectful of her opinions.[8]

Sadly, Florence Killilea died at the young age of 29 in 1931 from a heart attack that came after a blood infection and other related issues. Newspapers hailed her as being one of the boys. Players were shaken by her death, including pitcher Denny "Dinty" Gearin. He said the Brewers tried to win for her sake because they admired her and loved her ever-genial personality.[9]

The turnaround of owner to owner to owner wasn't the only upheaval at Borchert Field. Petitioners demanded the removal of the park in the 1930s, citing expanded seating capacity as a reason it was a nuisance.

Borchert Field with lights, which were installed midway through the 1935 season. Neighborhood homes are clearly visible beyond the right field fence (National Baseball Hall of Fame Library, Cooperstown, New York).

Dozens of ballpark neighbors joined together to fight, yet the park and team stayed in place. Shortly after Bob Uecker and Bud Selig were born, lights were installed at Borchert, to the delight of fans and the chagrin of neighbors.

Bud Selig has maintained in interviews that he attended around 40 Brewers games a season during his childhood, starting with his first game in 1937.[10] He wasn't part of the "knothole gang" of kids who would peek through knotholes in the outfield fence to see the games. Marie Selig always had seats for her boys. Bob Uecker, on the other hand, often had his eyes pressed up to a knothole after riding his bicycle eight blocks to the park.

Uecker and Selig were a bit too young to revel in the 1936 championship Milwaukee Brewers team. Milwaukeeans had been waiting since 1914 for their home team to win the American Association pennant, and they weren't disappointed when the Brewers turned in a 90–64 record. The team followed the season by navigating through a new playoff structure that led to the "Junior World Series." The AA representative Brewers would face the International League champion Buffalo Bisons to mirror the major league World Series. The Brewers knocked off the Bisons, four games to one, to emerge as the overall champ.

It would take another seven years for the Brewers to again win the pennant. By then the team was owned by the very colorful Bill Veeck, who bought the team in 1941 at the age of 27. His father, William Veeck, Sr., was originally a sports writer who became the Chicago Cubs president after his columns came to the attention of owner William Wrigley, Jr. Young Bill Veeck worked for the Cubs as a popcorn vendor, groundskeeper, and ticket salesman. Veeck stayed in Chicago until he got into a partnership with former Cubs player and manager Charlie Grimm to snatch up the Brewers. The 1940s version of the Brewers and Borchert Field under Veeck's leadership were about to get a lot more exciting—and zany.

Veeck claimed to have 11 bucks in his pocket when he got to Milwaukee.[11] But Veeck was the type of guy who didn't need deep pockets because he had creativity and craftiness on his side. Decades later, Bob Uecker came to be called "Mr. Baseball" by peers and fans, but Bill Veeck had the nickname first in Milwaukee. And it was for good reason as Veeck worked hard to come up with some of the craziest promotions to fill seats while simultaneously building a strong team. In 1942 he was named *The Sporting News* "Executive of the Year." Veeck was as perfect a fit for the 1940s as Otto Borchert was for the 1920s. He wanted to provide a diversion for fans during World War II and was by all accounts a success.

Veeck realized that third-shift workers were an important segment of the population that had a hard time attending Brewers games. Veeck visited war factories, where he heard the same story over and over—people on the overnight shift would come to games if they started at an earlier time. Veeck brought morning baseball to Milwaukee by scheduling a few 10:00 a.m. games. His first morning game handbill announced advance tickets for .75 and an increase to .85 if purchased day of game. Entertainment was touted as being "screwy—but funny!"

Veeck strongly believed in the combination of baseball and entertainment, and he was constantly trying to up the ante from his last promotion.[12] Occasionally Veeck would do his giveaways unannounced. Fans never knew if they'd receive a live lobster or pigeon. Maybe a block of ice or a ladder would be in the offing. Everything from weddings to chickens became part of the Milwaukee Brewers experience.

Veeck even performed music with his band of baseball executives, which included left-handed manager Charlie "Jolly Cholly" Grimm on banjo and general manager Rudie Schaffer on the one-string can fiddle. Veeck went to town on the slide whistle. A barber shop quartet and a Dixieland jazz band also performed at home games. Veeck spent a lot of time interacting with fans—especially kids—just like Otto Borchert did two decades earlier. He also encouraged his players and coaches to joke around as a way to delight the home crowds.[13]

One of the best gags that Veeck ever pulled was on Grimm's 45th birthday in 1943. Before the game that night, a massive cake was carried onto the field by Brewers players. One by one, several dancing girls emerged from the cake. Grimm was shocked but was in for an even bigger surprise. Veeck told Grimm he should check the cake for yet another gift, and out came Julio Acosta, a left-handed pitcher Veeck just acquired.[14] It was an appropriate present, as Grimm just happened to need a left-hander for his pitching staff.

Owgust (pronounced Awgoost), the Barrel Man, was an important part of the Brewers image from 1942 until the team left town in 1952. Owgust had a tap for his nose and a beer barrel torso, which you'd think would automatically put him at an athletic disadvantage. Yet the Brewers made him a fun and exciting baseball Superman in their promotional materials. Images depicted him flying through the sky to catch a ball or swinging hard for the fences—always with a huge smile on his face. Owgust even appeared as Santa Claus in the Brewers newsletter (*Brewers News*) in December 1944.

GM Rudie Schaffer was given credit for bringing Owgust to life in the

1940s, but origins of a Barrel Man can be traced back to 1901, when the Brewers started playing in the American Association. A few cartoons appeared in the *Milwaukee Sentinel* with a risqué look to the Brewers hero. His tapper was located down low in the front and was used to get opposing pitchers drunk. The Barrel Kid that appeared in the late 1940s seems tame in comparison, but at the time no one complained about him subconsciously promoting underage drinking.

What made all the "screwy but funny" entertainment at Borchert Field even more enjoyable was the fact that Veeck and Grimm had a powerhouse team. Veeck was extremely good at acquiring players for Grimm. In turn, Grimm managed the club to three pennants in five years.

World War II brought a mandate for less travel for baseball teams from the Office of Defense Transportation. As a result, the Brewers held 1943 spring training in Milwaukee starting in early April. Many of the players were already in great shape from working at various blue-collar jobs relating to the war effort during the off-season. Veeck himself went to war as a Marine and was stationed in the Pacific. He had his right leg amputated below the knee after he was struck by a recoiling anti-aircraft gun.

Veeck found out while he was in the Pacific that Charlie Grimm had been lured back to the Cubs once again to manage the team. Grimm talked his longtime friend Casey Stengel into taking his managerial job with the Brewers, and this move angered Veeck. He wrote a letter to Grimm, noting seven reasons why Stengel should be fired, saying in point six that "I have no confidence in his ability and rather than be continuously worried, I'd rather dispose of the whole damn thing."[15]

Veeck needn't have worried. Stengel led the Brewers to the 1944 American Association pennant. Veeck admitted he was wrong about Stengel, but it was too late. Stengel got wind of the nasty letter and called it a day as the Brewers manager. Veeck returned from the military in 1945 and called it quits too, selling the Brewers for a $275,000 profit. Not too long afterward, he became a minority owner of the Cleveland Indians and went on to use countless promotional ideas through a colorful baseball career that spanned another 35 years. He was posthumously elected to the Baseball Hall of Fame in 1991.

Milwaukee had another team playing at Borchert Field near the end of the Veeck era. The Milwaukee Chicks were added to the All-American Girls Professional Baseball League for the 1944 season. The Minneapolis Millerettes came into the one-year old league at the same time. The AAGPBL was founded by Chicago Cubs owner Phillip K. Wrigley, with the teams residing in Midwestern cities that generally didn't have a major league team. The league and the Rockford Peaches team were immortalized in the 1992 fictionalized movie, *A League of Their Own*.

The Chicks were a dominant team in the league and had Max Carey as their manager. He was a future Hall of Famer who won a World Series with the Pittsburgh Pirates in 1925. The Chicks led the league in batting average, stolen bases and runs scored, plus tied for first in home runs. Their 70–45 record gave them the right to play a seven-game, post-season series with the Kenosha Comets, and the Chicks won the set.

Yet despite their powerful season, the Chicks went the way of many other successful teams of the first half of the 20th century—to another city. They cited many factors for their departure to Grand Rapids, Michigan, for the following season. The Chicks didn't have a lot of community support as most locals were only interested in seeing the Brewers play at Borchert Field. High ticket prices were another reason for keeping fans away from the park. Well, that's when the Chicks did play home games at Borchert. The Brewers were at home during the Chicks playoff series, so the Chicks were forced to play the whole series at Kenosha's Lake Front Stadium.

Bud Selig has stated that he doesn't recall attending any Milwaukee Chicks games.[16] He continued going to Brewers games though the 1940s and has always looked back fondly on the many great teams and players he saw in those days. He had several favorites with the Brewers, but especially Hershel Martin. Selig said, "I'm the only one on Earth left who remembers him. They sold him to the Yankees in 1945. I became a Yankee fan, and quickly became a Joe DiMaggio fan, because Hershel didn't last too long."[17]

Martin mostly played in the minor leagues, and the switch-hitting slugger had great success with the Brewers, where he was voted Most Popular Brewer by the fans. He wound up playing with the big league Yankees due to the number of players enlisted in the military during World War II. Selig would get to see his favorite team in person at age 15, but not Martin, his favorite player, who by then was a player/manager in the minors.

Young Bud Selig was about to experience baseball games on a much larger scale than at Borchert Field as he spent a summer in the Big Apple. Marie Selig took her son on a six-week summer trip to New York in 1949, a journey that changed his life forever. His 15th birthday was a magical day, starting off with the amazing sight of the Yankees playing the White Sox in Yankee Stadium. That night Marie took him to see the play *South Pacific* to wrap up what Selig years later called a wonderful birthday.[18]

Marie and Bud also saw Giants and Dodgers games at the Polo Grounds and Ebbets Field. The city was baseball's capital, and Bud was becoming a student of the game, even occasionally attending games without his mother. Some days, Marie would go to a museum while Bud visited one of the ballparks.

The Seligs tried in vain to see the Yankees play the Boston Red Sox at Fenway Park that summer. The game was a sellout and they couldn't get in, so instead they visited a few Boston museums and Harvard University.

Selig's first major league game actually happened in 1944 when his parents took him to Wrigley Field in Chicago. He had been listening to Cubs games on the radio, as they were the closest big league team to Milwaukee. As with the later New York trip, seeing Wrigley Field for the first time would only strengthen his love of the game. Selig recalled, "My parents took me down and we went to the ballgame. What a thrill that was to me.... Wrigley Field, when I walked in there, I'll never forget the thrill. The green grass, the ivy, everything. It was exactly like I thought it would be."[19]

Selig had a childhood friend named Herb Kohl who also grew up to be a prominent local businessman and have a place in Wisconsin sports team ownership. After college, Kohl eventually became president of the Kohl's grocery and department store chain. Later he became a United States Senator and owner of basketball's Milwaukee Bucks franchise. Back in the 1940s, he was just a teenage sports lover and Selig's buddy. Their friendship would last a lifetime and was cemented in those early years by trips to games at Wrigley.

One such drive led them to seeing the Brooklyn Dodgers and Jackie Robinson break the color line in Chicago. It was May 18, 1947. "We sat in the upper deck and we were the only white fans up there," Selig said. "There was so much electricity and drama."[20]

Borchert Field was in a state of decline by the time Selig and Kohl attended the Jackie Robinson game at Wrigley. The park was old and outdated, and even though Bill Veeck had cleaned the place up during his ownership tenure, the best years were in the past. Part of the roof blew off in 1944, damaging nearby homes and injuring over two dozen fans. Not even a fresh coat of paint from Veeck's crew could disguise the fact that Borchert was the oldest park in the American Association.

After World War II ended, talk turned to a replacement for Borchert. Local officials and fans expressed the desire for a modern, more comfortable facility. A decrease in the use of public transportation to reach

Borchert Field led to an increase in vehicle traffic on the streets near the park. The need for a large parking lot or structure was apparent if a new ballpark was built.

Wisconsin celebrated its 100th year of statehood in 1948, and a nonprofit group called the 1948 Corporation sprang to life with a goal to revitalize Milwaukee in celebration of the anniversary. Many large public works were planned, including a library, downtown sports arena, zoo, museum, and ballpark. The community leaders and businessmen later became known as the Greater Milwaukee Committee. Many of their plans would take years to unfold, like the construction of a new baseball park. Discussions to build something "big league" had been hot and cold since the early 1930s.

The American Association Brewers became a Boston Braves affiliate in 1947, and naturally Braves owner Lou Perini was a big supporter of the proposal to build a Milwaukee ballpark. Perini told the Milwaukee Athletic Club to get ready to become a major league city within five years.[21] The city ultimately approved Milwaukee County Stadium, and ground was broken for the new ballpark on October 19, 1950.

Many locations were considered for the ballpark, including what later became Wisconsin State Fair Park before the Story Quarry site in western Milwaukee was selected. Korean War steel shortages would slow construction at times for the $5 million, publicly funded ballpark (which is $44.2 million in current costs adjusted for inflation). The end result was a simple design without many extras found in other stadiums—including the lack of bleacher seats at first. Hunzinger Construction Company did the stadium work, with Osborn Engineering of Cleveland serving as project architect. Osborn had designed Yankee Stadium, Fenway Park, and Comiskey Park.

When it became apparent that construction would be completed on County Stadium in time for the 1953 baseball season, city officials decided Borchert Field would no longer be necessary. Two years were left on the lease the city had with Idabel Borchert, but the city got around that snag and bought her out for $123,000. The city of Milwaukee may have overpaid her because a 1937 assessment had the property valued at only $73,000.

Milwaukee Mayor Frank Zeidler, Brewers general manager Red Smith, and Idabel Borchert burned the lease between games of a Brewers doubleheader on August 26, 1952. Fans sang "Auld Lang Syne" as the ashes were taken away by a horse-drawn hearse, and the curtain came down on 50 years of baseball history.

It was the end of an incredible run for the grand old ballpark.

Two

Borchert Field to Bushville

The Milwaukee Brewers eagerly anticipated the opening of their new home. The team did its best to promote the move. Even the backs of schedules proclaimed, "Watch for Brewer Opening in Milwaukee County's New Stadium!" Drawings of the stadium eventually surfaced in Brewers programs, but city officials were less interested. They had no intention of letting the Brewers ever play in County Stadium and pushed it as a big league ballpark, sending out brochures about Milwaukee to major league team owners.

After baseball ended at Borchert in 1952, crews worked quietly to clear the stands and equipment from the site. Early proposals for the site bounded by N. 7th, N. 8th, W. Burleigh and W. Chambers Streets included a school, expressway, housing project, and playground.

At first the land was used as a park for children called the "Borchert Field Tot Lot," but by 1963 the Tot Lot was gone to make way for Interstate 43. Today Borchert Field is remembered with a historical marker located in nearby Clinton Rose Park at northbound North 5th Street and West Burleigh Street. Roughly 150,000 cars pass daily over the spot that was once home to Borchert Field.

The Brewers began to sell tickets for the 1953 season, including a scheduled home opener with the St. Paul Saints on April 15. General manager Red Smith and the rest of his front office moved into County Stadium. As the season approached, it looked like the minor league Brewers would indeed be the stadium occupants, much to the dismay of local leaders and fans who thought Lou Perini was dragging his heels on possibly moving his big league Braves to Milwaukee.

Baseball franchises were not known to move from city to city like their minor league counterparts. The last move was a half-century earlier when the American League Milwaukee Brewers skipped town for St. Louis and became the Browns. Ironically, those same Browns were now more of a joke than an actual baseball team, and former Brewers owner Bill Veeck was having a rough go of turning the Browns into a respectable club. He was going up against the beloved Cardinals and their longtime fan base.

St. Louis baseball fans flocked to Sportsman's Park for Cardinals games. Most viewed the Browns as a glorified minor league team and had no interest in Veeck's promotional antics. Veeck thought he could bring the Browns back to their original home in Milwaukee, where baseball fans loved his wild promotions.[1] His timing was perfect because in late 1952, baseball Commissioner Ford Frick and team owners met in joint session and adopted a rule that required a team desiring to move to obtain only three-fourths of its own league's approval along with the minor league involved.

Meanwhile, Lou Perini had been offered $500,000 to move the Brewers out of town by a Milwaukee business committee—essentially "get out of the Browns way" money. Perini knew that owning the Brewers gave him territorial rights to baseball in the city, so he told the committee no thanks. He had already planned a move of the Braves to the city and had the other owners on his side. Perini later admitted that he was forced into sudden action by Veeck, and he originally had no intention of moving his team until the following year.[2]

Veeck was just the wrong guy at the right time. Most major league owners thought Veeck's promotions were better suited for the minors and didn't think much of him as a major league owner. When Veeck told the other owners he'd like to move the Browns to Milwaukee, they voted him down.[3] The Browns played one more season in St. Louis before Veeck was forced to sell his stake in the team. He had no leverage in keeping the team, having already sold Sportsman's Park to the Cardinals, thinking he'd be able to move the Browns easily.

A week after Veeck was shot down by the other baseball owners in his quest to bring major league baseball back to Milwaukee, a new vote was held in St. Petersburg, Florida, regarding the Boston Braves. The National League owners unanimously approved the proposed franchise relocation, and the news officially broke on March 18, 1953, although newspapers had already been printing rumors of the move for a few days.

Perini noted the lack of fan support in Boston when he announced his intention to move the Braves to Milwaukee.[4] Certainly, few could blame him after the Braves hit a lowly attendance mark of 281,278 in 1952 and finished in seventh place. It was a stunning fall from the franchise peak with a NL pennant in 1948 and nearly 1.5 million in attendance.

Two. Borchert Field to Bushville

The Braves had been in survival mode more often than not since a near-bankruptcy in the Great Depression. Perini initially bought into the team prior to 1941 as part of a large group. By 1944, the group narrowed to Perini and two other stockholders. The franchise needed a boost after stumbling on the field and at the gate due to the war. Perini and his partners were contractors who saw baseball as another business challenge, and they rebuilt the team in short order, only to see everything unravel.

Management and players started bickering during 1948 after Perini doled out a $52,000 bonus to pitcher Johnny Antonelli, a recent high school graduate. Some players revolted and demanded increases in salary, while others became angered after the season over the amount of credit manager Billy Southworth received for the 1948 pennant.[5] Southworth took a paid leave of absence from the team in late 1949, but returned the following season and managed through 1951.

While the wheels were coming off in the clubhouse, Perini purchased Braves Field, which had been under lease. His goal was to expand seating capacity to 50,000, but estimated losses of $580,000 in 1952 put an end to that idea. Money had already been poured into Braves Field for other improvements, such as a $75,000 electronic scoreboard and neon foul poles.

The final season culminated with Perini and his brothers, Charles and Joseph, buying up all the remaining stock held by minority stockholders. Members of the press speculated that Perini was either buying out his co-owners to ease their suffering, or paving the way to sell or move the franchise.

On the surface, it didn't seem as though a hometown owner like Perini would want to move his team. He grew up in Boston and had a large family to consider. Despite those factors, the only thing that made sense economically was to move the team. Only 500 season tickets had been sold for the upcoming 1953 season, making Perini's decision even easier.

Perini expected much better attendance in Milwaukee after witnessing the loyalty the locals had to their minor league Brewers team. He revealed, "I can't operate successfully from a financial standpoint in Boston. There is only room for one club in Boston. It is no longer a two-club city."[6]

Both the Braves and Red Sox were long-standing teams in Boston. The Braves had their origins in 1871 as the Boston Red Stockings, a charter team in the National Association of Professional Base Ball Players. This team and the ones that followed are arguably the longest-running professional sports franchise in North America. This fact didn't equate to ticket sales or success in the standings for the Braves—they were outdistanced by the Red Sox in those areas.

Viewpoints were beginning to change amongst baseball's insiders. More franchise moves were anticipated. Brooklyn Dodgers president Walter O'Malley declared, "You see more territory being drafted than you can shake a stick at. This will set up a chain reaction."[7] His Dodgers would be just one of the teams relocating in the coming years, partially due to the successful move of the Braves to Milwaukee.

Perini discussed changes in the population of major cities over the previous 75 years with the press. Besides Milwaukee, he felt that San Francisco, Los Angeles, and Montreal were major league-ready.[8] Perini's opinion was prophetic as baseball would see ten relocations and eight new franchises in a two-decade period.

The American Association Milwaukee Brewers would never play a game inside what they believed to be their ballpark. Instead, they moved to Toledo, Ohio, and became a new incarnation of the minor league Mud Hens after a five-year absence of that team. While the previous Mud Hens were affiliated with the St. Louis Browns, the new club remained a part of the Milwaukee Braves organization. Meanwhile, the parent club had just three weeks to get ready for their first big league season in Milwaukee.

Milwaukee Braves team officials quickly settled into County Stadium and set an on-sale date of April 1, 1953, for tickets. The Brewers' Opening Day ticket holders were offered similar seating locations when Braves games went on sale, with an upcharge due to Braves seats having a higher cost. The Braves team itself was still in spring training in Florida when news of the sale broke. Many of the players rejoiced at the opportunity of potentially playing in front of more fans than ever before.[9]

The fan response didn't disappoint—the home opener sold out a week before the game. The last of the Opening Day tickets—roughly 7,500 bleacher seats—were placed on sale in advance and were quickly gobbled up. The NL waived a rule limiting bleacher sales to the day of the game due to the high demand for tickets.

The time couldn't have been more perfect for big league baseball to return to the state. The Green Bay Packers had foundered for nearly a decade and held a third stock sale in 1950 to prevent bankruptcy and/or a move to another city. Milwaukee had an NBA team in the Hawks, but they spent four seasons in last place and moved to St. Louis after 1955.

Wisconsin residents were ready to support their new local team, and 10,000 fans turned out at the train station to greet the players and coaches.

A red carpet stretched from the train tracks out into the street, where players climbed into convertibles. They drove along a five-mile parade route where an estimated 60,000 people enthusiastically cheered and waved signs.

The players eventually made it to County Stadium and participated in limbering-up drills for an hour. Three thousand fans were allowed to watch the workout—far more than the attendance of any game the Brewers played at Borchert Field in their final season. The response to the new stadium was overwhelmingly positive from players and fans.

A public rally at the Milwaukee Arena capped off the day, but rain and hail kept attendance down to 5,000. Several city and state officials were on hand to welcome the team. Lou Perini thanked Milwaukee for the incredible reception and announced a new director for the club—Fred Miller, president of Miller Brewing Company. Miller received accolades for helping to bring the team to the city.[10]

The initial tune-up game against the Red Sox lasted only two full innings before being called due to rain. The early afternoon contest drew 9,596 fans who spent an hour under the grandstand before the umpires cancelled the game. The second exhibition was completely abandoned well ahead of the start time. A 30-mile-an-hour wind blasted into County Stadium, making for an extremely chilly day.

The Braves flew to Boston after the rainouts and played a weekend farewell set against the Red Sox. Both games were settled by 4–1 scores, with Boston winning the first game and Milwaukee the second.

The Braves had an odd schedule to start the season. They would play one game on the road in Cincinnati on April 13, then fly to Milwaukee for their home opener against the Cardinals the next day. After two days off, they would be back in action at Cincinnati for a game, followed by a return trip to Milwaukee for two more games with the Cardinals.

The traditional Opening Day game held each year in Washington, D.C., was rained out, leaving the Braves and Cincinnati Reds as the only teams playing that day. Milwaukee won their first big league opener by a final score of 2–0. Max Surkont pitched a complete game and gave up just three hits in a winning effort. It was a far cry from the last Milwaukee major league opener the Brewers played in 1901. Those Brewers held a 13–4 in the ninth inning over Detroit, but the Tigers scored ten runs in the bottom of the inning to win, a record which still stands as the greatest ninth-inning comeback in major league history.

The Braves returned to Milwaukee for their home opener against St. Louis, and a partly sunny morning greeted early visitors in the County

Stadium parking lot. Fans lined up early to be among the first in the ballpark when the gates opened at 11:30. They were treated first to the Braves conducting batting practice, before St. Louis took their turn at noon.

Infield practice was next—first for the Braves at 12:30 and then the Cardinals at 12:45. Both teams retreated to their respective clubhouses around 1:00 to make way for the pre-game ceremonies. Sports announcer Earl Gillespie introduced team owner Lou Perini, who passed the microphone to Commissioner Ford Frick. NL president Warren Giles also spoke briefly and congratulated the citizens of Milwaukee for building County Stadium, which made it possible for the Braves to move to the city.[11]

Government officials on hand included Milwaukee Mayor Frank Zeidler and Wisconsin Governor Walter Kohler. The players made their way to the first and third base foul lines as the capacity crowd gave a standing ovation. They remained standing as a Marine color guard marched to the flag pole in right-center field. A flag was raised and then lowered to half-mast as a bugler played "Taps." The flag went back to full mast for the playing of the "Star Spangled Banner."

Anticipation for the first pitch ran high through the crowd as the starting lineups were announced. Umpires and managers met briefly at home plate and broke up so the game could start at 1:30. Solly Hemus moved into the batter's box to become the first batter in County Stadium. Home plate umpire Jocko Conlan bellowed "Play Ball," and the game was underway after an opening pitch from lefty Warren Spahn.

The game went ten innings and had a dramatic conclusion. Billy Bruton hit a long drive that bounced off Cardinals outfielder Enos Slaughter's glove and landed beyond the outfield fence for what was thought to be a home run. An argument ensued when umpire Lon Warneke thought it was possible the ball either succumbed to fan interference or bounced over the fence. Slaughter later said he rammed his elbow on the fence and thought he had a chance to catch it on a second stab, but a fan grabbed the ball and ran off.[12]

Braves manager Charlie "Jolly Cholly" Grimm argued his case and Warneke changed course, awarding Bruton the homer, and the Braves walked off with a 3–2 victory. Just a year earlier, Grimm had been promoted to Boston Braves manager after leading the minor league Brewers for a successful second stint, including a second American Association pennant in 1951.

Bud Selig made it to the first Braves opener even though he was attending the University of Wisconsin–Madison. He and the thousands of other Braves fans were extremely passionate about everything that happened on the field on County Stadium's opener. They even cheered for foul balls and the appearance of the grounds crew.

Milwaukeeans were hungry for major league baseball, and fans came out to the ballpark in record numbers. It didn't matter that most attendees weren't familiar with the players early on. Johnny Logan, Eddie Mathews, Andy Pafko, Warren Spahn, and Lew Burdette among others would later become household names.

In the beginning, eager fans gobbled up tickets with little regard to who was playing—they were just showing support of their hometown team. It took only 13 home games for the 1953 Milwaukee Braves to eclipse the entire 1952 Boston Braves attendance total.

Outsiders didn't think the Milwaukee Braves could continue selling tickets at such a fast clip. Yet the locals knew better—they had supported a minor league team for 50 years through two world wars, the Great Depression, and the decline of what was once a top minor league facility.

Bodies kept coming through the gates to the tune of 1,826,297 fans, pushing the Braves to a National League attendance record in 1953. Even the popular Brooklyn Dodgers couldn't compete with those numbers, as they wound up in second place in the NL with 1.1 million fans. The New York Yankees won their fifth straight World Series (a record that still stands) and led in AL attendance with 1,537,811, also well behind the Braves total.

The popularity of the Braves helped the total attendance increase slightly for all MLB teams combined from the previous season. Only Brooklyn and Philadelphia saw an uptick in attendance; all other teams went down at the gate.

Some teams were lucky to get anywhere near a million fans each season throughout the Braves' peak years in attendance. The Braves annually sold a million tickets before the season even started. County Stadium initially opened with a 28,000-seat capacity with room for overflow. The city swiftly moved to toss $1.5 into the pot for more seating. Additional bleachers were constructed, and eventually the capacity grew to 44,000.

County Stadium continued to evolve during the Braves years. Several trees were planted in dead center field early on beyond the fence as a batter's eye. The grove was called "Perini's Woods" and was a bit better visual for batters than the parking lot.

Wrigley Field wasn't the only big league ballpark where outsiders could see a game for free. Bleachers were placed outside the National Soldiers Home Veterans Administration Hospital. The hospital's staff and patients watched games from this right field corner vantage point.

Local businesses showed their support of the Braves with freebies like beer, gas, clothing, and restaurant meals. These giveaways were estimated at $100,000 over the course of the first season alone. Besides giving items away, businesses also hung banners proclaiming their love of the Braves.

The fans were rewarded with a winning team right away as the Braves cruised to a 92–62 record in the first season. Eddie Mathews emerged as a big star due to his major league-leading 47 home runs in 1953, but the team itself also garnered a lot of national attention. An annual year-end *Associated Press* poll voted the Braves the "Surprise Story of 1953" due to their abrupt move from Boston, league attendance record, and pennant chase.

Young Henry "Hank" Aaron reached Milwaukee the next season—on April 13, 1954—and didn't immediately show signs of becoming one of the game's greatest players. He went 0-for-5 in his first game, and it took him another ten days to hit the first of his 755 career home runs. Prior to joining the Braves, Aaron had already played in Wisconsin with the minor league Eau Claire Bears.

Bob Uecker signed with the Braves in 1956 and also spent time with the Eau Claire Bears. All those years of watching games at Borchert Field and playing Milwaukee sandlot baseball paid off. Uecker has joked over the years about his dad paying the Braves $3,000 to sign him—but it was the other way around. Like Aaron, Uecker would also make his big league debut on April 13—but it would be eight years later—in 1962. Seeing the Braves come to town before he left for the service, and later signing with his hometown team, were indeed special moments for Uecker.

The Braves broke the attendance record in 1954 and led the NL in attendance until 1959, when the Los Angeles Dodgers became the top draw. No team eclipsed the 2,000,000-fan mark in a single season until the Braves did it in 1954. The team was an annual success at the gate with over 2,000,000 fans attending each season from 1954 through 1957.

Aaron and so many other great Braves players spoiled the fans with their winning ways. The team was always in the National League pennant conversation. John Quinn was viewed as a star general manager for constructing a deep farm system that kept churning out star players while augmenting his roster with a few shrewd trades. Even though the club backpedaled in the standings in 1955 and 1956, the fan support didn't diminish.

The Milwaukee Braves were truly a 1950s baseball version of a Cinderella story. By 1956 the team was on the verge of a World Series appearance, finishing just one game behind the Brooklyn Dodgers for the National League pennant. Fred Haney was the new manager, having replaced Charlie Grimm during the season. The Braves posted a 92–62 record, the same as their first season in Milwaukee. The difference was that the Dodgers chokehold on the league started to loosen up. The players, front office, and fans could feel the team was on the verge of greatness.

One of their most ardent fans, Bud Selig, graduated from college that year with a double major in political science and American history. Although he contemplated sticking around Madison to teach, he instead signed on for a short hitch in the army. After the army, Selig took a postgraduate accounting course at the University of Wisconsin–Milwaukee. Selig hated accounting but never cut classes—at least until late in the Braves' 1957 season.

The Braves reached the pinnacle of success in 1957, capturing the National League pennant with a 95–59 record. The St. Louis Cardinals finished a distant second, eight games back. The Braves' pennant-clinching win came on September 23 over the Cardinals when Hank Aaron hit a home run in the 11th inning.

Selig said one of his favorite County Stadium memories was cutting class to attend that historic game, even though he wound up sitting in an upper deck, obstructed view seat. He recalled, "I said, 'I can't miss tonight' ... and am very happy today that I did that. Those kind of things make great memories."[13]

In the World Series, the Braves faced the dominant New York Yankees, who had home field advantage. It was a daunting task because the Yankees were "always" in the World Series in those days, having played in eight of the last ten, winning seven. The Yankees were heavy favorites to win the championship, yet the Braves managed to beat them in seven games.

A rush of excitement rippled across Wisconsin not felt in the world of sports since the Green Bay Packers captured the NFL Championship in 1944. Wisconsinites gathered around their radios and televisions to cheer for their beloved Braves. The fanatical support continued when roughly 2,000 fans gathered at the airport to see the team off when they headed back to New York for the final games in the Series.

All the games in Yankee Stadium drew crowds above 60,000—well above what Milwaukee County Stadium could hold. As such, Braves players experienced a larger national spotlight for their efforts in the Series. Lew Burdette completed and won all three games he started and was named Most Valuable Player. Manager Fred Haney said, "If he could cook, I'd marry him."[14]

Several of the New York papers heaped praise on the new champions, while back in Milwaukee a celebration unfolded that hadn't been seen since V-J Day. Congratulatory messages rolled in from city mayors, prominent business leaders, and celebrities. Even Yankees manager Casey Stengel spoke highly of the Braves organization, in particular Haney and Burdette.[15]

Stengel hadn't been as pleasant prior to the World Series, calling Milwaukee "bush league."[16] According to the *1956 Baseball Almanac*, "bush" was defined as "distinctly below major league caliber." Stengel had either forgotten his stint as manager of the minor league Milwaukee Brewers—or he chose to ignore those days. It didn't take long for the local press and fans to pick up on the snub. Milwaukee became known as Bushville, yet some local fans and players took pride in the name. A huge banner reading "Bushville Wins" was unfurled during the Braves' victory parade.

The Braves had another great season in 1958, again winning the

In 1957, an estimated 750,000 people jammed Milwaukee's streets and airport to welcome home the world champion Braves, who had dispatched the Yankees in seven games (National Baseball Hall of Fame Library, Cooperstown, New York).

National League pennant by eight games. They returned to the World Series, but this time lost to the Yankees in seven games. The Yankees actually had to rally from a three games to one deficit, and in the process, became just the second team to do so in a World Series. The baseball landscape was changing as the Yankees were now the sole team in New York. The Dodgers had moved to Los Angeles, and the Giants relocated to San Francisco prior to the season.

The following season featured the last visit the Milwaukee Braves made to the post-season, as they finished the season in a tie for first place with the Los Angeles Dodgers. Milwaukee lost the playoff series in two games to the Dodgers, who then defeated the Chicago White Sox in the World Series.

The campaign started off with a front office shakeup. Owner Lou Perini added former Reds manager Birdie Tebbetts as executive vice president and, as president, Joe Cairnes—who had no baseball experience. General manager John Quinn decided to take an offer to run the Philadelphia Phillies after the front office got a little too crowded for his liking. Quinn's departure and the Braves' final run to the post-season signaled the beginning of the end of a great Milwaukee franchise.

While the 1960s Milwaukee Braves teams were not as dominant on the field as in previous years, they did wind up being the only major league franchise to play more than one season and never have a losing record. Despite finishing with an above-.500 record each season, attendance began to drop off significantly, with several factors attributing to the decrease.

The Braves couldn't get closer than five games behind the Pittsburgh Pirates after early August 1960. Even though the team won more games in 1960 than 1959, there was a noticeable decline in attendance in August and September as the Pirates pulled away to win the pennant. The season attendance fell under 1.5 million for the first time.

The Milwaukee County Board also prohibited fans from carrying six-packs of beer into County Stadium in 1960. Many of the fans were brewery workers who had gotten the beer for free on the job. They simply weren't willing to pay at the concession stand for something they could get for free. By 1961 the ban had been lifted, but many of the fans continued to stay away. The team fell to fourth place, and crowds averaged less than 15,000 a game. It was the last year the Braves drew over 1,000,000 fans, and they dipped to ninth out of 18 teams in total attendance.

Some of the lack of interest in the team can be attributed to burnout from the success of the 1950s teams. The Braves had long drawn double the population of the Milwaukee metropolitan area, and no other team in baseball could make such a claim. Bus trips catered in fans from around the state of Wisconsin as well, particularly from the western and central areas of the state. When the Minnesota Twins moved from Washington in 1961, they played to a total of 1.5 million fans, many of whom came from Wisconsin.

A resurgence of the Green Bay Packers also drew fans away from the Braves. The 1960 Packers posted an 8–4 record under second-year coach Vince Lombardi and lost in the NFL Championship Game. As an attendance comparison example, the Midwest Shrine Game exhibition between the Packers and Chicago Bears on Saturday, August 27, 1960, drew roughly 10,000 more fans than the Braves-Phillies game the previous Sunday. Not even Warren Spahn on the mound could fill the ballpark when fans had other choices in how to spend their money.

Spahn and other longtime stars like Hank Aaron and Eddie Mathews mixed in with young players developed in their farm system in the 1960s. The front office also had a willingness to pay to acquire proven players like infielders Roy McMillan and Frank Bolling. Yet the Braves were eclipsed by powerful National League teams like the San Francisco Giants, Los Angeles Dodgers, St. Louis Cardinals, and Cincinnati Reds. Those great teams made the Braves look simply good in comparison.

Cleveland experienced a similar drop in attendance in the 1950s despite the team consistently finishing no lower than second place between 1951 and 1956. They peaked with 2.6 million fans in 1948, but only drew 1.3 million in their 1954 season when they posted a 111–43 record. Just two years later, the Indians only saw 865,467 fans come through the Cleveland Stadium turnstiles. A simple explanation for the lack of attendance is that fans were frustrated at seeing the New York Yankees win pennants every year besides 1948 and 1954.

Even the successful Yankees teams saw their average attendance decrease from 27,000 a game to 20,000 from 1950 to 1959. When the Dodgers and Giants pulled up stakes and headed west, both were drawing fewer than 15,000 fans a game. As old landlocked ballparks in downtown areas lost appeal, MLB turned to the television medium to attract fans. The 1950s were ripe with baseball on television firsts, such as the NBC broadcast of the 1955 World Series entirely in color for the first time.

Owner Lou Perini initially didn't trust that television broadcasts of Braves games would help promote attendance.[17] He flat-out refused to allow any games on TV, just as Otto Borchert did with his Brewers on radio back in the 1920s. Perini relented by the early 1960s and realized money could be made through sponsorships and advertising.

It was too late for Perini to make such a move, as he lost money on the Braves in 1962 for the first time. His construction company, however, had been growing and went public in 1961. Shareholders were not happy with the performance of the baseball sector and voiced concerns. Couple all this with Perini owing a reported $1.5 million in back taxes, and it was becoming apparent that he'd probably need to get rid of the team.

He sold the Braves on November 16, 1962, to a Chicago group called the Lasalle Corporation, led by 34-year-old insurance industry executive William Bartholomay. Perini received $6.2 million in the sale after pulling $7.5 million in profits from 1953 through 1961. He kept a ten percent interest in the franchise and remained on the board of directors.

It wasn't long before the new ownership group began courting the city of Atlanta as a possible destination for the Braves. Some joked that Bartholomay didn't let the ink get dry on the paperwork before announcing his intentions to move the team.[18] But Bartholomay was completely serious in what he wanted to do with the franchise. His dream was to become the first man to bring a baseball team to the Deep South, even if he emphatically denied such a desire early on.[19]

Bob Broeg, sports editor of the *St. Louis Post-Dispatch*, wrote a story shortly after the 1963 All-Star Game speculating that a Braves move to Atlanta would happen within two years if the team didn't see a boost at the box office. Broeg pointed to an Atlanta delegation at the All-Star Game pitching to both the Indians and Braves as future residents of Atlanta.[20] Bartholomay and President John McHale both responded by saying the idea of relocation held no weight, and they were working to revive the baseball interest and attendance at home.[21]

Atlanta was growing quickly and had a larger television market than Milwaukee. The city of Atlanta responded favorably to the possibility of having major league baseball, and with the backing of Mayor Ivan Allen, Jr., Atlanta Stadium was built within a year. The stadium had 52,000 seats with a cost of $18 million, and it officially opened in 1965.

Rumors swirled about a possible Braves move to Atlanta throughout the summer of 1964. The Milwaukee County Board worked up a new contract by late September in a last-ditch effort to retain the Braves. Board members agreed to hand over authority over concession prices and full revenue from sales. The proposal meant that an additional $250,000 annually would go to the Braves. The Joseph Schlitz Brewing Company also offered to increase payments for radio and television rights by $125,000. The potential for additional revenue from these sources wasn't enough to turn around a decision that had been in the works for some time.

The new ownership group eventually went public in October and asked the National League for permission to relocate to Atlanta. Their request was granted, but the NL forced the Braves to finish out their stadium lease, and this meant playing a lame duck 1965 season in Milwaukee. The team still attempted to leave early, even offering a $500,000 buyout to Milwaukee County, which was promptly refused unless the NL promised Milwaukee an expansion team. But the NL wouldn't budge. Another $500,000 buyout was offered later and was also turned down.

When news broke of the request to shift the franchise, newspaper columnists barked over the mixed signals the ownership group had been sending to Wisconsin fans while surveying other cities as possible destinations. Cities considered included Atlanta, Dallas-Fort Worth, Seattle, and Oakland. Monte McCormick of the *Wisconsin State Journal* wrote, "The cloak of honest wooing was ripped off in Chicago Wednesday and replaced by one of contemplated deception."[22]

McCormick interviewed Bill Veeck in a separate article, and the longtime baseball team owner didn't pull any punches in his trademark style. Veeck said he wasn't against making money, but saw money as a reason why baseball had been getting a black eye recently.[23] Of the Braves move, Veeck commented, "It's wrong, it's greedy, it's indicative of the trend in baseball today."[24]

Milwaukee Mayor Henry Maier also referred to a black eye for baseball over the circumstances of the move. He said if anyone had illusions that baseball was just a sport rather than a business, the Braves move would remove those illusions. Maier called out Braves ownership for not only breaking a contract commitment with the county, but also for ducking a moral commitment to the community.

Some prominent Milwaukee businessman formed a group called "Teams, Inc." in reaction to the upcoming Braves relocation. Their main purpose was to get the major leagues to give them a new expansion team to replace the Braves. Initially Ben Barkin and Edmund Fitzgerald were the leaders of Teams, Inc., but eventually Bud Selig emerged as a key member of this organization and later became the president of "Milwaukee Brewers Baseball Club, Inc."

When the Brewers group became incorporated and applied for a franchise in 1965, there was some overlap of members between the two groups. The Brewers application said owners would not include non-residents of Wisconsin or exceed ten members for the foreseeable future.

The membership of the group would change by the time of the purchase of the Seattle Pilots in 1970. Others who were involved in the 1960s included Ralph Evinrude, Bob Uihlein, Jr., Oscar Mayer, Irwin "Irv" Maier, Duane Bowman, Herbert Kohl, John Murphy, Jack Winter, and Robert Cannon. Like Selig, Fitzgerald, and Barkin, these men were also business executives and highly regarded civic leaders.

Ben Barkin was a nationally known public relations executive who co-founded Milwaukee's Great Circus Parade in 1963. His public relations firm grew to be the largest in Wisconsin. Barkin worked for religious harmony, raising money for Protestant and Catholic causes and the United Jewish Appeal. Barkin, like Selig, was Jewish.

Edmund Fitzgerald was the chairman of the Cutler-Hammer Company, an industrial electrical equipment manufacturer. He gained the nickname "Little Ed," as a way of distinguishing him from his father, also named Edmund Fitzgerald. The elder Fitzgerald was the source of the name of the SS Edmund Fitzgerald, the Great Lakes freighter ship that sank in 1975. The ship was popularized by the Gordon Lightfoot song, "The Wreck of the Edmund Fitzgerald."

Ralph Evinrude was the board chairman at the Outboard Marine Corporation. His father developed the first commercially feasible outboard motor and owned a business called the Elto Outboard Motor Company, which later merged with Johnson Motor Company and became Outboard Marine. Evinrude joined the company after attending college at the University of Wisconsin–Madison and took over after his father passed away.

Bob Uihlein, Jr., became the president of the Schlitz Brewing Company in 1967. The Uihlein family had been running Schlitz since 1875, when Joseph Schlitz drowned. Uihlein also had an avid interest in polo and organized the Milwaukee Polo Club in 1949. In 1952, he purchased 60 acres of land to use for the club's playing fields.

Oscar Mayer was the hot dog magnate, not the actual hot dog. Selig remembers being nervous to meet Mayer and talk to him about becoming a financial stakeholder. Selig said he found Mayer to be a nice and kind man who loved baseball. Selig recalled, "When we were done, he came around his desk, shook my hand and said, 'I'm in. I look forward to being your partner.'"[25]

Irwin "Irv" Maier rose through the ranks to become Board Chairman of the Journal Company (Milwaukee newspapers) in 1968. He was a founding member of the Greater Milwaukee Committee in 1939, a group dedicated to building a baseball stadium, zoo, performing arts center, and museums. All of the proposed projects became reality. Maier was recognized with well over a dozen civic awards in his lifetime.

Duane Bowman made his mark in the dairy industry and was a Madison area civic leader. He had a background in baseball, first as a player and later an executive, with the minor league Madison Blues. Bowman helped launch the Madison Sports Hall of Fame in 1963 and was inducted into the Hall in 1967.

Herbert Kohl had worked as an investor in real estate and the stock market before starting his own investment company. He later became heir, with his brother, to a family-owned chain of grocery and department stores.

John Murphy joined the prospective ownership group as president of the Gateway Transportation Company, a family-owned trucking business in La Crosse.

Jack Winter founded Jack Winter, Inc., an early manufacturer of women's slacks. His company set trends in women's sportswear and operated 100 Clothesworks Stores, a nationwide discount chain.

Robert Cannon was Presiding Judge of the Wisconsin Court of Appeals and had been hired as Legal Advisor to the Major League Baseball Players Association in 1960. In 1965, Cannon was up for the job of Executive Director for the Association, but pulled his name from consideration as he'd need to move away from Milwaukee to take the job. His name was often brought up in the 1960s as a possible baseball commissioner.

The Teams, Inc. group came on board to help boost ticket sales prior to the final Braves season. The hope was that fans might support the notion of a future team in Milwaukee, even if they were bitter about the impending departure of the Braves. The idea worked, but just temporarily.

Three

You're All We've Got Now

When the Milwaukee Braves brought Teams, Inc. on board, the two entities reached an agreement whereby Teams, Inc. would receive a payout based on the number of tickets sold:

> 5 cents a ticket for the first 766,927 tickets sold (number matches previous low attendance mark)
> 25 cents a ticket for tickets sold between 766,927 and 1,000,000
> $1 a ticket for everything sold over 1,000,000

Teams, Inc. went to great lengths in their ticket sales drive, including reselling tickets their organization purchased for Opening Day. Another ticket team worked alongside Teams, Inc. featuring Braves manager Bobby Bragan and players Hank Aaron, Lee Maye, Denny Menke, and Del Crandall (before being traded to the Giants). Former Brave Johnny Logan also worked the phones. The groups teamed up to call former ticket holders—and even went door-to-door in frigid conditions to drum up sales.

Braves President John McHale called Bragan an inspiration and credited him for selling about 300 season tickets.[1] Bragan called the experience rewarding and pointed to Bud Selig's salesmanship as being a huge help in the campaign.[2] Selig sold at least 150 season tickets of his own.

The Braves front office also helped the cause by introducing new initiatives such as ten-game coupon books at a savings over single-game purchases, ten percent discounts on group ticket orders of 25 or more, and a decrease of prices for upper box seats. Another new, attractive feature was the ability of fans to charge tickets through a Braves arrangement with the American Express Company.

The new ideas and sales efforts helped, and the season home opener had the largest attendance of the final Milwaukee Braves season at 33,874. It took until the final series of the year for the Braves to play in front of truly large crowds, but it wasn't at home in County Stadium. They finished up the season in Dodger Stadium before crowds of up to 50,000 in early October.

Ben Barkin of Teams, Inc. let fans know early on that support of the team was tantamount to Milwaukee bringing another franchise to town. He affirmed, "This is a fight. The people of Milwaukee must realize the Braves need to be supported if there's going to be major league baseball in Milwaukee after this year."[3]

Lou Perini had the same viewpoint as Barkin. The former team owner called a boycott of the team a gamble that might ultimately ruin Milwaukee's chances for a future major league team. Perini predicted attendance falling off badly and Milwaukee being hurt in the long run.[4] Requests for support from both Barkin and Perini largely went ignored, as fans stayed away from the ballpark throughout the final season.

Bud Selig later insisted the Braves wouldn't have drawn 6,000 fans on Opening Day without the help of Teams Inc., but admitted the ticket drive didn't work after that due to the antagonism and hostility toward the Braves.[5] The hostility hit not only the Braves in the pocketbook, but also visiting teams and the National League. Paltry crowds for a two-game series with Houston in early May led to the Astros collecting a $633.30 check, while the NL took in just $133.24.

Not only was the attendance lackluster in 1965, there wasn't much evidence that anyone was listening to the games on the radio either. Braves ownership had already moved most of their actual baseball operations to Atlanta and started marketing the team there. This included providing some games on TV and radio. In Wisconsin there wasn't a true broadcast agreement—the games were provided for free to any radio station willing to put them on the air.

The Braves played their final home game in Milwaukee on September 22, 1965. Just 12,577 fans attended the 11-inning game, which was a sad ending to a previously exuberant chapter in Milwaukee's baseball history. Sandy Koufax was on the mound for the Los Angeles Dodgers, but even his star power didn't make a difference with the gate receipts. The game did have some great action, including a grand slam off Koufax by Braves second baseman Frank Bolling.

The small crowd loudly cheered longtime Braves stars Hank Aaron and Eddie Mathews. When Mathews came to the plate for his last at-bat, he was greeted with a two-minute standing ovation. "It shook the heck out of me," he admitted. "It was a typical Milwaukee crowd."[6]

Selig was sitting with Ben Barkin and Ed Fitzgerald of his Teams, Inc. group in the stands that day, discussing how to bring major league baseball back to Milwaukee. An older woman approached Selig and asked if he was indeed Bud Selig. When Selig responded that he was, she pointed her finger at him and uttered, "You're all we've got, Bud, don't fail us."[7]

Selig says what the woman told him is the essence of what baseball means to people: "I've always said to people coming into baseball to always remember that we're lucky; we're the guardians of this sport for this generation. That's a privilege, don't ever forget that."[8]

Just as when Borchert Field was put to rest, fans again sang "Auld Lang Syne" when the game ended. The Braves lost, 7–6, and left for a final ten-game road trip. The team moved all their offices to Atlanta immediately after the season's final game.

Even though the fate of the Braves' location had been decided by ownership and the league, an argument between those factions and others played out in court. The first judicial decision was issued in October 1964, by Circuit Judge Ronold A. Drechsler. He granted a temporary restraining order to keep the Braves from leaving Milwaukee. It was the same day the Braves board of directors voted to seek permission from the National League owners to move to Atlanta.

The Braves' move prompted the State of Wisconsin to file an antitrust suit against the team and the National League, demanding that the Braves stay put unless and until Milwaukee received an expansion team. It took until early March 1966, for the proceedings to begin.

Bud Selig and Ben Barkin didn't waste time waiting for the court case to begin and visited New York in January 1966. Selig said, "We are available, of course, should anyone in baseball want to talk to me."[9] But Selig and Barkin didn't get very far—National League President Warren Giles later claimed he didn't even know they were in town.

Meanwhile, Braves owner Bill Bartholomay continued to maintain that the Braves would open the 1966 baseball season in Atlanta Stadium on April 12, 1966.[10] The players started preparing for the season and reported to spring training with the roster listed only as the "1966 Braves." Yet each player wore a blue cap with a white "A" on the front, and all the pennants flying read "Atlanta."

Manager Bobby Bragan was clearly ready to move on from being booed by Milwaukee fans angry with Bill Bartholomay.[11] Braves fans did get to jeer Bragan in late May when the Braves played in Chicago against the Cubs. Busloads of Wisconsin fans did everything from looking for tomatoes to throw the skipper's way to simply hurling verbal insults. Even Bud Selig and Duane Bowman from his ownership group made the trip to see their former club, and according to reports, did not antagonize Bragan, who quipped, "Me get cheered? I'd probably faint."[12]

The change in location to Atlanta also coincided with a change in team hitting philosophy. Bragan had the Braves hitters working on small-ball skills in spring training, such as bunting, moving runners over, and dealing with force plays. "You sit waiting for the long ball and it never comes,"[13] Bragan asserted.

The Braves featured Felipe Alou, Eddie Mathews, Hank Aaron, Rico Carty, and Joe Torre in the top half of their lineup. Bragan admitted that most of those hitters had never seen a bunt sign in the three years he had managed the team. So they got ready for their home opener on April 12 with the mindset that the hitters would be more than a one-dimensional power outfit.

Torre had a history with Selig going back to their first meeting in 1960. Selig's car dealership had provided a car for Torre's older brother Frank, and then Joe bought a car from Selig. It was the start of a lifelong friendship, like what Selig grew to have with Hank Aaron.

As the new Atlanta Braves worked to get ready for the season, back in Wisconsin the antitrust trial moved through many twists and turns. Defense lawyers opposed a state proposal that testimony from former Milwaukee Brewers minor league owner Bill Veeck should be admitted in the case. Testimony from Veeck in late December came just before a temporary injunction from Wisconsin Judge Elmer Roller ordering the team to play in Milwaukee until a replacement franchise could be obtained. Judge Sam Phillips of Atlanta also issued a temporary injunction calling for the Braves to play games that season in Atlanta.

In his testimony, Veeck said expansion to include a Milwaukee team in the National League before the 1966 season was "feasible and possible." Veeck's opinion was contrary to NL officials saying it couldn't be done. As an example he cited the 1961 expansion of Washington and Los Angeles. The expansion draft happened less than a month after both teams were awarded franchises in late 1960. The 1961 season opened on time without issue.

Bartholomay acknowledged both injunctions from Judges Phillips and Roller in interviews. Yet he maintained, "The Braves fully intend to honor our contract with the Stadium Authority and all our larger obligations to the citizens of Atlanta, of Georgia, and the entire southeast, as the Braves have always honored our agreement with the county of Milwaukee."[14]

Playing games anywhere other than Atlanta Stadium would be a direct breach of the court order, according to Bartholomay, and he added that the Braves might ultimately need to choose which court to obey. Cubs owner Philip K. Wrigley suggested the Braves split their squad and play half their games in each city.[15] His solution, of course, never came to fruition as the Braves started selling tickets in Atlanta only for the upcoming season.

Judge Roller was interested in a quick trial with baseball season rapidly approaching and didn't want a repetition of testimony such as Veeck's. Yet the trial dragged on and on. Roller asked Braves attorney Earl Jinkinson and league counsel Bowie Kuhn to work with their clients to see if the court could settle the dispute with a league representative.[16] Roller already had been advised by the state and defense that his ruling would undoubtedly be appealed in the United States Supreme Court by the losing side.

Kuhn was a member of the New York law firm Willkie Farr & Gallagher and went on to become baseball's commissioner in 1969. At age 42, he was the youngest commissioner in baseball history. As counsel in the Braves case, he railed against Judge Roller's order calling for the National League to expand to 11 teams for the 1966 season. He warned that doing so would cost millions of dollars and bankrupt the Braves.[17] Someone on the state's side drew up a schedule of games for 11 teams and introduced it in court. Kuhn responded by calling the schedule bunk, plain and simple.[18]

Bud Selig had an opportunity to come to the stand and testify that he and nine other Wisconsin businessmen could pull together $4,500,000 for a new major league expansion franchise if the Braves did in fact play games in Atlanta. He said each member of the group would put up $150,000, another $1,500,000 would be obtained via a bank loan, and $1,500,000 would come from revenue.[19] Selig based the revenue figure on 800,000 in attendance, expenses reported by the Braves, and the California Angels' expenditures in 1961 as an expansion franchise.

Braves attorney Earl Jinkinson asked Selig if his group could come up with $11 million—the same amount as the Houston Sports Association spent in buying the Astros. Selig responded that his group was not building an Astrodome, and additional money depended on the player-stocking program offered.[20]

Selig estimated player salaries for a first season at $335,000, and $100,000 each would cover scouting, a farm system, and bonus payments initially.[21] These costs would rise to a maximum of $1,000,000 annually after three years.

Although Selig said California Angels Treasurer Frank Leary, among others with the organization, had been cooperative when Selig visited the previous summer, the defense flew Leary in as a rebuttal witness.[22] The defense wanted him to analyze Selig's prospectus to show a lack of finances and understanding of the issues in acquiring and operating a major league club.

Leary had his doubts that Milwaukee would draw 800,000 as a first-year expansion club, but he agreed with the $335,000 estimate for first-year player salaries.[23] Leary testified that scouting, players' salaries, and farm system costs all increase considerably after the first two or three years. The Angels' cost for player salaries had climbed to $960,000 after six years.

Alleged harassment also was an issue in the trial. County Board Chairman Eugene Grobschmidt was given credit for livening up the court proceedings after he admitted in court that he called owners of the Braves liars.[24] When asked if he had advocated continued harassment of the team and a boycott by fans, he denied the charges. A newspaper article had quoted Grobschmidt as calling Bartholomay and Braves president John McHale "liars."[25] Grobschmidt said, "I don't recall that. I referred to 'em as liars so many times that this is probably one of them."[26]

Grobschmidt and McHale had a contentious history going back to when the news first broke of the Braves' intention to move. The Braves were in sixth place at the time, and to Grobschmidt and others, it looked as though they were throwing games to make it easier to justify relocating. Grobschmidt claimed in televised remarks that the Braves were capable of playing better baseball. McHale threatened to sue Grobschmidt for slander if he didn't retract the statement, but that never happened.[27] "They won ten straight after that,"[28] Grobschmidt stated after being questioned in court about those earlier remarks.

Grobschmidt was a longtime backer of major league baseball in Milwaukee who was very vocal about not allowing the minor league Brewers to inhabit County Stadium. Before the Braves moved to Milwaukee, he commented that $5 million hadn't been shelled out to build a ballpark for a minor league team.[29]

Others were not so kind when it came to supporting baseball in Milwaukee. Hall of Fame member Jackie Robinson came to town to speak in front of 500 guests at the Milwaukee Boy's Club recognition dinner, and he didn't hold back on commenting on the trial and the business of baseball. He said he couldn't see baseball returning to Milwaukee, even if expansion happened.[30]

Robinson expected Milwaukee to be boycotted by baseball team owners, and the city wouldn't get a new team. He said the owners held Milwaukee in the same regard as renegade owner Bill Veeck—they didn't want any part of either one. While Robinson saw the Braves leaving town as morally wrong, he called it a matter of business.[31]

Robinson offered his firsthand opinion of Dodgers owner Walter O'Malley moving the team to Los Angeles from Brooklyn in 1958. He said, "When the Dodgers left Brooklyn, people cursed O'Malley all the way to Los Angeles. He just laughed at them—all the way to the bank. The Braves owners have left Milwaukee for Atlanta, and they will be laughing too."[32]

Robinson predicted changes coming to baseball no matter which way the court ruled in the Braves case. He expected more consideration to be given to fans and cities with major league teams—but not Milwaukee. In his opinion, the trial results would prove nothing, even if the case moved to the Supreme Court.[33]

Finally, after a seven-week trial including some nights and weekends, the court was ready to render a verdict. The day after the Atlanta Braves played their season opener, Judge Roller found the Braves and National League in violation of Wisconsin antitrust law for taking the Braves out of Milwaukee without providing a replacement team. Roller ordered the Braves to return to Milwaukee if the league failed to submit an expansion team plan for 1967 by May 16.[34]

To say William Bartholomay was less than amused by the decision is a vast understatement. "There is as much chance of the Braves playing in Milwaukee this summer as there is the New York Yankees,"[35] he asserted. Bartholomay quickly moved to an appeal filed by league counselor Bowie Kuhn, expressing the idea that state courts did not have jurisdiction over a national sport.

Atlanta's Opening Day featured the Braves in a matchup against the Pittsburgh Pirates, while back in Milwaukee the community braced for its first season without professional baseball since 1883. Some fans traveled to Atlanta to support their team, while others stayed home after finding they wouldn't be receiving better seats than the new local fan base. The Milwaukee travelers weren't needed as 50,671 fans packed Atlanta Stadium for the home opener.

The Pirates beat the Braves, 3–2, in a thrilling 13-inning battle. Braves hurler Tony Cloninger pitched a complete game in a losing effort, giving up homers to Willie Stargell and Jim Pagliaroni. Stargell's blast came on a high breaking ball in the 13th inning, after watching Cloninger record a dozen strikeouts. Joe Torre accounted for both Braves runs by clubbing two homers.

It was a sad ending for the home crowd on an otherwise perfect evening. The crowd fell just 222 short of capacity, and the fans attending enjoyed stellar weather conditions. Recent exhibitions against the New York Yankees were chilly in contrast to the comfortable opening night atmosphere.

Back in Milwaukee, there had been a threat of rain the previous overnight. Workers remained busy at County Stadium, as if they were preparing for the typical excitement and fanfare that a home opener brings. Groundskeepers removed the tarpaulin from the infield, covered as a precaution if rain did arrive. They carried the tarp to the outfield and carefully smoothed over the base paths. Other workers placed green padding on the outfield walls as if they were preparing to protect Henry Aaron from a collision. The stadium would be ready in case its wayward team came home, which of course didn't happen.

The Braves remained in Atlanta, where the team experienced an up-and-down campaign. Manager Bobby Bragan was fired in August and replaced by Billy Hitchcock. Wisconsin baseball fans felt like they had the last laugh after Bragan hit the unemployment line. He had choice words about Milwaukee after the Judge Roller court decision, saying he'd never return even if the court said he had to—not even for all the cheese in Wisconsin.[36]

Atlanta stormed to a 20–8 record in September under Hitchcock. Despite leading the National League in runs scored, they finished with an 85–77 record, good enough for fifth place behind the champion Los Angeles Dodgers. The era of Atlanta baseball had officially begun.

Judge Roller stayed his earlier court order directing the Braves to return to Milwaukee from Atlanta or the NL to provide an expansion franchise. This was pending an appeal to the Wisconsin Supreme Court. Braves' attorney Earl Jinkinson made a motion for a new trial based on 36 separate grounds.

In a short statement to the court, Jinkinson said, "We sincerely believe the court has misinterpreted the decisions of the United States Supreme court and the Wisconsin Supreme Court." Jinkinson had some harsh criticism at the "kooky, nutty idea of the attorney general and his staff that baseball when played in Milwaukee does not violate the antitrust laws but when played outside Wisconsin it does."[37] Jinkinson commented that baseball was an interstate business, thereby making all of baseball outside the jurisdiction of Roller's court.[38] The case was the first to hold baseball in violation of a state anti-trust law.

The court action was far from over, as the Wisconsin decision was appealed to the U.S. Supreme Court. A 4–3 vote went in favor of not reviewing what had been decided in the state of Wisconsin. Atlanta legally had the Braves. Selig and Fitzgerald declined to comment, while Barkin said he was only speaking for himself (not the Brewers group or Teams, Inc.) when he said they must abide by the high court's decision.[39]

If the issue of team location and the antitrust case wasn't complicated enough, that was just the tip of the iceberg. Milwaukee County itself owned the stadium. The county filed a similar lawsuit in Federal court to the state case. They claimed the Braves, the National League, and its clubs were in violation of Wisconsin statutes and federal antitrust laws in their actions to relocate the team.

Bill Veeck again popped up and commented on the situation, saying that baseball could potentially undergo a radical realignment with expansion to Oakland, Seattle, and Buffalo. In his opinion, the Braves should remain in Milwaukee with a sign at County Stadium 200 feet long and 20 feet wide announcing that the team was open under new management.

In the end, no combination of court rulings could keep the Braves in Milwaukee. In early April 1966, Milwaukee County Stadium sat mostly silent for the first time since opening in 1953. Other than what continued to play out in the courts and press, it was a quiet time in Milwaukee baseball history, save for the occasional stadium employee listening to an Atlanta Braves game on a transistor radio.

When the Braves left Milwaukee, this was the first time a franchise move left a major league city without at least one team. After teams in Philadelphia, Boston, New York, and St. Louis left for other locations during the 1950s, at least one franchise remained behind. The so-called "Ford Frick rule" that came about when Commissioner Frick and major league owners loosened rules allowing franchises to relocate in 1952, paving the way for the Braves to move to Milwaukee, came back to make it just as easy for the team to leave town.

For the most part, Milwaukee baseball fans had a hard time getting over the departure of their hometown team. Some went down the path of bitterness and resentment. Even the 1970s/'80s TV show *Happy Days* occasionally referenced the Braves, as the program was set in Milwaukee. In a season 11 episode, avid fan Howard Cunningham sadly says he can't believe the Braves are moving to Atlanta.

Once Bud Selig came to the realization the Braves were gone and there was nothing he could do to bring them back, he turned his attention to the next best thing—purchasing an existing club with the intent of relocating it to Milwaukee—or talking baseball's power brokers into giving the city an expansion club. Selig was in it for the long haul, but unfortunately for him, four long years of countless disappointments were on the horizon.

Selig made his first of several trips to the major league owners meetings in October 1965, where he begged repeatedly for an expansion franchise or to be first in line to purchase an existing club. This particular meeting was held in the Edgewater Beach Hotel in Chicago. When Selig wasn't inside the conference room with the owners, he could often be found loitering in the hotel lobby. "We'd look behind a potted palm, and there would be Buddy,"[40] baseball executive Peter Bavasi joked.

Selig found himself generally not welcome at baseball owners' meetings. Many owners simply referred to him as "that Buddy guy from Milwaukee."[41] American League President Joe Cronin had little time for Selig and once asked him what he was doing at their meeting.[42] Yet it's entirely possible the owners and executives may have listened to Selig had he been lobbying for baseball to place a franchise in any other city other than Milwaukee.

Ironically, one of the hot topics at that first owners meeting Selig attended was who should replace Ford Frick as baseball commissioner. Little did the executives know that the guy they spurned for the remainder of the decade would one day become their commissioner. Another key topic at the meeting was finalizing a $30.6 million contract with NBC covering three years of game broadcasting rights. Not on the table for discussion was any sort of league expansion.

"Baseball didn't want to come back here under any circumstances," Selig said. "We'd go to baseball meetings and we were treated like we had leprosy."[43]

In early December, Selig and three other members of his potential ownership group flew to Miami Beach, Florida, on a mission to speak with baseball's owners about expansion. Selig was joined by Edmund Fitzgerald, Duane Bowman, and Robert Uihlein, Jr. Selig, Bowman, and Fitzgerald were still minority owners in the Braves. They started off with a two-hour session with National League team owners.

President Warren Giles of the NL believed the group didn't have the financial resources needed to field an expansion club—in his mind, $8 to $10 million. Giles felt there was no animosity toward the group, but one unidentified owner said someone should tell the group the facts about operating a baseball club.[44]

The next day, AL President Joe Cronin again met them with a flat-out refusal, later commenting that expansion in 1966 was absolutely impossible. While he did find the Milwaukee contingent to be good people overall, he also chuckled and said the league would take their application under advisement. The league basically took everything under advisement, according to Cronin.[45]

Owners cited the lack of administrative personnel, players, and a farm system in refusing expansion.[46] A formal application from Dallas-Fort Worth for an expansion club was also rejected for the same reasons. The Dallas-Fort Worth group also dated their application November 1— too late for formal consideration. Commissioner William Eckert gave a final assessment of possible expansion by saying it might be years, not months, before additional clubs were added.[47]

Selig's group disagreed with Eckert, Cronin, and Giles and spoke of their baseball potential, explaining that they felt they had the financial stability to own and operate a major league franchise.[48] Selig had $4.5 million available because the ten businessmen in his group promised to put up $150,000 apiece and they also had a $1.5 million loan commitment from two Milwaukee concessionaire companies. The Joseph Schlitz Brewing Company had agreed with the group on radio and television rights, but numbers weren't provided.

Bud Selig, shown here in 1975, spent five years leading the fight to bring major league baseball back to Milwaukee (National Baseball Hall of Fame Library, Cooperstown, New York).

A comparison that Selig often drew between his group and previous expansion clubs was having a stadium lease and the television/radio rights. He pointed to the expansion franchises of 1961 and 1962 as carrying only the necessary financial commitments initially.[49]

Selig remained upbeat after the meeting and acknowledged to reporters that everyone was polite and attentive.[50] Selig's mood changed when he was asked if he attended the meeting because he expected the request for a franchise would be denied, thereby strengthening the antitrust suits the state and county had against the Braves and major league baseball. He finished by saying his group was far from discouraged and they would meet to assess everything that happened in Florida.[51] "I'm an incurable optimist," Selig said. We're going to keep plugging for a franchise. We're all hopeful something will happen in the future."[52]

An article appeared in *The Sporting News* on December 18, 1965, in which Selig described how Milwaukee had been rejected for a new club. While the other businessmen in Milwaukee Brewers, Inc. were highly regarded in the community, it was becoming clear that Selig was the leader and mouthpiece for the group. He did the bulk of presenting arguments to baseball executives and consistently made himself available to the media for comments.

Selig's efforts to bring major league baseball back to Milwaukee were honored at the annual Diamond Dinner of baseball writers at the Pfister Hotel on January 23, 1966. A record crowd of 875 saw Selig receive the Sam Levy Award, named for the late writer of the *Milwaukee Journal*. A long list of speakers highlighted the evening, including Bob Uecker, Johnny Logan, Edmund Fitzgerald, and Chicago White Sox owner Arthur Allyn.

For Allyn, it was an opportunity to state an opinion and begin to make amends for being responsible for the Braves leaving town. Allyn emphasized his belief that baseball is both a monopoly and a business, and as such, should be subject to antitrust laws. In Allyn's mind, any monopoly such as baseball had a deep responsibility to its fans, and the fans in Milwaukee shouldn't be deprived of major league baseball.[53]

Allyn said the predicament in Milwaukee was entirely his fault. The Braves ownership group headed by William Bartholomay and Thomas Reynolds previously held 46 percent of the White Sox. Allyn said, "I, like a fool, bought out the share and made it possible for them to come up here and move your club to Atlanta." He continued, "I'm sure that if I could get the opportunity again I'll never let them out of my grasp."[54]

The gala evening gave fans hope that baseball would return to Milwaukee, but it wasn't quite enough for fans like Selig to get over missing their beloved Braves. An often-told story by Selig involves the first Atlanta Braves home game radio broadcast. Selig was driving and pulled off to a gas station to listen to the beginning of the game. "I tuned in to the legendary Bob Prince out of Pittsburgh," Selig remembered, "and he opened by saying, 'Greetings from Atlanta's Fulton County Stadium. We're a long ways from Milwaukee, Wisconsin.'"[55]

At that point, Selig couldn't hold in his sadness and began to cry uncontrollably. One of the gas station attendants came over to check if he was all right. While the encounter with the female fan at the final Braves home game who begged him to bring baseball back to Milwaukee was a driving force, this moment also haunted and pushed Selig through the next few years.

Selig found another ally at the 14th annual Diamond Dinner of baseball writers in January 1967. Winter weather kept *The Sporting News* Editor and Publisher C. C. Johnson Spink from attending the dinner, but his speech was delivered by Bob Inserra, manager of the publication's Chicago office. A transcript was published in the February 4, 1967, edition in Spink's "We Believe" editorial column.

The speech had a play on "We Believe" with a list of things believed by Spinks concerning the transfer of the Braves to Atlanta. He believed the sale of the team to William Bartholomay should never have happened, and a group of Milwaukee residents should have had the first crack at buying the franchise. Other beliefs were that the new owners had the legal right to relocate the team, but major league baseball did not have the right to leave Milwaukee without a team.

Selig responded with a short letter to the editor, published in the April 1 edition. He said, in part, "I feel you have made a significant contribution in creating a new feeling of working in a constructive and cooperative manner that will facilitate the securing of a major league baseball club in Milwaukee."[56]

With local backing from other civic leaders and people with a national voice such as Spink, Selig kept plugging along. He was willing to try anything to bring a new franchise to town, so his group kept their application with major league baseball active throughout the remainder of the 1960s.

One new and unique idea was to bring a single major league game to Milwaukee—even if it wasn't a new local team and was a seemingly meaningless exhibition game. The Brewers group talked Chicago White Sox officials into holding a game against the Minnesota Twins at County Stadium on July 24, 1967, a Monday night. It wasn't the greatest timing for either team, as Chicago had a doubleheader in Kansas City the day before, and Minnesota was traveling between Anaheim and New York.

The seeds for a contest between the two clubs were planted the previous season with a Class A game at County Stadium between their affiliates. The Appleton Foxes and Wisconsin Rapids played a regular season game on August 27, 1966, with permission from the Midwest League. A crowd of 4,532 saw the game originally scheduled for Wisconsin Rapids. While this was 3,000 more than a typical home game, attendance fell below expectations. The two teams shared expenses and gate receipts.

Selig's group had interest only in hosting minor league teams—not owning them, despite a report to the contrary by *New York Post* columnist Milton Gross. He wrote that Selig had been in New York on July 29 to make arrangements for ownership of a Triple A club, putting his group at the forefront for a major league expansion club in 1969 or 1970. Selig said the story held no merit, and his group never had a thought about owning a minor league team. He had been in New York but denied speaking to anyone about baseball matters.[57]

By the next spring, the Brewers group got ready to host the Twins/White Sox game on a much higher level of public interest. Due to early clamoring for tickets to the exhibition, tickets went on sale in mid–May, three weeks ahead of schedule. Braves season ticket holders from 1964 and 1965 were allowed an early opportunity to purchase tickets in their previously reserved seat locations. A downtown ticket sales outlet was opened in a card shop a week later due to initial sales being so brisk.

Selig was exuberant over the interest in the game and told reporters that phone calls and letters had come in from all points of the state.[58] The response was a far cry from the Braves' lame duck season, when Selig himself had to call season ticket holders to get them to renew. Even big league ticket prices of $3.50 for box seats and $4.50 for mezzanine boxes didn't deter fans from snatching up tickets.

County Stadium remained ready for game action on a day's notice. Roughly $200,000 had been spent on an improvement program since the final Braves game, according to stadium manager Bill Anderson.[59] The county park commission asked later in the summer for money to be placed in the county board's budget to start replacing wooden seats in the stadium with plastic or fiberglass.

It was money well spent in the minds of the Milwaukee Brewers, Inc. group, as they predicted an expansion team would be theirs by 1970. Edmund Fitzgerald believed that as long as the group remained baseball-conscious and kept in the public eye, they had a legitimate shot at a team. Fitzgerald pointed to Selig's spring training trip to Florida as making a positive impact on the group's efforts.[60] Selig made the rounds and spoke to as many executives as would listen. The discussions led to the Twins/White Sox exhibition game being scheduled. This put the city of Milwaukee and the potential ownership group back in the line of sight of major league baseball's top brass.

Two men at the top of the pack, Commissioner William Eckert and AL President Joe Cronin, accepted invitations to the game. The Brewers group made the announcement of their special visitors at a luncheon on

June 23 and were proud to note advance ticket sales of 20,000 for the exhibition. Besides that game, they also had an opportunity to promote an upcoming international soccer match at County Stadium.

White Sox general manager Ed Short and business manager Rudie Schaffer represented their club at the luncheon. Short said the White Sox didn't need to promote the game because Milwaukee had long before proven itself as a major league city. In another show of friendship between the Sox and Brewers group, Short restated his franchise's opinion that Milwaukee should land the next expansion club.[61]

The largest crowd ever to attend a game in County Stadium watched the White Sox beat the Twins, 2–1. The ballpark officially held 43,768 — yet 51,144 came through the turnstiles and proved Wisconsin still had a strong baseball fan base. Over 3,000 spectators watched from the outfield, where they were roped in. The largest paid crowd ever to see a sporting event there was treated to an impressive fireworks display after the game.

Instead of cheering for Braves players like Hank Aaron, Warren Spahn, Johnny Logan, and Eddie Mathews, fans were happy just to see former Braves reliever Don McMahon in a White Sox uniform. After nearly two years, they were happy to see major league baseball, period. The Brewers ownership was in turn starting to feel the vibe from fans turning from bitterness to disappointment and disillusionment over not having a team of their own.

The two important guests of the Brewers group were able to see firsthand that Milwaukee was still a viable major league baseball city. Judge Robert C. Cannon of the Brewers group met Cronin and Eckert at the airport. They had attended Hall of Fame induction ceremonies at Cooperstown, New York, before flying to Milwaukee for the exhibition game.

Well over 5,000 fans were turned away because of the already oversized crowd.[62] This contributed to a traffic backup and travel delays to the stadium for Cannon, Cronin and Eckert. "An impressive sight," Eckert said.[63]

Twins owner Calvin Griffith was equally impressed and told the press that he would propose a franchise for Milwaukee at the summer owners meeting. He also said he'd cast a vote in favor of a move by the Kansas City Athletics to Milwaukee if owner Charlie Finley ever brought up the subject. When asked if baseball's owners could ignore such a large turnout, Griffith stated, "Hell no. I thought 20,000 to 25,000 would be a hell of a crowd."[64]

Commissioner William Eckert did give the owners a blueprint for expansion, but he noted there wasn't a sense of urgency to make it happen earlier than 1970. While Eckert mentioned being impressed by the crowd in Milwaukee and the condition of the ballpark, he said he wouldn't give Milwaukee preferential treatment if expansion did happen. Cronin chimed in with congratulations to Milwaukee for an impressive turnout and stated it would be hard not to consider the city seriously in expansion talks.[65] It was anyone's best guess as to when these talks might be.

Four

A Team That Didn't Exist

Expansion wasn't the only subject on the minds of the Milwaukee Brewers group. Vice president Edmund Fitzgerald hoped that besides landing a pro baseball team, the group would also acquire the rights to basketball, hockey, and soccer franchises. He noted that it could be a real pot of gold if just one organization ran all the ticket sales and promotions for multiple teams in Milwaukee. Fitzgerald said he found it strange that with 112 to 115 professional sports teams, Milwaukee didn't have a team of its own.[1]

Despite applying for a franchise in the United Soccer Association, Milwaukee would not have a pro team until the Wave arrived in 1984 to join the American Indoor Soccer Association. The Milwaukee Admirals (originally Wings) joined the American Hockey League in 1970, but they were not owned by the Brewers group.

Bud Selig told the press to expect the Brewers group to be very active in the future.[2] They made plans to attend the World Series and the following year's All-Star Game, while continuing to plead their case with baseball officials. It was too late in the season to plan another exhibition, so the group worked to pay the Twins and White Sox an estimated $30,000 each from the gate receipts. As sponsors of the game, the Brewers group took an estimated $25,000 to help pay expenses the group put toward the game.

Milwaukee Brewers Baseball Club, Inc. was aptly named, especially in the wake of missing out on bringing other professional sports to the city. The group members pressed on with the goal of landing just an expansion baseball team, although for a brief moment around the time of the successful exhibition, it looked as though an existing team might be moving to town.

The Sporting News published a story two days before the Twins/White

Sox exhibition, detailing the offer Kansas City owner Charlie Finley pitched to Milwaukee County Executive John Doyne to move his team. *The Sporting News* declined to name its sources for this information, and Doyne later denied having any conversation with Finley about such a move.[3]

According to the unnamed sources, Finley would pay no rental on the lease of County Stadium until attendance hit 900,000. The second year, the mark would drop to 750,000 and continue to slide downward over the life of the lease. Finley would also receive concession profits, but the county would keep monies from parking.[4] Schlitz Brewing Company also had a hand in luring the A's as they offered a $500,000 TV contract.

Finley had reportedly given up on trying to move the Athletics to Oakland because he couldn't land a local television or radio contract. Finley reportedly had been willing to sell 49 percent of his club's stock to the Milwaukee group.[5] The price tag was well within range as Finley valued the A's at $8,000,000. The sticking point in making a deal turned out to be absentee ownership. Selig's group wanted 51 percent of the stock, and that caused Finley to drop the negotiations.

Even if the sides reached agreement, it didn't appear that Finley had the seven votes from his fellow owners to approve a franchise switch. The Chicago White Sox were named in *The Sporting News* as a solid "yes" vote, and this enraged owner Arthur Allyn, who said he was not on Finley's side.[6]

As quickly as the potential move to Milwaukee surfaced as a story, another report came to light about potential TV and radio contracts in San Francisco for Finley's team. He looked across the bay from Oakland to sign a three-year deal for $1 million for 81 television games each year and $1 million for all radio broadcasts over the three years.

The American League moved quickly to shut down the story about the A's relocating. President Joe Cronin said the subject would not be discussed at the early August league meeting. He called it not fair to the players and fans to talk about moving a franchise during the season.[7]

Selig denied that anyone from his group had contact with Finley. In speaking with *The Sporting News*, Selig reminded everyone that his ownership group preferred to land an expansion franchise with full local ownership.[8]

One of the men who orchestrated the Braves move to Atlanta agreed about a Milwaukee team needing local ownership. Former Braves president John McHale had since been working as an aide to Commissioner Eckert. In interviews held at the August owners meeting, McHale called himself an expansion-minded person and hoped to see a blueprint drawn up for additional teams. He had been in communication with Selig and Fitzgerald and acknowledged being in favor of baseball in Milwaukee.[9]

Things were quiet after the owners meeting until mid–September, when Selig announced that his group had contracted with the Chicago Bulls of the National Basketball Association to hold three games at the Milwaukee Arena.[10] One would be an exhibition with the Boston Celtics just prior to the regular season, and the other two would be regular league games.

County officials had gotten on board with the efforts to bring pro teams permanently to Milwaukee and floated the idea of building a modern sports arena next to County Stadium. The downtown Milwaukee Arena had been built in 1950 and was still in good shape, but had a schedule loaded with non-sports events. A new arena would solve the issue, according to county officials.

Selig's childhood friend, Herb Kohl, led the basketball venture. Even though the Brewers group expressed delight in organizing the Bulls games, they had yet to formally apply for a pro basketball franchise.[11] The NBA had added two cities in the previous three seasons and remained committed to further expansion by 1970.

Milwaukee did get its expansion club, but it was awarded to the Milwaukee Professional Sports and Services, Inc. ownership group. Wesley Pavalon and Marvin Fishman led the group that brought pro basketball back to Milwaukee after a 13-year absence. The contest-named Bucks played their first game in October 1968. Kohl did eventually get his team when he bought the Bucks in the mid–1980s in an effort to block anyone else from acquiring the team and moving it out of Milwaukee—a familiar scenario to local sports fans.

Selig focused on baseball rather than basketball when he spoke at a Rotary Club luncheon in late September. He told the local crowd of 300 that he didn't agree with the theory that Milwaukee was an inferior television market. According to Selig, rights fee possibilities were better than those offered in Washington, Pittsburgh, Kansas City, Cincinnati, and St. Louis.[12]

Selig denounced critics who called Milwaukee a cheap town. The true test for Selig had been the Twins/White Sox exhibition, where concessions sold at a record level. The Brewers group used a scale that averaged seating and concession prices across major league baseball in determining what to charge fans. The Brewers group claimed not to have heard a negative word about the exhibition game, specifically the pricing.[13]

Another argument Selig brought up was the claim about Milwaukee not supporting a losing team. He cited the Pirates dropping from 1,700,000 fans in their pennant-winning year of 1960 to an attendance of 759,000 four years later. The Red Sox had a similar high number as contenders but fell to 652,000 as a losing team. Selig said it proved that no matter the city, everybody loved a winner.[14]

Even though some teams such as the Pirates and Red Sox had decreased attendance, in 1966 25,182,209 fans attended major league baseball games—an all-time record. Selig said, "Baseball is a very lively corpse, indeed. I, for one, would welcome this so-called moribund activity back to Milwaukee with great excitement."[15] Selig reiterated his group's stance of wanting to secure an expansion team and not being interested in stealing another city's franchise. He believed the key was to intensify efforts and present a saleable package to baseball that kept the Brewers ahead of the competition.[16]

Within a month, Selig went from a passionate presentation to not having a comment for reporters.[17] The Brewers had franchise applications in front of both leagues but lost out on an American League franchise. The AL allowed Charlie Finley to move his Athletics to Oakland from Kansas City. Finley had purchased a controlling interest in the Kansas City Athletics in 1960, and in similar fashion to when the Braves were sold, started looking to relocate the team right away. After seven years, Finley finally got his wish, and the A's were headed to Oakland.

As a result, the league voted to expand to Seattle and Kansas City, filling the void in the city left by the Athletics' departure. It wasn't what the owners had planned in the first place. AL President Joe Cronin met with a Kansas City delegation to break the bad news about the loss of the Athletics. Senator Stuart Symington (D–Mo) blew up and frantically debated Cronin through a long conference.[18]

Symington threatened to have baseball's antitrust exemption revoked, so the owners put their heads together and offered expansion to Kansas City and Seattle in 1971. This wasn't good enough for Symington who didn't think Kansas City should wait that long for the Royals to begin playing. The owners responded by moving the expansion up to 1969.

Symington predicted, "Oakland will find it's the luckiest city in world since Hiroshima."[19] Symington also called Finley one of the most disreputable characters ever to enter the American sports scene.[20]

As for the city of Seattle, owners were licking their collective chops over placing a team in the Pacific Northwest. Seattle had been experiencing steady population growth for 30 years, hosted the 1962 World's Fair,

Four. A Team That Didn't Exist

and had a long and rich aviation history. The Museum of Flight was established in 1965 to rave reviews and a steady stream of visitors. Seattle had long been associated with air travel, going back to 1910, when William Boeing purchased Heath's shipyard on the Duwamish River. It became Boeing's first airplane factory and led him to incorporate his company a few years later, just before the U.S. entered World War I.

Major league baseball had one condition for Seattle: King County was required to construct a domed stadium within three years. In the meantime, the new team wouldn't have a choice but to play home games in the sorely out-of-date Sicks' Stadium, a minor league complex.

Max Soriano and his brother Dewey initially led the franchise ownership, Pacific Northwest Sports, Inc. On the surface, it looked like nothing could go wrong in the third-largest metropolitan area on the West Coast. The Cleveland Indians had even flirted briefly with the idea of relocating to Seattle in 1964.

"I was happy as heck," said Dewey Soriano." You don't sleep very much, I'll tell you that, because you want to get going and you want to get players that can really help your club."[21]

An outcome of the two teams joining the sport was a reorganization of each league. The leagues split into two divisions—East and West. It was decided that the two divisional winners would meet in a five-game playoff after the regular season to determine who would move on to play in the World Series.

It came out later that Milwaukee was never under serious consideration by the AL for a team when Seattle and Kansas City were awarded franchises.[22] White Sox owner Arthur Allyn and Twins owner Calvin Griffith reportedly backed Selig to no avail.[23] Rep. Henry Reuss, D–Wi, also voiced support as he wired Commissioner Eckert prior to the meeting and demanded expansion to 24 MLB teams, including Milwaukee. Reuss pointed to higher nationwide population to support and stock four new teams with players.[24]

Reuss was onto something in the possibility of further expansion, as a lot of money could be reaped by adding more clubs. The 20 teams in 1968 received about $300,000 each from television revenue. With a new three-year NBC Game of the Week contract in 1969, the 24 teams would receive roughly $400,000 each.

With expansion, the new AL teams had a jump on drafting players first. It was thought that the National League might respond by considering expansion at their November meeting. The Brewers group sent a telegram to NL President Warren Giles and requested a chance to present their case. They followed up by mailing a packet with material supporting their application and request to the league office, as well as sending telegrams to Commissioner Eckert and all NL owners.

The group clearly needed to be proactive with swift action, as Dallas-Fort Worth appeared to be the main threat to Milwaukee. They had a proposal for a new stadium on the table that could turn the tide their way. San Diego appeared high on the list with a new $28 million stadium but didn't have much in the way of radio/TV prospects.

The Brewers group kept plugging along on all fronts while they waited for the NL meeting. They negotiated with Arthur Allyn to have nine regular season "home games" and an exhibition game during the 1968 season at County Stadium. It would be the first time since 1956 that a team would play regular season games in a city other than its home. The Brooklyn Dodgers played a handful of NL games that year in Jersey City, NJ.

Both sides would benefit from this distinctive agreement. The Brewers group would continue to host baseball in a stadium that was only being used for two "home" Green Bay Packers games each season and a handful of other events. The White Sox would most likely have better attendance than at their real home. The team had its 17th consecutive winning season in 1967, but attendance at Comiskey Park remained under one million fans for the second straight year.

Allyn reminded fans that he had no plans to move his team to Milwaukee, while Selig stated that a ten-game schedule would not interfere with a new franchise, should one be granted.[25] All of the games were planned as night contests. The AL approved the proposal without much opposition. Executives from New York and Detroit initially had concerns about alienating fans in Chicago, but voted for Allyn as a courtesy. The only vote against came from Baltimore's ownership, but Allyn claimed they were upset with him about another matter.[26]

The games gave Selig's group a welcome diversion as news came back from the NL that no representative from a city seeking a franchise would be welcome at their November meeting. When the owners met in Chicago, they chided the American League for allegedly breaking the rules and discussing league expansion on their own in October.[27] President Warren Giles said, however, the NL would not contest the AL's expansion plans to Seattle and Kansas City.[28] He did comment that rules called for a joint meeting between leagues before any commitment or action be taken to expand.[29]

Giles called the NL meeting an informal preparation for a joint meeting between leagues in Mexico City on November 30. No vote or action

Four. A Team That Didn't Exist

was taken for NL expansion at the meeting, but Giles remarked that there was no sentiment for expansion, and he believed the owners were prepared to go into the joint meeting and talk intelligently.

The Brewers group expected to be invited to attend the MLB meeting in Mexico City at the end of the month. In the meantime, they fielded calls from people interested in tickets for the slate of 1968 games. They announced that the White Sox would play the Cubs in an exhibition game on April 6 to kick off the Milwaukee season.[30]

As the Mexico City meetings got closer, it started to become apparent that expansion wasn't in the cards. When news hit the papers, it wasn't surprising that the league had tabled the discussion for a later date. The NL thanked the AL for a good discussion centering on its expansion plans and had a harmonious meeting, according to Commissioner Eckert.[31] Each city seeking a new franchise had a representative on hand, but this wound up being strictly for informational talks. None were allowed to make a formal presentation to the owners.

As a weary 1967 wound down, the Brewers group could at least celebrate a good response to the scheduled White Sox games. Over 2,000 season tickets were sold in the first two weeks. Single games would go on sale in the New Year. Informal polling found that 50 percent of the season-ticket buyers were not season-ticketholders when the Braves were in town, but the price for a ten-game schedule was much less. Ticket prices were again lining up with the major league average, with mezzanine box seats the most expensive at $4.50 each.

By the time the 15th annual Diamond Dinner rolled around in late January, season-ticket sales were closing in on 7,000 with no signs of slowing down. Selig and Fitzgerald both expressed optimism that Milwaukee might have a team by 1969.[32] A capacity crowd of 650 gathered to honor a team that didn't exist for the third year in a row.

Richard H. O'Connell, GM of the Boston Red Sox, dropped a bombshell before the dinner. He revealed that Kansas City Athletics owner Charlie Finley had planned two years prior to propose playing one-third of his 81 home games in Milwaukee.[33] Finley spoke to each AL owner on an individual basis but never brought it up officially in a meeting. O'Connell thought it would have been a good idea on an emotional basis for the city with no team.[34]

Fitzgerald and Selig were featured speakers that evening and kept the crowd engaged. Fitzgerald talked about widening an already large circle of friends in baseball throughout 1968.[35] Selig announced that season-ticket sales for the White Sox games would continue until March 1 and that everyone had a stake in the future of a full-time Milwaukee team. It was a critical time in the city's sports history, in Selig's mind, and he believed further proof would improve their chances as a future MLB city.[36]

Some of the proof came on March 7 when the Brewers sold a ticket to their 10,000th customer, just three days after single game tickets went on sale. There was a bit of a delay in starting the single game offerings due to the overwhelming response for season tickets. The Brewers and White Sox held a celebration at the County Stadium ticket office, complete with a cake with "10,000" on the side.

The milestone had significance for the White Sox. Total sales for the ten games had reached 120,000. In Chicago, sales had reached 300,000 tickets for a total of $1 million. The record sale had been close to $1.5 million in 1960, and the White Sox figured it would be surpassed due to the renewed interest in the team and the partnership with Milwaukee.

Within two weeks of the celebration, Selig traveled to Miami, where the NL's three-man expansion committee held a meeting. They didn't make a recommendation to the league, but instead decided to prepare a report to present to the league at a special meeting scheduled for April.[37]

The Brewers ushered in the 1968 season with an open house at County Stadium the Sunday prior to the Sox/Cubs exhibition. An estimated crowd of 5,000 came out to kick off "Take Me Out to the Ball Game" week in Wisconsin. Even a chilly day after an early-morning rain didn't dampen spirits. Fans eagerly scooped up an additional 1,800 tickets for the exhibition game, plus 600 more season tickets were sold for all ten White Sox games.

The fans were able to go on a guided tour that took them behind the scenes to the press box, dugouts, home clubhouse, bullpen, and scoreboard. While much of the day centered on the stadium, former players Harvey Kuenn and Johnny Logan were on hand to sign autographs and take photos with fans.

Conditions were even worse when the White Sox and Cubs took the field on April 6. The temperature topped out at 46 degrees with a brisk, 17-mile-an-hour wind that blew in off Lake Michigan, knocking the chill index to between 30 and 35 for much of the afternoon. A crowd of 20,759 diehards turned out and stayed through ten innings before the White Sox claimed a 3–2 victory.

Selig voiced satisfaction with the turnout on such a frigid day.[38] The goal was 30,000, but walk-up sales were slow due to the weather. Everyone hoped for a warmer spring day on May 15, when the White Sox were scheduled to play the California Angels.

Four. A Team That Didn't Exist 65

While the Brewers worked on ticket sales for that game, they received some encouraging news. Judge Robert C. Cannon of the Brewers group spent time in Chicago, where NL owners met in late April. They ultimately decided expansion could happen in 1969—with one catch—the owners needed unanimous agreement on two cities.[39]

At that point there were five cities seeking a franchise, but only Milwaukee and San Diego had ballparks that were deemed ready for major league games. In Cannon's opinion, that meant Milwaukee was halfway home to obtaining a team.[40] Selig refused comment until the Brewers group could organize while they waited for the next meeting of NL owners.[41]

Selig did have an opportunity to comment on the fight to bring baseball back to Milwaukee when he was honored at the Variety Club luncheon on April 24. He was crowned "King for a Day" and received a plaque for his efforts. Civic leaders voiced their approval of Selig's work, and former Braves shortstop Johnny Logan saluted him with a poem.

Selig said, "I wouldn't want anyone to think this has been a one-man effort. I feel some embarrassment, lest anyone have the mistaken idea that I've been doing this all alone." He added, "It has been an up-and-down experience, frustrating in some cases and fraught with disappointments."[42]

Yet another huge disappointment would soon land in Selig's lap, but before that happened, he enjoyed another decent turnout at County Stadium for the White Sox/Angels game. Weather again kept the crowd down below the goal of 30,000 fans, as 23,510 came through the gates on a Wednesday evening. Tornado warnings and expected rain hurt walk-up sales, but the total still doubled the largest Chicago home game attendance so far that season—11,546.

Those who saw the game were able to witness the first AL regular season game in Milwaukee since the city's brief 1901 franchise. Others were able to watch the game on TV as a local station had an agreement to carry 127 White Sox games, including all of those at County Stadium.

Excitement from the game subsided as the Brewers group anxiously awaited the NL owners' meeting. San Diego appeared certain to receive a franchise because they had a sparkling new stadium and tycoon C. Arnholt Smith sitting on a diverse mountain of assets that the other applicants couldn't match.

Walter O'Malley of the Los Angeles Dodgers backed San Diego and pushed for the other franchise to be further east than Dallas-Fort Worth.[43] O'Malley's opinions and influence carried a lot of weight at meetings, and the Brewers believed he would lobby for their group due to his partnership with Schlitz Brewing, specifically group member Robert Uiehlein.[44]

The Union Oil Company dumped sponsorship of Dodgers games, and O'Malley had no choice but to return millions of dollars of advance payments. Uiehlein and Schlitz came to O'Malley's rescue. Schlitz also had sponsorship deals with the Houston Astros, San Francisco Giants, and Chicago Cubs. Judge Roy Hofheinz of Houston appeared ready to vote any team into the league other than Dallas-Fort Worth because he didn't want another team cutting into his radio/TV revenues, the richest in baseball at the time.[45] The Schlitz sponsorship could potentially send his vote Milwaukee's way.

Not every team owner had been jumping for joy over the possibility of expansion. Bob Carpenter of Philadelphia had been anti–Milwaukee because he didn't care for the lengthy court proceedings when the Braves left town.[46] However, O'Malley spoke to him the previous month at the meeting that brought a unanimous vote for 12 teams.[47]

Philip K. Wrigley of the Cubs commented that Carpenter had been the most vocal against expansion, but he wasn't the only NL owner not ready to go all-in on adding teams. Wrigley didn't wholeheartedly favor expansion but believed it was inevitable. His biggest concern centered on how leagues would be aligned with expansion and the possibility of watered-down rivalries.[48]

The meeting had been scheduled for May 22 in St. Louis but was switched to Chicago the following week, when the AL owners also had a meeting there. The *Milwaukee Sentinel* reported that the city's baseball fate was on the line.[49] The paper obtained a copy of a brochure created by Selig's group that was titled "The Milwaukee Market—Ready Now for Major League Baseball." It had been distributed to National League owners a couple of weeks ahead of the meeting and served to compare the cities vying for a new team.

National League president Warren Giles later confessed that the voting process over expansion cities had been lengthy and took at least 18 ballots before a unanimous agreement was reached.[50] After five hours of deliberation, the ten owners had a decision and awarded San Diego and Montreal franchises. Giles said, "All five cities bidding made excellent representations." He added, "If we're going to expand, let's really spread it out."[51]

The owners agreed it was important not to add teams in the same general section of the country, and as a result with the addition of Montreal, baseball would be an international sport for the first time.[52] The choice had been unexpected, as many pointed to political pressure from New York, Texas, and Wisconsin. Montreal also had been without a baseball team since 1960, when it was a farm affiliate for the Brooklyn Dodgers.

Montreal received unanimous backing first according to the owners, and some stated that it was not a compromise to keep out Dallas-Fort Worth or Milwaukee.[53] The view was that Montreal had a brighter long-term future than the other applicants. While the city did not have a big league park, it could build a domed stadium without needing a municipal vote.

Judge Robert Cannon joined Bud Selig as representatives for Milwaukee, and Cannon admitted being stunned over Montreal being selected. He felt that baseball should take care of its own cities in the states before expanding to a foreign city. Cannon said, "Had the two Texas cities, or even Buffalo got the spot we'd have no hard feelings. But we just can't accept this decision on Montreal."[54]

When questioned about why Milwaukee wasn't chosen, Giles responded succinctly that the city was only 85–90 miles away from two major league clubs in Chicago. Giles had stated the need to study expansion for a minimum of three years at the Mexico City meeting. He had talked about at least getting some sort of timeline in place for expansion. Somewhere in the intervening four months, Giles completely changed his mind. He felt the long-term plans the owners and expansion committee put in place were solid.[55]

Selig was again crushed by baseball's owners when Giles stepped to a microphone to announce the new franchises in San Diego and Montreal. He swore Giles was going to say Milwaukee when the "M" formed on his mouth.[56] Selig had no idea what the Brewers might do next, as the group had put all of its efforts toward expansion. He could only console himself in the Brewers' resiliency and having youth on his side.

Reactions from Milwaukee residents and politicians ran the gamut from apathy to bitterness. A general sense of lost respect for baseball hovered over the city. Milwaukee County board chairman Eugene Grobschmidt had been a critic of the Braves move to Atlanta, and he didn't hold back on offering his opinion that Montreal should not have been given a franchise. He also thought the only way to get a franchise back to Milwaukee would be to steal a team from another city.[57]

Lamar Hunt and Tommy Mercer of the Dallas-Fort Worth group also left the meeting dejected, but vowed not to give up. Mercer said they would look at other ways to get into big league baseball, which led reporters to speculate that the foundering Cleveland Indians might want to look for a new home in Dallas-Fort Worth or Milwaukee.[58]

Commissioner Bowie Kuhn commented a year later that Milwaukee was just outcompeted in their attempt at gaining an expansion team. Kuhn called Milwaukee a good major league city but felt the timing was wrong. Kuhn added that he couldn't see a scenario where additional expansion would be possible, and he refused to give any public advice to cities seeking purchase of an existing club.[59]

As June rolled around and the Brewers planned their next move, reports again surfaced that Arthur Allyn had been considering a move of the White Sox to Milwaukee. Allyn again scoffed at the suggestion, and AL president Joe Cronin stepped in to squelch the rumors.[60] Selig told sports editor Lloyd Larson of the *Milwaukee Sentinel* that the Brewers would not be a party to luring an established club away from another city.

Selig said, "We will go after an established franchise only if it becomes crystal clear the owners want to dispose of it and the city where it is located no longer is interested in keeping it there."[61]

Larson also interviewed Edmund Fitzgerald and surmised that the two men didn't see the time and effort devoted toward the franchise bid as a failure. Fitzgerald felt gains had been made in the previous two years, and they actually had 80 percent support from owners in both leagues.[62] Selig and Fitzgerald vowed not to give up and approached the future with confidence.

The immediate future involved the continued schedule of White Sox games at County Stadium. While the team didn't play well and managed a dismal 1–8 regular season record at their home away from home, the real results were at the gate. The crowd sizes ranged between 18,748 and 42,808—an average of 29,366 per game. But the total numbers told the true story—246,478 fans saw those nine games. The attendance for the exhibition game in poor conditions also was encouraging at 20,759 fans. In 58 Comiskey Park games, the total attendance was 539,478—or 9,301 fans per game.

Selig even brought back the Beer Barrel Man logo from the 1940s American Association Milwaukee Brewers promotional materials. The logo was featured prominently on programs and pins sold at all the games. It was a big hint toward what any new Milwaukee team would be named and what their mascot might be.

When the Twins returned to County Stadium in 1968 to play the White Sox, their owner, Calvin Griffith, offered his opinion about more games in Milwaukee. He was in favor of the White Sox playing double the games in Milwaukee and scheduling a full series with opposing teams rather than one-off games. Griffith said the low crowds in Chicago meant

Four. A Team That Didn't Exist

the team would most likely lose money when factoring in money to the visiting teams along with meal and hotel bills.[63]

Griffith even suggested the Chicago Cubs play some night games on weekends in Milwaukee to meet the demands of fans crying out for night baseball. Cubs owner Philip K. Wrigley had offered the previous August to bring his team to Milwaukee for an exhibition if the details could be worked out. This never happened as the Brewers group continued to focus on their relationship with the White Sox.

The White Sox's home away from home agreement continued in 1969 with an increase in games, but to just 11 rather than the expanded schedule that Griffith suggested. The Sox played to a 7–4 record that season. Attendance dropped in 1969 to an average of 18,019 per game, but this still tripled the average game attendance at Comiskey Park. Some blamed lousy weather for the drop in attendance, but other factors were clearly at work as season ticket sales dropped from 11,000 to 7,500.[64]

Selig cited the hope of getting an expansion team being gone in 1969.[65] The last hope to bring a team to Milwaukee until baseball owners brought up expansion again would be to purchase an existing team. While the White Sox looked to be a leading candidate, with the Washington Senators and Cleveland Indians as other possibilities, the expansion Seattle Pilots emerged as the Brewers' prime target.

Seattle had a history with minor league baseball that went back even further than Boeing, and it paralleled Milwaukee's baseball history. The Pacific Coast League was founded in 1903 as a merger between the Pacific Northwest League and the California League. The Seattle team was known as the Clamdiggers during their stint in the Northwest League, but changed the name to the Indians upon entering the new PCL. The team was a contender in 1906, yet it wasn't enough to avoid contraction as the league went from six teams to four. The team was revived in 1919, again as the Indians in the expanded eight-team league. It took a few years, but the Indians finally won their first PCL pennant in 1924.

The Indians played in Dugdale Field until 1932, when it burned down on Independence Day. Officials determined arson as the cause of the fire and declared the ballpark a total loss. Dugdale had a large capacity for a minor league park at 15,000—especially considering it had been built in 1913.

The Indians moved to Civic Stadium and played six seasons there until being purchased by Emil Sick in 1938. He was the owner of Rainier Brewing Company and appropriately decided to rename his new team the Rainiers. Sick decided to put a lot of money into his new investment, which included building a new 15,000-seat stadium where Dugdale once stood.

Sick's Stadium officially opened on June 15, 1938. Interestingly enough, Jack Lelivelt, who had managed the American Association Milwaukee Brewers, was in the dugout as manager of the Rainiers, and he stuck around until 1940. The Rainiers played to exceptional results in their new home, finishing first from 1939 through 1941, and they captured the PCL pennant from 1940 through 1942. Despite finishing in third place the following two years, they went on to win the post-season title series each season.

The crowds at Sick's Stadium were so large that fans had to stand in the outfield. Many simply couldn't get in for games and watched from a hill close to the park. In what was considered the finest minor league sta-

A Rainiers baseball game at Sick's Stadium in 1940, two years after Emil Sick bought the team, which had been the Indians, and renamed it for his brewing company (courtesy University of Washington Libraries, Special Collections, Seattle Rainiers Baseball Team Photograph Collection, UW 15727).

Four. A Team That Didn't Exist

dium in the country, the Rainiers routinely led all teams in attendance—even those in larger markets like Los Angeles. Half a million fans came through the Sick's Stadium gates in 1940 to set a new PCL attendance record.

Emil Sick committed himself to more game promotions by the mid–1940s, but the team didn't need anything special to pull in more fans because they played so well on the field. Sick viewed the Brooklyn Dodgers as an example of a team offering entertainment in addition to the game.[66] Sick was aware that not everyone was interested in the technical aspects of the game. He said, "I believe that baseball is primarily a show. We can use more special nights, more bands, more hoopla to add to the excitement. And, as far as I'm concerned, Seattle will have that kind of baseball entertainment from now on."[67]

It turned out the Rainiers were about to enter a pennant drought, and the ballpark entertainment became a welcome sight for fans. The Rainiers finally won the PCL championship under Hall of Fame player turned manager Rogers Hornsby in 1951. The team took one more pennant in 1955 under manager Fred Hutchinson. He was one of several major leaguers who had played for the Rainiers during their history. Others included Wisconsin-born pitcher Ryne Duren and outfielder Vada Pinson.

The Rainiers were sold to the Boston Red Sox in 1960, and the Sox held onto the team for just five years before selling to the California Angels in 1965. The team was renamed the Seattle Angels to reflect their new affiliation. The final Seattle PCL pennant was captured in 1966. The league had expanded to include American Association teams and had been divided into Eastern and Western divisions.

Emil Sick passed away in 1964, before the final years and changes to his team. Members of his family took the ownership over, and Sick's Stadium had a name change to a plural possessive form—Sicks' Stadium. The family ownership didn't last long as the city of Seattle purchased the stadium in 1965, thinking the property would be used for a freeway. This didn't happen after it was determined the new Pilots franchise would play temporarily in Sicks' Stadium. The Rainiers went out quietly and finished in eighth place in 1968 as the Pilots prepared for their first season.

By late September of 1968, the Seattle City Council approved a $1.17 million contract that would allow remodeling and rental of Sicks' Stadium. The contract was not without controversy, as two council members tried to stall the agreement. They wanted to bring in consultants to analyze the deal to see if it was fair. The city expected to recoup the money between rental, salvage, and roughly $375,000 in admission taxes. The goal was to use Sicks' Stadium for about five years until a domed stadium could be constructed, and this new stadium had already been approved by voters. Local sports fans were excited to have another professional team in Seattle—the National Basketball Association added the expansion Supersonics in 1967.

The new Seattle baseball franchise needed a name. Dewey Soriano organized a contest in the spring of 1968, and the most popular frontrunners had ties to water and air: Skippers, Pilots, and Mariners. Even Rainiers ranked high on the list of 21,252 contest entries. The Pilots name emerged as the winner at the end of March, when the team's board of directors was announced.[68]

An early sign of trouble came with the board announcement of Cleveland industrialist William Daley as team president. Dewey Soriano had asked Daley to underwrite a large amount of the franchise's purchase price, and in return sold Daley 47 percent of his stock.[69] Soriano took over the chairman of the board position, while his brother Max moved into the president role of the Seattle Angels AAA affiliate.

The American League expansion draft held in October 1968, became characterized for "problem player dumping." Teams with players who couldn't be traded previously due to issues such as age or injury were left exposed to the draft. The Pilots and Kansas City Royals had no choice as to what players were available—only three regular players and two starting pitchers were on the list of 60 names to choose from. Some of the pitchers in the draft had a history of arm injuries, such as Pilots selections Wally Bunker and Steve Barber.

Many of the players chosen by Seattle were skilled veterans, but in some cases their skills had declined. Don Mincher of the California Angels and Tommy Harper of the Cleveland Indians were the number one and two draft picks by the Pilots. Even though Mincher was selected first by the Pilots, he was coming off a season where he was beaned and didn't come back quite the same hitter with California.

Seattle did wind up picking a few players who went on to have great careers—namely Lou Piniella, Marty Pattin, and Mike Marshall. Kansas City leaned more toward acquiring younger players, yet still had little option but to round out their roster with veterans based on what the other teams made available.

The National League draft for Montreal and San Diego also had player dumping issues. But no matter what the players had for a skill set or injury history, each would cost $175,000. The cost for 30 players added up to a grand total of $5.25 million. Seattle general manager Marvin

Four. A Team That Didn't Exist

Milkes commented, "This draft is just the start of things. We'll make deals later."[70]

Milkes wasn't kidding. By the time the Pilots ended their short time in Seattle, Milkes had traded 11 of the 30 expansion draftees for 18 other players. A roster in a constant state of flux proved to be the least of the franchise's worries, as far deeper troubles loomed ahead.

Five

The Pilots Take Flight

Marvin Milkes' first real baseball job was as a batboy and clubhouse attendant for the Los Angeles Angels of the Pacific Coast League. He became a baseball executive in the mid–1940s as an assistant general manager with the Fresno Cardinals, in the St. Louis farm system. When he hired Milkes at age 23 for the job, Cardinals owner Sam Breadon asked him if he wanted to work 14 hours a day and take all the heat for losing. Milkes replied that he was willing to do so, and Breadon told Milkes if he was that much of an idiot, he was hired.

Milkes went on to win *The Sporting News'* Minor League Executive of the Year Award (Lower Classification) in 1956 with the Cardinals. He moved on to a GM job with the San Antonio Missions in Baltimore's minor leagues.

Milkes nabbed the job as assistant general manager of the big league Los Angeles Angels in 1961. The new franchise was part of an expansion in the American League, so Milkes got a lot of on-the-job training in putting a ball club together from scratch. By 1965 he was also overseeing the minor league Seattle Angels. Milkes' work with Seattle led him to the job as general manager of the new Pilots franchise. Owner Dewey Soriano hired him to shape the new ballclub as he had the Angels.

Milkes proved to be an aggressive GM during the Pilots lone season. Those close to him had many colorful descriptions of his personality and work ethic. Words like ruthless, rude, uptight, off-center, reckless, and controlling shed some light on how he was viewed by others. Milkes often agreed with the assessments and warned that he expected everyone to match his frantic pace. When manager Joe Schultz said before the season that he thought the Pilots could finish third in their division, Milkes held him to the statement.[1] While the team made it through the first half of the year just six games out of first place, the second half was a disaster, and their last-place finish turned out to be no surprise.

Five. The Pilots Take Flight

At times, it appeared Milkes couldn't make up his mind with the team roster. He moved players up and down from the majors to the minors and was relentless with orchestrating trades. Those close to Milkes couldn't decide if he was smart on judging talent or simply reshuffling the deck because he had a temperamental personality.

Lenny Anderson, a beat writer for the *Seattle Post-Intelligencer*, concluded that Milkes was the weakest link in the franchise and said he couldn't have scouted Joe DiMaggio.[2] Knuckleball pitcher and *Ball Four* author Jim Bouton has maintained that the players were judged based on personality and not on talent.[3] An example of this happened when Milkes traded future star Lou Piniella to Kansas City for John Gelnar and Steve Whitaker. Piniella went on to win the AL "Rookie of the Year" Award that season and played another 15 years in the big leagues.

Like Milkes, manager Joe Schultz also was in the midst of a long baseball career. His father had been a major league outfielder from 1912 to 1925, and this influenced Schultz toward a career in baseball. He debuted as a catcher for the Pittsburgh Pirates in 1939 and got into coaching when his playing career ended ten years later. Milkes knew Schultz from working together in San Antonio in the 1950s.

Schultz got the job as the Pilots manager after serving as coach on many successful 1960s St. Louis Cardinals teams. Even though Milkes didn't make the official hiring announcement until the ninth inning of the seventh World Series game in 1968, those watching the game already knew that Schultz was on the way to Seattle. The NBC broadcast kept showing him coaching third base while broadcasters Harry Carey and Curt Gowdy acknowledged that he would be the first manager in Seattle Pilots history.

Schultz agreed to a one-year contract and had votes of confidence beyond those whom he worked with in the Cardinals organization. Brooks Robinson played for the 50-year-old Schultz in the minors and gave Schultz credit for much of his success.[4] Harry Dalton, director of personnel for Baltimore, believed Schultz inspired confidence and got the most out of every man on the roster. Dalton said, "He's the type of manager that makes every player think pennant."[5]

It turned out that Schultz was probably the best choice as skipper of the patched-together Pilots. Players for the most part liked his personality, and he pretty much tried to keep things loose and let everyone have fun. A few players said he wasn't a very solid tactical manager and that most of the actual instruction came from the coaching staff.[6] Schultz was busy making sure coolers were well-stocked with Budweiser beer for his team. Schultz used "Pound that Budweiser" as a main catch-phrase. Win or lose,

Schultz loved his Bud and wanted to share that love with his team. He later became a larger-than-life character due to Bouton's book—but he wasn't always portrayed in the best light.

The Pilots began marketing tickets to home games in local newspapers during January 1969. Loge box seats were $4.50, and reserved seats cost $3.50. Fans using mail order forms were instructed to include 25 cents to cover shipping and handling costs. The prices sound low by today's standards but were actually the highest major league ticket prices in 1969. When fans came out to Sicks' Stadium and found out what they paid for, many didn't return.

Sicks' was a shadow of its former self and had fallen into disarray. The once stately ballpark was like Milwaukee's Borchert Field prior to demolition—but in this case, there wasn't a major league stadium ready for baseball. The Pilots needed to increase seating to 30,000 before Opening Day due to their franchise agreement, and construction on bleacher seats started the same day Opening Day tickets went on sale. It was a race against time that the workers had little chance of winning.

By the end of the first week of February, tickets for individual games had been on sale for two weeks. Dewey Soriano expressed optimism that despite the cold weather, renovations to Sicks' Stadium would be done before the home opener.[7] Temps had been hovering around the freezing mark in Seattle, but the sounds of bulldozers, saws, and hammers continued. Contractors estimated that most of the work would be done by March, and Soriano could get league approval shortly after that.

Players reported to spring training in Tempe under Schultz. The skipper already had an idea in mind for his starting rotation, but the position spots were up for grabs, particularly in the outfield. Eight hurlers had a combined 34–31 record the previous season, led by Gary "Ding Dong" Bell at 11–11.

Schultz kicked off camp with a standard split-squad workout in preparation for the team's first game on March 7. A pension dispute lingered over baseball, and some players were late in arriving to camp. As they rolled in to their new team, many spoke to reporters about the opportunities that came with playing for an expansion club. Utility man Chico Salmon said, "I'm as good as anyone the Pilots have. If I get a fair chance, I will be a starter. I'm going to lose the utility man tag."[8] Schultz continued to extol the virtues of his team to anyone who would listen, and predicted a third-place finish. "We can let our starters pitch as far as they can, then go to our bullpen. And it is a good one."[9] As for his batting lineup, Schultz said, "We should score some runs. We certainly have the potential."[10]

Five. The Pilots Take Flight

Seattle christened a new, 6,000-seat facility at their spring opener against Cleveland. The park had been rushed to completion just in time for game play. The Pilots pounded out 16 hits and drew eight walks in a 19–3 rout. From there, camp turned into business as usual while the team got ready to open the season in California against the Angels on April 8.

The city of Seattle rolled out the red carpet before the Pilots' first home game on April 11. Several hundred fans lined a parade route called "Welcome Lane" that was used after the Korean War to welcome home soldiers. The route spanned the airport to downtown Memorial Plaza, located close to Seattle's City Hall. Bands played and made the celebration even more festive.

Schultz was presented a key to the city at a special ceremony at Memorial Plaza, and Governor Dan Evans also gave GM Marvin Milkes a bat made of Washington wood. Players and team staff were escorted off to a luncheon to celebrate their arrival. The Pilots players, management, and fans were ready for baseball. Sicks' Stadium, however, was not quite ready for occupation.

Public fanfare leading up to Opening Day momentarily overshadowed the continuing seat construction at Sicks' Stadium. Just 19,500 seats were ready for the game, but even though the franchise agreement for seating capacity wasn't met, the team remained in place. Workers were still placing seats on Opening Day, and some fans had to wait until the third inning to come into the stadium. It took until June to reach a 25,000-seat capacity.

Seating wasn't the only problem at Sicks' Stadium. Water pressure was an issue for any crowd above 8,000 people—and only got worse as the game went on. Often nothing happened if a toilet was flushed after the seventh inning. On the positive side, a new scoreboard had been installed prior to the opener. New lights and fences were added to make the experience more enjoyable for fans. If nothing else, the collection of characters who made up the Pilots roster did make the season more interesting for those following the team.

Not only did the team have a guy like Bouton scribbling notes that would later make up his groundbreaking book, the team also had a speedy third baseman in Tommy "Tailwind" Harper. Many baseball fans had yet to hear of Harper—but they sat up and took notice after he stole 73 bases that season. Schultz gave him the green light to steal whenever he liked, saying that Tommy was completely on his own on the bases.[11]

Power came from first baseman Don Mincher in the form of 25 home runs. Tommy Davis finished a distant second to Harper in steals with 19, but he led the team in runs batted in with 80 and had the highest batting average (.271) of anyone that played more than 100 games. Davis' statistics illustrate the severe lack of team offense, as he didn't even play a full year in Seattle—Milkes traded him to Houston at the end of August.

The Pilots started slow and played to a 7–11 record in April, but fared much better in May and even put together a modest five-game winning streak. They stayed within shouting distance of a .500 record through the first three months, as older guys played back to form and younger players like Mike Hegan developed quickly. Other than the obvious issues at Sicks' Stadium, external distractions hadn't come to light yet. Even though the stadium itself left a lot to be desired, a few players commented that they really enjoyed playing in a place with such a beautiful backdrop as Mt. Rainier.

As fans got to know the team better, they naturally picked out their favorite players. Possibly one of the oddest fan clubs of all time popped up due to the actions of a Seattle disc jockey. Robert E. Lee "Bob" Hardwick started the Ray Oyler Fan Club after discovering that Oyler had mostly hit under .200 in his career. The club was dubbed the "S.O.C. I.T. T.O. M.E. .300" Club. This was an acronym for "Slugger Oyler Can, In Time, Top Our Manager's Estimate and hit .300." Over 15,000 fans joined the club and raised Oyler to cult status. They even set him up with an apartment and car. Oyler responded by hitting a career-high seven home runs, but fell well short of a .300 batting average at just .165 over 106 games.

Pitchers did not fare well in hitter-friendly Sicks' Stadium. Gary Bell started on Opening Day and threw one of the best outings in the park, winning 7–0. Yet Bell and other Pilots couldn't help but notice the short porch in left field—a hitter's dream and a nightmare for pitchers. When catcher Jerry McNertney toured the field prior to the home opener, he told reporters that he couldn't decide if he liked the short porches or not, as it would be good for him offensively but not for pitchers.[12]

Wisconsin-born Gene Brabender had the most wins on the staff in 1969 with 13, but might possibly have been better known for drinking beer between innings while pitching a shutout against the Royals. Since the team had a hard time winning games, there weren't a lot of save opportunities for relievers. Diego Segui led the team with 12 saves while posting a 3.35 earned run average. Jim Bouton, John Gelnar, Bob Locker, and John O'Donoghue were also bright spots in the Pilots' bullpen.

The Pilots also played in a ballpark during the 1969 season that didn't have a true home team –Milwaukee County Stadium. The Chicago White Sox scheduled one of their 11 "home" games there against the Pilots on the night of Monday, June 16. A preview article that ran in the *Milwaukee Journal* just days before lauded the Pilots for looking better than the 1962 expansion New York Mets team that won just 40 games and set the 20th-century major league record for fewest wins in a season. Mike Hegan was acknowledged for his great hitting and Tommy Harper gained praise for stealing bases. Manager Joe Schultz received credit due to the outstanding job he did with the collection of players picked up in the expansion draft.[13]

The 1969 draft happened just days before the Pilots played the White Sox. The Pilots had their first chance to draft young players just starting out in baseball, as opposed to the mostly veteran guys thrown into the expansion draft the year before. With their picks, the Pilots chose Pat Osburn, Gorman Thomas, Jim Slaton, Gary Martz, Bob Coluccio, and Bob Hansen. All of them would go on to play in the majors, although Martz had just a cup of coffee in left field for the Kansas City Royals that consisted of one inning and one at-bat. Osburn chose to sign with the Cincinnati Reds, while Thomas, Slaton, Coluccio, and Hansen worked their way through Seattle's and later Milwaukee's minor leagues to play eventually for the Brewers. Thomas and Slaton became fan favorites and huge contributors during the Brewers' peak years as pennant contenders.

The Pilots completed a trade with the Chicago White Sox shortly after the draft. They flipped pitchers, with reliever Bob Locker going to the Pilots for Opening Day starter Gary Bell. When Locker put on the Pilots uniform and later appeared in the County Stadium game, little did he or many other players know they'd be back in Milwaukee the following year as the Brewers. A total of 13,133 paying customers plus 2,950 members of the Milwaukee Brewers "Knothole Club" came out to see their "home away from home" White Sox. They should have given all their attention to the opposing Pilots team that was a bankruptcy away from becoming permanent Milwaukee residents.

Rookie pitcher Billy Wynne earned his first career win that day for the White Sox, 8–3. He went the distance and worked around eight hits, four of which came from Don Mincher and the hot-hitting Mike Hegan. Harper had a rough night with three errors at second base and three strikeouts. The White Sox extended their Milwaukee winning streak to five games but were still a game behind the Pilots in the standings. "I don't know what it is," said White Sox manager Don Gutteridge. "If I could, I would take this stadium back to Chicago and nail it down."[14]

It was just one game and one loss. The Pilots players and fans saw a .500 season as a lofty goal, but at that point it was thought 70 wins was entirely possible. That many victories would match the first-season expansion team record set by the 1961 Los Angeles Angels. The achievement would not be lost on Pilots GM Marvin Milkes, as he was the assistant GM in 1961 with the Angels.

Schultz remained optimistic about his team's fortunes. "Playing every day has to make them better," he had proclaimed in spring training.[15] Unfortunately, this was the case for just a few players and not the whole team. More forgettable nights just like the one in Milwaukee were on the horizon.

Reality started to set in for the Seattle Pilots somewhere around midseason. The players knew it would be an uphill battle playing against powerful teams like the Minnesota Twins and Oakland A's. Yet the Pilots somehow held their own in the American League West standings through June. The team sat just six games out of first place on June 28 before injuries and poor play unraveled their early success as they staggered to a 15–42 record over the course of July and August.

General manager Marvin Milkes kept wheeling and dealing throughout the dog days of summer while the team plummeted in the standings. He picked up catcher Larry Haney in a trade with Oakland just before the team's wheels came off. Next, Milkes bought veteran pitcher George Brunet from the California Angels to join the Pilots rotation. A few weeks later, he shipped Jim Bouton to Houston for pitchers Dooley Womack and Roric Harrison. Bouton would have to continue compiling his *Ball Four* book with the Astros, while Harrison toiled in the minors and Womack pitched to a 2.51 earned run average for the Pilots over 14⅓ innings down the stretch.

Milkes didn't just focus on acquiring pitching in August and September. He kept shopping in the Houston Astros aisle, nabbing outfielders Sandy Valdespino and Danny Walton in exchange for Tommy Davis. He also purchased infielder Fred Stanley from Houston. These moves probably didn't resonate with baseball fans in Milwaukee when they appeared as one-liners in the sports page. The names Valdespino, Walton, and Stanley would get a lot more Milwaukee media attention in 1970.

The players who had been with the Pilots all along started hearing rumors of payroll troubles. Dewey and Max Soriano knew they were in trouble financially by May, but it became more of a pressing issue as the summer dragged on. The first human walked on the moon while the Pilots were busy dropping a couple of games to the Minnesota Twins—with both losses by pitcher John Gelnar. The landing was played on the Sicks' Stadium loudspeaker, turning into one of the few highlights of an otherwise disastrous season.

Five. The Pilots Take Flight

The Seattle Pilots are the only team in the modern era to have played only one season in a city (National Baseball Hall of Fame Library, Cooperstown, New York).

When August rolled around, the Pilots spiraled out of control and lost 19 of 22 games. They had a 15-game losing streak at home and finally beat Kansas City in early September to halt the carnage. Rumors of a move to Texas were swirling, and the local press turned on the team. The *Seattle Post-Intelligencer* ran a snarky headline after the Kansas City victory that gained coverage in other media outlets: "Pilots Win 1 Straight."[16]

Newspapers also covered the security of Joe Schultz's job as manager of the club. In published articles, Milkes said, "Some say a manager who is loved by players and fans alike should be retained. I'm not conducting a love-in."[17]

Milkes commented that he and Schultz had yet to discuss anything beyond the current season, but he did want to decide on a manager for 1970 before the World Series started. Milkes still believed he had built a club capable of finishing in third place.

As the team spiraled out of control, they finally had their only locally televised game of the season. The game on August 31 at Tiger Stadium was carried on KING-TV. One other game had been televised nationally but was blacked out in the Seattle area. Television outlets originally scoffed at the package offered by Dewey Soriano–$15,000 a game for 20 games. Later, when the price was lowered to $5,000 a game, the stations still questioned whether they could get enough sponsors to cover costs.

Back in Milwaukee, the Brewers group focused on the cash-strapped Chicago White Sox. The Allyn brothers put money back into the team prior to the season to boost sagging attendance. They were fighting a negative public perception of the neighborhood close to Comiskey Park that went back to the riots after Martin Luther King's assassination the previous spring, even though the unrest happened five miles from the stadium. Lights were installed around the exterior of the park and in the parking lots at a cost of $100,000.

Additional money was spent on artificial turf which ultimately covered only the infield. The Allyns couldn't come up with the $300,000 needed for the outfield. They did cough up the money to have wire outfield fences installed that shortened the dimensions. Teams scored 12 percent more runs at Comiskey than at the average park in 1969. This was a stark contrast to 1950–68 when they scored 9 percent fewer runs than average. The improvements did little to offset the poor play of the 94-loss White Sox, and attendance dipped to 392,762. An 11-game schedule in Milwaukee brought in nearly half that amount.

Newspaper articles appeared about the inevitable move of the Sox to Milwaukee. Selig and his cohorts decided the time was right to try to purchase the team from the Allyn brothers. Arthur Allyn claimed he had all but three votes necessary to authorize relocation, but it was later learned that at least six owners were against the move.[18]

The Brewers were proactive and flew representatives to each AL city to plead their case with team owners. AL president Joe Cronin responded by telling the group to cease and desist trying to buy an existing franchise.[19] In a further counter-move, Commissioner Bowie Kuhn passed on a directive to club owners that he should have knowledge of any potential club sales, and these would only happen with his approval.[20]

According to Arthur Allyn, the Brewers had offered $13,000,000 for the White Sox, which fell $1,000,000 short of his asking price.[21] Lamar Hunt of the potential Dallas-Fort Worth ownership had called numerous times, but never officially put an offer on the table.

John Allyn wasn't fond of the sale idea and told his brother to call a meeting with the seven-man board of directors of the Artnell Corporation to discuss the matter.[22] Instead, Arthur Allyn bent to pressure and sold his shares in the team to his brother. What was a surprise to many fans was that both brothers had equal shares in the team, but Arthur had acted as spokesman. Neither brother could have completed a sale of the team without getting approval from the other one.

Arthur Allyn had grown tired of watching his franchise fall apart and decided to go into semi-retirement, save for being an entomologist with a $250,000 butterfly collection. His brother knew worse days could be ahead but vowed to keep the team in the Windy City.

Selig's attempt to purchase and move the team was officially off the table. Other than the White Sox games at County Stadium, it had been a very quiet year for the Brewers group. The unraveling of the Seattle Pilots kick-started the group back into action.

Distractions took their toll on the Pilots and Seattle throughout the season's final month. William Daley clearly wasn't happy with the low attendance numbers. Despite not being the majority stockholder, Daley had a large stake in ownership, so he voiced his displeasure to the press. He warned the city's populace to attend games or he'd move the team.[23] No one responded to that threat as fans largely stayed away from the ballpark. Supposedly Daley had promised $8 million to the league to support the team, but the league didn't make him follow through and spend the money to help keep the team afloat.

Daley did say he'd give Seattle one more season to support the team, but he couldn't say what would happen after that. He blamed the press for the franchise's shortcomings. This didn't sit well with *Seattle Times* writer Hy Zimmerman, prompting him to write a fiery column telling Daley to take his ball club and go home. Zimmerman didn't hold back, pointing out that a good reporter wrote for fans, not for a ball club.[24]

After Zimmerman ripped into Daley, the baseball executive began to think keeping the team in Seattle might not be in his best interests. Bud Selig received a tip from American League owners to start negotiations to buy the Pilots, so off to Seattle he went in September. News stories were published citing insider sources with knowledge of the Pilots' impending move to Milwaukee. These articles even mentioned the team being rechristened as the Brewers.

Other rumors of a possible move to the Dallas-Fort Worth area circulated, centering on Lamar Hunt buying the team. Hunt claimed to have made no efforts toward a purchase, nor did he have any familiarity with Seattle's ownership.[25] Daley later denied that he was selling his shares of the Pilots to Hunt.[26]

The Pilots ended their season in last place with a 64–98 record. The expansion Kansas City Royals had bested Seattle by five games. Poor attendance has often been mentioned as a reason why the Pilots failed to remain in Seattle after just one season. While increased revenue from higher attendance may have helped their cause, the Pilots didn't have the lowest attendance in the majors that year. San Diego, Philadelphia, and the Chicago White Sox had lower gate numbers for the season. In fact, it would take until 1974 for the expansion Padres to eclipse what Seattle drew in 1969.

Within a few days of the season's finale, Pilots president Dewey Soriano denied he would be replaced as president of the team. He also said that the status of GM Marvin Milkes remained unchanged. Soriano couldn't guarantee that the team would retain manager Joe Schultz for the 1970 season.[27] Milkes said coaches had not yet learned whether they would be rehired, and he knew it could put them into an awkward position. Yet by the following week, Milkes announced the dismissal of coaches Sal Maglie and Ron Plaza.[28]

Negotiations between Selig and the Seattle ownership shifted to Baltimore during the World Series. There was a difference in opinion as to what the franchise was worth. The Sorianos wanted $13.5 million, and Selig offered $9 million. They eventually came to a momentary agreement for $10.8 million—until Daley and the Sorianos shifted direction and denied that a deal ever was in place. Selig returned to Milwaukee again without a franchise, figuring that it was his last shot and that the Brewers ownership group wouldn't stay together much longer. Selig said later he felt it was yet another wild goose chase.

The Brewers organization went on yet another dead-end excursion in making three unsuccessful attempts to purchase the Washington Senators that fall. Robert Cannon began negotiations with the Senators ownership group and made an offer of around $10 million. The Senators turned down the offer because they wanted the new owners to stipulate that the team wouldn't be moved. The Brewers moved on, appointing former Braves star Eddie Mathews as vice president in charge of public relations and promotions.

In late October 1969, AL president Joe Cronin took a deeper look at where the Pilots might be playing in the upcoming season. Cronin met with representatives from the city and the state of Washington. Mayor Floyd Miller talked Cronin into having the meeting, as he was convinced Seattle could continue to support major league baseball.[29] But Cronin didn't have complete support from local taxpayers. Citizen groups were popping up who were opposed to a proposed $40 million domed stadium.

"The plight of the Pilots, it seems to me, is due to poor management and has no bearing on the city's wish to enjoy major league baseball,"

Five. The Pilots Take Flight

Miller concluded.[30] Hy Zimmerman offered his opinion that Daley had made the situation worse by blaming the press for the state of the franchise. Zimmerman wrote, "The Pilots since their inception have been clothed in controversy, clad in contentiousness. It has been an up-tight organization and the press did not make it so."[31]

Around the same time as the meeting between Cronin and Miller, major league owners planned a joint meeting. However, vice president John Holland of the Chicago Cubs clarified what was on the agenda, saying the meeting was only to hear a report from the player relations committee on negotiations with the Players Association.[32]

The Pilots continued conducting business just like any other major league team. In November, Joe Schultz was fired as manager, which the skipper took as being part of the game.[33] Even though many had figured Schultz would be dismissed, for some it looked like a scapegoat move by Marvin Milkes to cover himself while potential new owners looked at the club.

Milkes had his credibility come into question in a related staff move. He stated that coach Frank Crosetti had been given an unconditional release from the team at his request and would probably be joining another team within a few days.[34] Crosetti fired back that he had heard about his dismissal on the radio when returning home from a fishing trip, and it was a lie that he asked to be dismissed.[35]

The news switched over a few days later to the hiring of Dave Bristol to manage the team. Although Bristol was just 36 years old, he had 3½ years of experience managing the Reds, plus a long background in baseball. He was let go by the Reds after the team collapsed at the end of the season and fell out of contention. Bristol immediately signed on as a coach for the Montreal Expos, who then let him speak to Milkes about the managerial opening.

Bristol had competition for the job in Billy Martin, also recently fired despite leading his Minnesota Twins to the American League West pennant. Martin told Milkes that he was sorry they couldn't work together but that he'd available to Bristol if he needed any information on the league and players.[36]

Bristol got to work on replacing Schultz's coaching staff in the final month of 1969. He tapped Wes Stock to be the new pitching coach and added Roy McMillan and former Twins manager Cal Ermer. Bristol added youth to his corps in 30-year-old Jackie Moore as catching coach. Even though Moore had just five hits in his brief big league career with Detroit in 1965, he went on to an over-40-year coaching career.

Schultz was named as a possible candidate to replace Martin in Minnesota, and he had gotten a thumbs-up from owner Calvin Griffith over how he handled running the expansion Pilots.[37] The Twins went in a different direction, and Schultz moved on as a coach with the other expansion team—the Kansas City Royals. The Royals had been busy celebrating former Pilots outfielder Lou Piniella being named the American League "Rookie of the Year."

Milkes celebrated as well with the press about his new young manager. He said the hiring of Bristol "should assure the baseball world and the fans this is a very stable organization."[38] He couldn't have been further from the truth on the state of the franchise.

Bristol and Milkes both had a realistic view of the Seattle players after their rough first season. Both men cited the New York Mets as an example of an expansion team who eventually built a contender. Yet neither he nor Milkes wanted to wait eight years for a pennant. Bristol explained, "We'll have to build from within. You can't trade your way to a pennant."[39]

Milkes kept working toward building a better ballclub throughout the off-season. In October, the Montreal Expos sent Seattle outfielder Floyd Wicker to complete a three-team trade started back in September. Milkes dealt pitcher Dooley Womack to one of his frequent trading partners, the Houston Astros, and sold them pitcher Mike Marshall. Just before Thanksgiving, Milkes purchased pitcher Wayne Twitchell from Houston, the last transaction the two teams would make during the off-season.

Milkes would close out the year by swapping pitchers with the Washington Senators—George Brunet for Dave Baldwin. Next he sent Ray Oyler and Diego Segui to Oakland and got infielder Ted Kubiak and pitcher George Lauzerique in return. Dick Simpson and Steve Whitaker were shipped to San Francisco just before Christmas for pitcher Bobby Bolin. In many of his trades, Milkes was showing that he wasn't afraid to deal away players acquired during the previous season.

Milkes also wasn't afraid to trade away most, if not all of his power hitting, much to the dismay of many Pilots fans. Even though first baseman Don Mincher slugged 25 homers in 1969—his fourth season with 20+ round-trippers—he was sent with infielder Ron Clark to Oakland. To his credit, Milkes got quite a haul back, especially considering that Clark was clearly a throw-in after hitting just .196 the previous season in a mostly backup role. Outfielder Mike Hershberger, veteran catcher Phil Roof, and pitchers Ken Sanders and Lew Krausse all headed to Seattle.

For a moment, Milkes diverted the attention from the team's shaky

Five. The Pilots Take Flight

future toward the actual roster. Milkes said that he couldn't neglect the ball club and felt he had upgraded the whole organization since its inception.[40] Milkes knew that Dallas-Fort Worth and Milwaukee were potential destinations for his team, and he offered to gladly move with the team if it was a good fit. But he acknowledged, "The American League hasn't told me anything. I'm just like Will Rogers—all I know is what I read in the papers."[41]

There were countless articles about the Seattle Pilots for Milkes to read in the papers. The franchise started 1970 in free-fall mode toward insolvency and an inevitable sale. Seattle theater owner Fred Danz hit a roadblock trying to purchase the team early in the year. Newspaper headlines announcing Danz as the new Pilots owner started appearing in November, but those proved to be premature—and eventually incorrect.

Pilots principal stockholder William Daley had met with Danz over the course of several days in Cleveland. Daley was expected to cut his stock in the Pilots from 60 percent back to 30 percent to make way for Danz to take over the franchise. Dewey and Max Soriano and Cleveland natives Greg Devine and Alan Fritchey were rumored to be giving up their shares in the team as part of the deal. The new ownership group led by Danz would therefore have 70 percent of the team, which would be controlled by Seattle interests. Daley expressed happiness that such a deal might come to fruition and hinted that the sale would be completed before the end of the year.[42]

The Danz group needed to put together an adequate money package and meet a tight deadline. The Bank of California had loaned Pacific Northwest Sports, Inc. $3.5 million toward keeping the Pilots afloat. Danz met resistance from the bank in carrying the loan forward; the bank maintained that it would cover only $750,000. Seattle mayor Wes Uhlman stepped in to try to mediate the financial tangle with the bank but didn't think it was a good loan from a banker's standpoint.[43]

Danz continued to remain confident the parties could work out the finances so the Pilots could remain in Seattle. He remained upbeat when baseball executives including AL President Joe Cronin and Commissioner Bowie Kuhn decided to visit early in January to consider the problems surrounding the troubled franchise. Danz felt that exposure of the issues warranted a visit.

Cronin and Kuhn spent an hour meeting with Danz and left by saying the burden was on the purchasers and that they weren't in Seattle to solve anything. They called their visit a fact-finding mission to review the financial state of the franchise. Cronin said the AL had the utmost belief in the city of Seattle supporting its team, but gave Danz a deadline of January 22 to finalize the purchase of the Pilots franchise.[44]

To garner support, Danz announced a special three-year ticket sales campaign. Danz said the ticket drive needed to raise at least $1 million to encourage local bankers to loan his group the $3.5 million the previous ownership group borrowed from a California bank.[45]

In another last-ditch move, Danz and a group of 20 Seattle businessmen met with Lloyd Nordstrom, president of the Seattle Central Association. They discussed a financial package that Danz believed would keep the Pilots in Seattle, but the details were never quite worked out, and Danz missed the January 22 deadline set by Cronin.

The situation in Seattle began to be felt outside baseball. Boston Patriots President Bill Sullivan went on record as saying the Pilots troubles were hurting Seattle's chances of acquiring a pro football team. The Patriots were considering leaving Boston for lack of a suitable stadium, but Sullivan no longer had Seattle high on the list due to the baseball issues. He claimed to have received offers from three Seattle groups to purchase the Patriots.[46]

Kuhn spoke at the Wisconsin Baseball Writers Association's 17th annual Diamond Dinner on January 18 and told the crowd about the serious situation in Seattle. He mentioned the possibility of a franchise transfer and said that Milwaukee would be given serious consideration for relocation of the franchise—but he couldn't guarantee anything. Kuhn told the record crowd of 710 that Milwaukee had a friend in him, and he would tell them when to give up hope in getting a new major league team.[47]

A few players from the 1957 Milwaukee Braves team and former general manager John Quinn were honored at the dinner. Representing the Braves were Felix Mantilla, Johnny Logan, Hank Aaron, Frank Torre, Andy Pafko, Billy Bruton, and Lew Burdette. Quinn noted the background of success in the city and felt it would be a logical choice for another franchise.[48]

Selig swore to continue fighting for baseball in what he called the largest metropolitan market in the nation without a major league team. Milwaukee's population at the time made it larger than at least three cities that had a team. Baseball was a priceless asset to a community as far as Selig was concerned.[49]

It didn't take long for the press to jump all over Kuhn's remarks. On January 21, the *Chicago Sun Times* reported that the Pilots would be transferred to Milwaukee within 72 hours. The newspaper stated that a deal had been signed for $11 million transferring the team to the Brewers ownership group, and an announcement would be made shortly. Daley chimed in shortly thereafter and mentioned how impressed he was by the people in Milwaukee, which would be a fine place for the Pilots.[50]

Not to be forgotten, Lamar Hunt of the potential Dallas-Fort Worth ownership group popped up and said he was cautiously optimistic about moving the Pilots to Dallas-Fort Worth. He declined to start celebrating until he landed the team.[51]

A freelance Seattle promoter named Fred Ruge threw his hat into the potential ownership ring. Ruge insisted that his requests to purchase the Pilots had largely been ignored by major league baseball. He claimed that at least 22 national firms had pledged monetary support, but he wouldn't name these firms until the league agreed to a meeting.[52] Ruge sent a telegram to AL President Joe Cronin outlining his plans for the team, which included building a domed stadium with private funds at the site of the 1962 World's Fair. Ruge's attempts at purchasing the Pilots also went by the wayside. Cronin maintained that "we are bending over backwards to keep the franchise in Seattle."[53]

Six

The Pilots Crash Land

Whether the team remained in Seattle or moved elsewhere, AL owners were generally adamant about not allowing a bidding war for the team to break out. The owner of the Kansas City Royals, Ewing M. Kauffman, was preparing to chair a four-person committee at the late-January AL owners meeting. "The asking price is $8.8 million," he divulged. "We've done this so William Daley and the Sorianos will make less than half a million profit. They don't deserve a profit. They didn't stay in there and pitch."[1]

Many of the owners at the meeting expressed resistance to the team pulling out of Seattle. However, not everyone agreed. Chicago White Sox owner John Allyn thought it would be best if Seattle moved the club to Milwaukee.[2] Oakland A's owner Charles Finley had the opposite opinion and stressed that it was up to someone in Seattle to come up with an idea.[3] Finley later proposed a temporary move of the team to Milwaukee until Seattle's domed stadium could be built, but this idea met with resistance and quickly went by the wayside.[4]

Finley had a good friend in Oakland airline executive Edward Daly, who briefly threw his hat into the ring as a purchaser for the Pilots as January ended. Daly met with several AL owners and checked into the Pilots' financial situation, but he didn't go much further as a potential owner.

Within a few days of the AL meeting, the league backtracked and granted an extension of February 6 to the ownership group led by Fred Danz. The extra time did not help Danz come up with the lowered asking price for the franchise.

Seattle Mayor Wes Uhlman jumped back into the thick of the ownership arguments. He had city lawyers construct a lawsuit after the Danz ownership deal fell through. While Uhlman said it was a last resort to keep the Pilots in Seattle, he threatened the league and Pacific Sports Inc.

Six. The Pilots Crash Land

with a multi-million-dollar lawsuit if the team moved. Ulhman called the $40 million bond voters had approved for a domed stadium a huge reason for the lawsuit and warned that a damage suit could follow a franchise move.[5] The city of Seattle filed a "specific performance suit," asking Pacific Northwest Sports, Inc. to fulfill the remainder of its five-year lease agreement. Uhlman quipped that any new owner buying the team would also be buying a lawsuit.[6]

AL owners reconvened on February 10 in Chicago to find a way to keep the Pilots in Seattle. League President Cronin again acknowledged the many problems faced, including the long-term financial viability of any potential local ownership group.[7]

The league went on to turn down an application for the team's operation by a civic group led by hotel executive Edward Carlson. Carlson said his group had met all the commitments for purchase of the franchise.[8] They had $1.5 million to match $1.5 million from owner William Daley in a limited partnership, plus $2.75 million in working capital, and renegotiation of the $3.5 million owed to the Bank of California was set up. Carlson expressed disappointment in having the application turned down, but believed the group had achieved its objective of keeping the team in Seattle.

Dewey Soriano had fully expected the AL owners to approve the sale of the team to Carlson and considered himself done with the team. He pledged to continue to try to solidify the team and squelched rumors surrounding the state of the franchise.[9] Unfortunately for Soriano, the rumors would only increase, and he wound up in one of the hottest seats of all those concerned with the team.

Valentine's Day brought a change in Seattle's front office. Fred Hamey, former GM of three clubs, was picked by the AL to be the "overseer" of Pilots operations. Marvin Milkes was elevated to the position of executive vice president and general manager of the club. Milkes said that Hamey would not interfere with operations, and Hamey's primary function would be to provide reports back to the league.[10]

The Pilots also announced drastically reduced ticket prices and an emphasis on family attendance, but this announcement was not without controversy. The ownership group headed by Fred Danz sold $300,000 worth of tickets under the old prices. Milkes said Danz was in Arizona, but when he returned, they needed to work on getting purchasers tickets at the new prices.[11]

Tickets that sold for $6 were reduced to $4.50. Loge tickets that sold for $4.50 were reduced to $3.50. Reserved seats were cut 50 cents to $3.00

each. General admission seats were also cut 50 cents, to $2.00 for adults and $1.00 for students. The Pilots also announced a family ticket plan.

Players began trickling into Tempe Diablo Stadium for spring training, uncertain of what ownership group might have control of the team come the start of the season or what city they would call home. The new roster additions worked to fit in with one-season "veteran" Pilots players as new manager Dave Bristol ran his first camp. The first spring game was on March 6 against the Cleveland Indians at Tempe. Radio announcers Bill Schonely and Jimmy Dudley again were at the microphone for what they hoped would be another season of Pilots baseball.

Even though it was baseball time in the Valley of the Sun, the players and coaches were understandably thinking about things beyond the diamond. New manager Dave Bristol found himself in the difficult position of having to motivate players who weren't sure if they'd get paid or where they should line up living arrangements. Bristol's background with star players in Cincinnati such as Pete Rose, Johnny Bench and Tony Perez had him well-prepared for the situation at hand. So he worked to control what he could, such as shaping the regular season roster.

Bristol hoped the players would be able to adjust quickly and move on if the team flipped locations. But he agreed it was a very touchy time for his team. "It's been tough on them," Bristol confessed. "You can't tell a man forget about the home front and worry about your job. That's a tough situation no matter what you do for a living."[12] But the team didn't revolt or sit out. They kept practicing and playing through March while the ownership battles raged on.

Commissioner Bowie Kuhn circled back and contacted Edward Carlson in mid-month. Carson's idea of operating the Pilots as a non-profit franchise had been shot down by AL owners in February by an 8–4 vote. While Kuhn hoped the non-profit franchise option could be revived, Carlson basically told him "thanks but no thanks" in a telegram.[13] The economic analysis on which the Seattle proposal was submitted to league owners in Chicago had become completely invalid, according to Carlson. Kuhn didn't continue down this path, and the idea was shelved. Later Kuhn would admit the league should have pounced on the initial offer from Carlson.[14]

The league then loaned the existing Pilots franchise $650,000 for operations, with no deadline on repayment. Another possibility was discussed and dismissed—the league operating the team as a trustee. It was decided that it was better to put money toward the current ownership rather than having a group overseeing the franchise.

Six. The Pilots Crash Land

Bill Daley said the money would go toward paying for spring training contracts and bonuses, but it didn't stretch very far, as so many outstanding bills needed to be paid.[15] Insiders were predicting a minimum of $1.7 million in losses for the upcoming season. Daley admitted that he'd be taking a tremendous loss by keeping the team in Seattle for the coming season. Daley commented, "I'm not so sure we'll be a moneymaker in 1970 or 1971, but when we get the domed stadium I'm sure we'll be profitable."[16]

Meanwhile the Pilots looked increasingly likely to move with each passing day. Pacific Northwest Sports, Inc. filed a petition in U.S. District Court to order a sale. Provisions of Chapter 11 of the Federal Bankruptcy Act were used in filing the petition, and Federal bankruptcy referee Sidney Volinn was assigned to hear arguments in the matter. The Bank of California had grown tired of waiting for the $3.5 million they were owed by Pacific Northwest Sports, Inc. When the bank demanded an immediate repayment from the broke ownership group, it was the final blow that set the bankruptcy in motion.

To transfer the club ownership and move to another city, it was necessary for nine of 12 league owners to vote yes. The only team with veto power would be the White Sox, who were close enough to Milwaukee to invoke territorial rights. The owners easily approved the transfer. White Sox owner John Allyn said, "We have never voted against the moving of a franchise to Milwaukee or anywhere, and I do not intend to do so at this time."

With no practical local ownership group in sight, AL president Joe Cronin made a call to Bud Selig and gave him his blessing to buy the Pilots. Selig later divulged that he had been calling everyone connected to the Seattle situation since the previous fall, but no one had returned his calls. He said, "Then, on March tenth, Joe Cronin called. He was actually friendly on the phone. I thought, well, maybe...."[17]

Even though the writing was on the wall for a franchise move, legal action started before the move was a done deal. Lawyer Alfred J. Schweppe kicked off the resistance on March 13 by filing a city suit meant to enjoin the Seattle-to-Milwaukee move.[18] The Soriano brothers pleaded with Schweppe to call off the suit so they could sell the Pilots to Selig, or their only option would be to file reorganizational bankruptcy. Schweppe said his beef was with the AL and its owners, not the Sorianos.[19]

Florida Circuit Court Judge James Bruton, Jr., told the American League not to move the Pilots to Milwaukee.[20] He signed a temporary restraining order that would restrain the league and owners from any action until all legal questions were settled. This order was filed initially by noted lawyer William L. Dwyer on behalf of Washington State against professional baseball. AL owners met in Tampa on March 18, presumably to agree to fold things up in Seattle. They were handed restraining orders as they walked across the hotel lobby to the conference room.

Damages of $80 million for the city and state were requested under the state's antitrust laws if the team moved. Seattle Mayor Wes Uhlman insisted it was up to the league to pay for the mistake of placing a club in Seattle that was substantially underfinanced. Ulhman was realistic and expected the team to move, but hoped to recover damages that protected the city and taxpayers.[21]

Eventually the number of legal cases dropped to just the bankruptcy case and the State action. King County and the City of Seattle joined the State's case. Dwyer was seeking $32 million in damages in his lawsuit. One of Dwyer's many arguments revolved around the league allowing the team to leave town in the face of local ownership offers. He contended that MLB had also considered an illegal agreement between the Pilots and vendor Sportservice in making its decision.[22]

Sportservice had fronted $2 million in start-up money to the Soriano brothers when they were originally awarded the franchise. The Sorianos in turn allowed the giant concessionaire exclusive rights at Sicks' Stadium, which was a privately-owned facility. This wasn't legal because a local law prohibited such an arrangement. Vendors were to bid for the rights to sell in a private facility. Sportservice, however, could follow the team to Milwaukee because County Stadium was publicly owned.

Dewey Soriano had previously told Sportservice that the Pilots might have to go somewhere else if Sportservice couldn't be in Seattle's future domed stadium.[23] Dwyer believed the team was removed during enforcement of an illegal dealing arrangement, and any sort of tying contract was a violation of free trade.[24] It would take years for Dwyer's suit to be settled, with many more arguments based on many legal theories. By 1972, the Ninth Circuit Court of Appeals called Dwyer's mix of federal and state claims a legal tour de force that most laymen could not understand.

AL owners responded to Bruton's restraining order at their meeting by telling attorneys to proceed with all possible speed in lifting legal restraints barring a move of the Pilots franchise. AL attorney Alexander Hadden read a lengthy statement and said he would attempt to remove any legal barriers as soon as possible.[25]

The league also decided in the meeting not to support the Pilots financially beyond the $650,000 already handed over for spring training

Six. The Pilots Crash Land

expenses. The discussion went on for seven hours, with Robert Cannon of the Brewers waiting in the wings for a glimmer of hope.

Just when it appeared things couldn't get any worse for the Pilots, the team lost its rights, title, and interest in their training facility. E. B. Smith, Vice President of Pilot Properties, Inc. and owner of the facility, said the club could use it on a day-to-day basis. Smith decided to cancel the contract because the club failed to comply with the agreement for the use of the facilities. Smith accused the club of being $500,000 in arrears in funding the facility and filed suit for damages in excess of $1.5 million.[26]

Smith knew that Pacific Northwest would be unable to fulfill its monetary obligations in bankruptcy. A huge stumbling block for Smith came in the form of Dewey Soriano being President of Pilot Properties, Inc. Not only that, Pacific Northwest Sports, Inc. owned 60 percent of Pilot Properties. Smith also needed to get in line for his money behind the Bank of California and Sportservice.

Sidney Volinn signed an order that changed the course of major league baseball in Seattle and Milwaukee. Volinn's order on March 22 lifted the restraints to sell the Pilots to Bud Selig's group—and this was meant to lead into a special hearing on March 30 where Volinn would decide if the sale would have merit. All the previous debates and attempts to put together a viable ownership group in Seattle together meant nothing to Volinn. He wanted a solid ownership group with enough money to cover the creditors owned by Pacific Northwest Sports, Inc. Not only that, he wanted Washington State and Seattle to show just cause why they would not interfere with the sale of the Pilots to Selig.

The legal struggle continued in King County Superior Court on March 23, where a flustered Judge Hugh Mifflin wanted to know what moving the team had to do with current ownership losing $1 million a year.[27] Seattle attorney Alfred J. Schweppe attempted to secure an injunction against the AL and Pacific Northwest Sports, Inc. to stop any sale to the Brewers. Mifflin clearly ran out of patience and cracked the whip on anyone who wandered too far from the topic at hand.

Seattle restaurateur Dave Cohn was one of the people called to the stand, and he testified that the asking price for the Pilots should be $5.25 million, not including what the current owners needed to pay off their debts. Cohn also believed there were still Seattle interests who could purchase the team, didn't name anyone, but said that, given 90 days, he could round up the money.[28] The hearing was recessed halfway through the day pending the outcome of the hearing before Volinn.

Max Soriano was the first witness to testify in Volinn's court regarding the negative cash flow, and he admitted to the team losing roughly $12,500 a day in a "catastrophic" financial situation. Soriano said, "It has been apparent for several months we would be unable to operate without the infusion of new monies."[29]

By new monies, Soriano meant millions—not the $650,000 the league provided. He went on to say that a conservative estimate of $4.3 million would be needed to get the Pilots through until spring training in 1971. This amount also covered an expected $1.55 million cash loss for the 1970 season. The Pilots had just $91,000 in the bank during the bankruptcy hearing.

Soriano also admitted signing a contract on March 8 to sell the Pilots to the Milwaukee Brewers Baseball Club, Inc. prior to April 1. He called the contract binding and said that it should be carried out pending the lifting of any legal restrictions. Soriano said his group was not in a position to sell the team to a third party, most likely in reference to Dave Cohn's claim that he could raise the funds to buy the team.[30]

Volinn said he would render a decision early the next week.[31] Despite the delay, Volinn gave the AL permission to vote on the sale of the team to Milwaukee because time was running out on the April 1 contract deadline Pacific Northwest Sports, Inc. had with the Brewers. Nine owners needed to approve the move, and there was a good chance the vote could come over the weekend by phone.

Until Volinn voiced a decision, he put a federal injunction in place, blocking the various lawsuits and the injunction that Schweppe had been seeking. Volinn warned that no one should believe the transfer of the team to Milwaukee was a foregone conclusion. He could potentially tell the league to take a different action and rule the sale out completely.

Reactions in both Seattle and Milwaukee heavily went the route of foregone conclusion. Fans in Seattle were justifiably angry and expressed their anger in many ways. Photographer Don Wallen placed a skeleton wearing a Pilots cap in sitting position on the mound at Sicks' Stadium. A six-foot effigy of Dewey and Max Soriano was hung in a Seattle mall with a note pinned to the dummy that said, "Thanks Max and Dewey."

Milwaukee shop owners placed signs in their windows welcoming the Brewers to their new home. One store even prematurely offered two box seat tickets to anyone who purchased a color television, but noted that a transistor radio would be given if the Pilots didn't move to Milwaukee.

Preparations were made at County Stadium if the court decision went Milwaukee's way. The grounds crew went to work on the four inches of

Six. The Pilots Crash Land

With the departure of the Pilots in 1970, the future for major league baseball in Seattle looked bleak. Here a skeleton in a Pilots cap sits within an empty Sicks' Stadium (courtesy University of Washington Libraries, Special Collections, Don Wallen Collection, UW 39661).

snow recently dumped on the ballpark. Stadium manager Bill Anderson called other preparations annual things his crew did to get the stadium ready for the season, and not specifically connected to the Pilots.[32] The grass needed work as it was still beat up from the previous year's Green Bay Packers games, and yard lines could not be completely removed by Opening Day, so they were visible to those in attendance.

In the front office, the staff got ready to handle ticket sales at a moment's notice. Lists of Braves season-ticket holders were circulated with the goal to place those fans in their old seats if possible. An unnamed source claimed that tickets for Opening Day had already been printed.[33]

As the final weekend of March arrived, several previews of the upcoming season hit newsstands. Pilots manager Dave Bristol called the attitude of the players a pleasant surprise. He also believed his pitching staff could surprise people.[34] If the pitching failed, though, he didn't have much of an offense to fall back on, as his outfield remained unsettled.

Players anticipated the change and gave away bats and helmets to kids, then started making calls to line up living arrangements in Milwaukee. A few, like pitcher Lew Krausse, were a bit too proactive in sending personal items ahead of time to Seattle. Years later, he admitted it was the biggest mess he'd ever been through in his life, and he'd never do it again for the $35,000 he made that year.[35]

Monday came, and some complications arose in Volinn's court. He expressed intrigue in a provision in the AL constitution that the league would take over a bankrupt club. Special state assistant attorney general William Dwyer adeptly pointed out that the AL now owned the Pilots due to the sheer fact that they were in bankruptcy court. Dwyer also argued that the club was not bankrupt because it now belonged to the AL, and the AL was not bankrupt.[36]

Dwyer and AL attorneys went back and forth over whether the league had pledged to keep the Pilots in Seattle through 1970. If this were the case, Dwyer said, a new owner could be found for the team. However, he acknowledged that once the team was gone from Seattle, it would be gone for good.

Milwaukee Brewers attorney Elwin Zarwell was present at the hearing but initially told Volinn he had no instructions from the group to appear officially on their behalf.[37] Volinn opened the proceedings by stating that if an offer were to be considered, it would make sense that someone be able to answer questions about that offer. He added that no offer had been attached to the petition by the Pilots, so in his mind there was no offer before the court.[38]

Zarwell asked for some time to contact the Brewers group for instruction, and by early afternoon he had been given clearance to answer questions on their behalf.[39] Tops on Volinn's list were questions about an agreement the Brewers had entered into leasing the spring training site in Tempe rather than purchasing it. He also questioned whether the AL had approved the transfer of sale, which Zarwell could not confirm.

Other last-minute hiccups included attorneys for Seattle promoter Fred Ruge making a pitch for their client to buy the team. Attorneys for the Pilots' radio network argued that the network had a $212,000 contract, which gave Golden West Broadcasting full veto power over any sale or transfer of broadcasting rights.[40]

Volinn recessed the hearing until the following morning at 9:00 a.m. He decided he wanted more time to consider the AL constitution and added that not all matters had been discussed.[41] The court never reconvened as Volinn approved the sale of the team for $10.8 million to the Brewers that night. He said it was obvious the Pilots couldn't pay their

Six. The Pilots Crash Land

debts and survive a second season in Seattle. The only other solution would have been to force the league to carry the debt, and Volinn did not believe this to be fair. "Every way we turn around, we have an assured $10.8 million offer from Milwaukee," Volinn expressed. "If we don't take that, we have nothing."[42]

Zarwell declared that the verbal statement was as good as written approval. It would take a $20 million bond put up by Washington State to bring forth a review of Volinn's decision, and that wasn't about to happen. A new Milwaukee baseball franchise was now a slam-dunk.

Volinn wisely appointed a receiver to oversee the aftermath of the sale. Any funds of the sale that were to be distributed needed to be on the order of his court. Max Soriano was elated to be out of the legal and financial mess. He expressed hope that someone else would come along and bring baseball back to the city in the approved domed stadium.[43]

The move of the Pilots opened baseball up to a fight over being exempt of antitrust laws. Dwyer promised that the city of Seattle and state of Washington would push on in their $82 million antitrust damage suit, which had already been filed in court.[44] The suit would proceed with the removal of the team.

As Volinn announced his decision in favor of the franchise sale, Selig was back at home in Milwaukee, pacing the floor. His phone rang at 10:15 p.m., and *Milwaukee Sentinel* sports editor Lloyd Larson delivered the news, exclaiming that they got the franchise.

After the brief phone call, the two men went in totally different directions. Larson acted quickly to get as much information as possible about the new Milwaukee franchise into the next day's paper—April 1—but it was no April Fools' Day joke. Selig stopped pacing long enough to collapse into a chair and cry tears of joy over what he says today was his proudest career accomplishment.

"It was a long, tough 5½ years with a lot of rejection, and a lot of sadness," Selig confessed. "Then the ultimate happened. Nothing will ever give me the satisfaction that [landing the team] did."[45]

The team's equipment truck left Tempe, but the driver didn't know if he was going to Seattle or Milwaukee. He was instructed to drive as far as Provo, Utah, before stopping for word on which direction to travel. When Volinn's decision became final, the truck took a right turn and headed northeast to Milwaukee.

The immediate celebration in Milwaukee seemed rather subdued. When the news broke, a few fans whooped it up at places like Ray Jackson's, the Sports Inn, Gene & Marcy's, and Bert's Tap. The bars weren't packed by any means since it was a Tuesday night. Some of the patrons that were out cheered and made plans to get to the stadium as soon as tickets went on sale.

Baseball fans at home called radio and television stations in Racine and Milwaukee to ask if what they had heard about the team moving was true. The stations reported that their switchboards became jammed due to the huge volume of calls.

Not everyone concerned with the team shared the same happiness. First baseman Mike Hegan had serious personal issues when the team moved. He had purchased a home in Seattle the previous winter for his family and had yet to spend a day in the dream home. Pitching coach Wes Stock also had Washington property and hoped the team would stick around, but acknowledged that he had to go wherever the club went.[46] Others such as speedster Tommy Harper did not have those issues, but he believed the Pilots should have one more year to straighten out their problems.[47]

As for learning about the franchise move, pitcher Dave Baldwin states, "I went out on the field one morning, looked at the scoreboard, saw that 'Milwaukee' was taped over 'Seattle.' I thought it was a prank. It wasn't."[48]

Bristol hoped the players would be able to adjust after the season started.[49] He sized up the team by saying he thought the pitching and defense were good, but the hitting was spotty. Unlike his predecessor, Joe Schultz, Bristol refused to predict a third-place finish. Bristol considered 70 wins a good season and thought his team could make things interesting at the very least.

Left behind in the shuffle were the many Sicks' Stadium employees facing unemployment. They quietly packed mementos of the Seattle Pilots to ship to Milwaukee, including batting helmets, caps, T-shirts, and mascot dolls. They also dealt with the issue of no-longer-needed concession supplies for Opening Day.

The second annual Pilots pre-season luncheon at the swanky Olympic Hotel ballroom wasn't cancelled despite the lack of a team. Sponsors decided it should still go on and would have the feel of an Irish wake, which seemed like a wise move after just 15 people attended the event. Mayor Wes Uhlman made an appearance but had shifted his focus from the plight of the Pilots to preventing a city-wide garbage strike.[50] In the background, the hotel worried about loss of revenue for rooms being held for the California Angels, who should have been in town for Opening Day.

While those who were left behind lamented the loss of their home

Six. The Pilots Crash Land

team, players, coaches, and executives began to look forward to their new home. Milkes expressed sadness in leaving behind Seattle after being an executive there for five years, but was beyond happy to keep his general manager job. He looked to the future by saying, "You know, I've never been to Milwaukee."[51]

Selig didn't sleep the night he won the Seattle franchise in bankruptcy court. There wasn't time for sleep—he and his ownership group needed to get ready for a morning press conference. They also had to get moving on hiring people to staff a formerly empty ballpark. Could they sell tickets fast enough to pack Opening Day? They had so many unanswered questions, but finally the question of franchise ownership had been settled.

Selig got a huge motivational boost the following morning when he arrived at Milwaukee County Stadium. Former Green Bay Packers coach Vince Lombardi sent a telegram with the message: "Congratulations on getting a team you worked so hard for."[52] Selig kept the telegram, and it eventually hung on the wall of his Milwaukee commissioner's office.

While Selig had become well-known in Wisconsin, not everyone was familiar with him. Reliever Ken Sanders says he didn't know any of the new ownership group.[53] When starter Marty Pattin saw Selig for the first time, he blurted to Sanders, "Hey, Jerry Lewis bought the team!"[54]

Sanders remarked in recent years that no one was sure how Selig would pay the team's salaries, which was a fair concern after the financial issues the Seattle Pilots experienced. He indicated that the combined salaries for the players and coaches came out to about $729,000.[55] Dick Ellsworth led the team with a $40,000 salary, with Max Alvis second at $30,000. Adjusted for inflation, today Ellsworth would make $247,666—well below the 2015 league minimum salary of $507,500. No matter the pay level, Selig felt confident his ownership group had enough financial strength to keep the franchise afloat in the long term.[56]

The front page of the Wednesday, April 1, 1970, *Milwaukee Journal* trumpeted the city being big league again. Selig still declined to celebrate fully. He was waiting to hear what he called comments of the other appropriate parties that would make the sale of the Seattle Pilots to Milwaukee Brewers, Inc. official.

One of the "appropriate parties" was bankruptcy referee Sidney Volinn. Back in Seattle, he held a meeting in his courtroom to sign papers officially transferring the team to Milwaukee. The verbiage in the court order had been deliberated over for nearly three hours by lawyers before they came to agreement. He signed the order for the sale of the Pilots to the Brewers at 7:50 p.m. EST, and this action opened the door for the state of Washington and city of Seattle to move ahead with their $82 million antitrust suit.

Milwaukee politicians were obviously much happier with the outcome of the bankruptcy hearing. County Board Chairman Eugene Grobschmidt also was excited but cautioned the public not to expect a contending team for at least a couple of years. Yet he did express hope that the new team could repeat the path of the New York Mets from expansion team to World Series champions.[57]

Grobschmidt mentioned that the county board had worked to approve a contract that would encourage the Brewers organization in bringing baseball back to Milwaukee.[58] The county would take parking receipts, but wouldn't take a cut of the concession or ticket sales until the team sold one million tickets.

Baseball weather was nowhere to be found when Selig's contingent arrived at the Pfister Hotel for a press conference officially announcing the Milwaukee Brewers franchise and its upcoming arrival in the city. Cold and snowy conditions ruled the day as Selig read a telegram from American league president Joe Cronin welcoming the Brewers into the league. Cronin sealed the move of the Pilots to Milwaukee by stating in the telegram: "On behalf of the American League, I want to convey my congratulations to your organization on its return to baseball."[59]

Selig joked that his organization was having the shortest season-ticket sale in baseball history, with ticket prices announced on the day of the press conference.[60] Selig's ownership group remained optimistic that sales would go well even with a short window until Opening Day.[61]

The club initially announced they would sell home game tickets only for the April games at the stadium. Lowest price tickets were $1 for Bleachers, $2 for Upper Grandstand and $150 for the season, $3 and $225 for Lower Grandstand, $4 and $300 for Lower Box, and $5 and $375 for Mezzanine. Game times were announced, with day games starting at 1:30 p.m., night games at 8:00 p.m., and twilight-night doubleheaders at 6 p.m.

The Brewers requested some schedule changes, with an April game being changed to a doubleheader in July. The Green Bay Packers caused two conflicts late in the season, but Selig said those issues would be dealt with later. He also reported that the team would only play day games during the month of April.[62]

Naturally there was a huge push to sell as many tickets as possible, mainly to eclipse the Pilots' poor attendance in 1969, but also to get beyond the one million mark. However, an advantageous deal happened to exist on the rental of County Stadium: if the team didn't draw one million fans, the rental cost would be just $1. If more than one million fans came through the gates, the team would pay the county five percent of gross admissions after taxes and other deductions. The percentage would rise to seven percent for 1.5 million fans and ten percent for two million or more.

A favorable financial picture appeared possible even if the Brewers did not meet their attendance goals. The Milwaukee Braves had claimed to lose money when attendance dropped below one million fans. However, many of the losses in the later years came from interest payments on the loans used by the Chicago syndicate to purchase the team. Depreciation on high-value players and a low-revenue radio/television package also were factors contributing to the losses on paper.

The Brewers' radio/television package would net more than double that of the Braves. Carrying a second-year roster made up of mostly expansion draft players meant a lower value rather than the championship players with the Braves. These factors plus the stadium rental provisions all meant a lower break-even point compared to the Braves.

Newspapers quickly updated all the remaining spring games on their sports pages to Milwaukee vs. the opposing team. Members of the media also noted how appropriately named the Brewers were—Wisconsin led the country in yearly beer consumption with 27.2 gallons downed per person (including children).[63]

Wisconsin media outlets started rounding up information on the new team and season. The *Milwaukee Journal* ran a large ad asking fans to follow their new big league club in the newspaper. Other Wisconsin newspapers scrambled to put staff writers in place to break down the Brewers roster and all the happenings in Milwaukee.

As big league baseball returned, Mother Nature still held a wintry grip over the state. Wisconsinites are generally used to "spring" merely being a word, a tease at times when winter skips straight to summer. The 1970 winter had been typical for Wisconsin, with each month getting a bit warmer than the last. When all was said and done, January in Milwaukee had an average temperature in the mid–30s—a veritable heat wave according to locals.

By March, the weather turned into tease mode, with a day that hit the upper 40s with sunshine. The warming trend didn't hold as temperatures plummeted heading into April and the announced return of baseball to the Cream City. To make matters worse, wind speeds increased and only reinforced the bitter chill.

The weather forecast called for more snow into the weekend prior to Opening Day with an expected high temperature in the upper 30s. By April 2, fans were driving in snow to County Stadium to buy season tickets. They arrived in five inches of snow in the parking lot and enormous drifts due to 50 mile-per-hour winds.

The poor conditions didn't keep fans from scarfing up tickets to see their new team in action. One ticket office worker used the word "bedlam" in describing the ticket sales to local media. The madness had just begun and wasn't about to let up.[64]

Selig had correctly gauged the initial interest level, as more than 1,000 season tickets were purchased on the first day of sales. Workers somehow found the time to sort, count, and make tickets ready for distribution the following day.

Milwaukee Braves fans had an opportunity to get their old season seat locations back for upcoming Brewers games. Priority was also given to Chicago White Sox season-ticket holders. Brisk ticket sales continued as the weekend passed and other work around the stadium took shape.

The concession stands were announced as cleaned and stocked on Sunday—and all Milwaukee beers would be on sale for Opening Day. A few changes to the Brewers ownership group were also announced, with two investors dropping out and seven new owners named. One of the new names was familiar—William Daley of the Seattle Pilots ownership group.

Jerome Holtzman of the *Chicago Sun-Times* claimed later in the summer that Selig and Fitzgerald made an 11th-hour trip to Boston to ask Daley for help in coming up with a down payment on the Pilots.[65] Selig later denied going to Boston and said 84 percent of the team was held by Wisconsin investors, the other 16 percent by Daley.[66]

A total of 23 partners made up the ownership group. Only $5.1 million of the $10.8 million used to buy the franchise in bankruptcy court came in the form of cash. The remaining money was in the form of notes provided by Northwestern Mutual Life Insurance Company and the Sportservice, Inc. stadium food vendor. Northwestern could potentially wind up as the sole owner if Selig and his individual partners decided to quit funding the team.

Selig had his team and ownership group finalized—but did his team have uniforms? It turned out a few prototypes were created a couple years back in case Selig nabbed a team. A few photos had already surfaced with those prototypes. One had pinstripes with navy blue script lettering—a nod to the old American Association Brewers uniforms. Another photo showed pitcher Marty Pattin modeling a jersey with capital letters and narrow stripes at the end of the sleeves.

Six. The Pilots Crash Land   105

With the tight timeline until Opening Day, there simply wasn't time to get the prototypes ready. The team went the route of "minor adjustments" and tore off the "Pilots" name from the jerseys and put "Brewers" on in its place. However, anyone looking closely could still see the outline of "Pilots" on the jerseys. For the caps, an "M" replaced the "S"—and, as with the jerseys, the caps kept the base colors of blue, gold, and white.

When the *Milwaukee Journal* published a team photo on Sunday, April 5, the caption said readers were meeting the Brewers—although players and coaches had on the Pilots uniforms. The photo had been taken in the latter stages of spring training, prior to jerseys being adjusted. Manager Dave Bristol had yet to finalize his roster, so by the time it was published, six players were noted as no longer with the major league team.

Bristol did set his starting pitching rotation a few days before the season opener, choosing all right-handers—Lew Krausse, Gene Brabender, Marty Pattin, George Lauzerique, and Bob Bolin. Only Brabender and Pattin were holdovers from the previous season. Krausse was tabbed for the Opening Day assignment.

The American League didn't institute the designated hitter in place of the pitcher until 1973, so the Brewers staff had another assignment—batting. The vast majority of the pitchers hit well south of .200 for the year, but Lauzerique, Bob Bolin, and Skip Lockwood did manage to hit home runs.

There wasn't as much certainty on the team when it came to the position players, as Bristol admitted only four spots were set—first baseman Mike Hegan, second baseman Tommy Harper, shortstop Ted Kubiak, and catcher Jerry McNertney. "I'd be lying if I didn't say I was looking for a center fielder," Bristol divulged.[67]

In a direct response to Bristol's need for an outfielder, GM Marvin Milkes pulled off two key moves just before the season opener. On April 4, he traded Frank Coggins and Ray Foster to the Cleveland Indians and received third baseman Max Alvis and outfielder Russ Snyder in return. The next day, he purchased outfielder Ted Savage from the Cincinnati Reds. Bristol knew Savage well from his managerial stint with the Reds. Snyder and Savage found playing for a second-year expansion team to be a great opportunity, as each appeared in over 100 games in 1970.

Most names on the roster would be unfamiliar to fans unless they had followed the Milwaukee Braves or the Chicago White Sox during the years they played at County Stadium. Outfielder Sandy Valdespino played in Wisconsin for the Appleton Foxes, but his stint there happened in 1958.

The old cry of stadium vendors that you can't tell the players without a scorecard seemed in the Brewers' case to be accurate.

The team wrapped up spring training in Tempe with a game against the Cleveland Indians. They were beaten soundly, 11–3, as Wisconsin native Gene Brabender took the brunt of the beating. Seattle/Milwaukee finished with a 13–15 spring record and prepared to head to their new home in the Midwest.

Seven

One Million or Bust

The team left spring training and flew to Milwaukee with a scheduled nighttime arrival, but were unaware of the large crowd waiting at the airport. The new Brewers were met by an estimated 8,000 fans waving supportive banners while singing "Take Me Out to the Ball Game." Many started lining up at 7:30 p.m. just to get a glimpse of the Brewers. High winds and a chilly spring rain stopped just before the team arrived.

Dave Bristol was the first off the team's charter flight at 10:07 p.m. He came down from the plane with stewardess Barbara Heimann on his arm. She was wearing a Brewers prototype uniform—a version that wouldn't be used in 1970. A photo of Heimann in the uniform and infielder John Kennedy greeting fans later ran in several newspapers. Heimann told the press the guys on the team were fantastic and fans would love them.[1]

Dozens of horn-honking cars followed the team's buses as they maneuvered through the downtown area to the Sheraton-Schroeder Hotel. Another 200 fans gathered at the hotel to greet their new team.

Normally Bud Selig was good for a well-thought-out comment, but he was clearly moved by the scene at Mitchell Field and could only say, "I think the crowd is amazing for a cold, rainy night like this."[2] He wasn't the only one taken aback by the rousing welcome.

General manager Marvin Milkes also couldn't quite comprehend the warm fan reception. He commented, "I can't believe people like this exist anymore. People have been calling the office, volunteering their services and offering their homes for use by players and their families."[3]

Milkes hoped the Brewers would be worthy of the fans and speculated that the reception would have a profound effect on his players.[4] Odds makers in Las Vegas didn't believe in the team's worthiness or any profound effects from being first in fans' hearts. When odds makers assessed the upcoming AL West pennant race, the Brewers and Kansas City Royals were placed as 100–1 shots. Baltimore and Minnesota were given the nod to win the AL divisional races.

Neither Milkes nor Bristol would predict a pennant for the new Brewers team. Milkes did pledge to help bring the Milwaukee community back to what everyone felt was the baseball capital of the world. Milkes said the bulk of the Pilots front office would remain intact, and a publicity department would be named later.[5]

The day after arriving, the team had a noon luncheon at the Pfister Hotel put on by the Metropolitan Milwaukee Association of Commerce. It served as an official welcome by the community to players and staff, and the 650 tickets sold out quickly at $5 each. The Association of Commerce gave an estimate at the luncheon that $8 million would enter the local economy due to the return of baseball.

After the luncheon, Bristol planned to showcase Milwaukee's new team to the press and other onlookers in one final tune-up for the season. He scheduled a workout for the team at County Stadium the following day and expressed optimism over the changes in the team's roster from the previous season. The new Brewers roster had only 14 players left out of 53 who had played in Seattle.

The roster turnover decreased the average player age. Not everyone was happy about the youth movement, especially relief pitchers Ken Sanders and Dave Baldwin, who were on the wrong side of the age level and were sent to the Brewers' AAA team in Portland, Oregon (Pacific Coast League).

The farm system also included affiliates in Clinton, Iowa (Midwest League), Newark, New Jersey (Rookie League), and a winter rookie entry in the Arizona Instructional League. Milwaukee had 148 players under contract, including those in Milwaukee to start the inaugural Brewers season.

On Tuesday, April 7, 1970, Bristol sent out the following lineup against the visiting California Angels for Opening Day:

      Tommy Harper   2B
      Russ Snyder   CF
      Mike Hegan   1B
      Danny Walton   LF
      Steve Hovley   RF
      Jerry McNertney   C
      Max Alvis   3B
      Ted Kubiak   SS
      Lew Krausse   P

Seven. One Million or Bust

The fans were treated to actual spring weather conditions even though many had trekked through snow and gusty winds to purchase tickets a few days earlier. Sunshine and a balmy (for Milwaukee in April) 57 degrees with light winds from the south made for a great opener.

Players for both teams were introduced by the voice of the Braves, Earl Gillespie. They received raucous cheers for several minutes as they ran to stand along the baselines. Gillespie acknowledged former Braves manager Fred Haney in his box seat, team president Selig, Mayor Henry Maier, and County Board Chairman Eugene Grobschmidt.[6] All four received thunderous applause.

The crowd split over their love/hate for Governor Knowles and Commissioner Bowie Kuhn, as each received as many cheers as boos. All agreed over their collective dislike for American League President Joe Cronin, as boos rained down on the executive.

The fanfare continued with Milwaukee County Executive John Doyne taking to the pitching rubber for the ceremonial first pitch. Doyne showed a strong arm with a strike down the middle to Brewers catcher Jerry McNertney, leaving fans and players on the cusp of a new Milwaukee baseball era.

The new era would be interrupted briefly after another "first pitch" by Brewers pitcher Lew Krausse to Sandy Alomar of the Angels (formerly of the Milwaukee and Atlanta Braves, 1964–1966). After the pitch, the ball was taken out of play and tagged for the National Baseball Hall of Fame in Cooperstown, New York.

Krausse didn't last long in the game itself, after being roughed up for four runs in three innings. The Angels cruised to an easy 12–0 victory. John Gelnar came on to pitch after Krausse but allowed four more runs without retiring any hitters. Krausse headed for the clubhouse and, before he knew it, Gelnar was in there with him. Bob Meyer gave up another three runs on five hits and a walk. Surprisingly, the Angels scored all their runs without hitting a home run. The Brewers helped them out by committing two errors.

Meyer recalls other factors beyond a mismatch that may have contributed to the one-sided loss. He states, "What most stands out regarding that game was our long workout the day before at the stadium. Dave Bristol, our manager, was all charged up and pushed us with a lot of running, etc. I think a lot of the guys were tired from that extended workout."[7]

Bristol didn't believe any of his players had anxiety issues, but rookie outfielder Danny Walton admitted to being shaky. The size of the crowd overwhelmed him, leading to a misplayed fly ball and butterflies in his first two at-bats.[8]

Milwaukee didn't do much to muster any offense as they collected only four hits—and three of those were by Steve Hovley. Andy Messersmith threw a complete game and struck out 11, making his win look easy. Bristol dejectedly asserted that Messersmith looked like Hall of Fame pitcher Walter Johnson. In retrospect, he said that Seattle had its expansion draft, and maybe they should have had another one for Milwaukee.[9]

First baseman Mike Hegan gave a tip of the cap to the fans for having unbelievable patience and still cheering for the team in the eighth inning when the score was 10–0.[10] Pitcher John Morris agreed, saying "The opener was electric. I felt privileged to be part of the franchise."[11]

The lack of offensive electricity was offset by a few fans taking matters into their own hands. They ran on the field with a banner or a roll of toilet paper and were apprehended by security. Nine juveniles between the ages of 13 and 17 were taken into custody by game's end. During the ninth inning, the uprisings got out of control, with fans streaming on the field and scuffling with attendants and the police, before being shut down for good.

Fans who remained in the stands displayed banners with messages such as "Go Braves No. 2" and "Go Sandy V," with the Sandy Valdespino Fan Club happy they could see their favorite player as a pinch-hitter.

Some fans were turned off by the 50 cents per cup charged for beer. Most beer drinkers needed to visit the concession stand for suds due to a shortage of vendors roaming the stands. One vendor was spotted serving up draft beer from a spigoted barrel.

Attendance came in at 36,107 for the contest—below County Stadium's capacity—but was considered a great number considering the short window for ticket sales and lingering winter weather. The total eclipsed the Braves' home opener in 1953 of 35,701.

Most of the fans remained until the end of the game despite the drubbing. When the game ended, it took roughly 45 minutes for the 8,000 cars to get out of the parking lot, with help from 22 deputies directing traffic.

The game had been broadcast on radio, with Merle Harmon and Tom Collins calling the action. Seattle Pilots announcers Bill Schonely and Jimmy Dudley were left behind when the team broke training camp in Tempe. Harmon and Collins would also double as TV voices for 26 games in 1970, with Milwaukee Bucks announcer Eddie Doucette assisting them in the booth.

In all, 16 players can lay claim to appearing in the first Milwaukee

Brewers franchise game. While he didn't make an appearance, infielder John Kennedy was happy to be in a Brewers uniform for their first game, as he had played in the last Braves game in Milwaukee. Coach Roy McMillan was also a link to the Braves, having been an infielder for the team from 1961 through 1964. He joined Bristol's coaching staff that included former Minnesota manager Cal Ermer, pitching coach Wes Stock, and bullpen coach Jackie Moore.

Pitcher Gene Brabender saw his childhood dream fulfilled when he stepped on the field at County Stadium before the game. His uncle had taken him to a Braves game at age 12, and Brabender later told his dad that he would one day play in County Stadium.[12] "Bender" became the first Wisconsin native to appear in a game for the Brewers. He grew up west of Madison near the small town of Black Earth on a farm, and baseball took him from milking cows, to a tryout and signing with the Los Angeles Dodgers.

Brabender went on to play three seasons in Baltimore (and won a World Series there in 1966) under future Brewers general manager Harry Dalton before being traded to the Seattle Pilots. He was legendary for his many pranks with the Pilots, such as nailing shoes to the floor and shooting darts with a blowgun in the general direction of his teammates.

Selig wasn't pranked on Opening Day, but a fan made him feel like the joke was on him. Selig recalled, "That was the only time in my life when I didn't give a damn if we lost."[13] He ran into a fan who had a different reaction. He pointed his finger at Selig and said, "You wanted a team in the worst way—and that's what you got!" Selig said, "I knew then the honeymoon was not going to last very long."[14]

The baseball honeymoon was officially over in Seattle as fans and the media processed through the myriad of reasons why the Pilots failed. Poor relations between the club and city officials, along with playing in an outdated minor league park, always made the list. Time and time again, the lack of equity capital in a start-up business rose to the top as what effectively ended the Pilots franchise.

On paper, the Pilots looked like a profitable endeavor—at least initially. William Daley recalled that a huge misstep happened due to a projection from Price Waterhouse that the Pilots would make $900,000 in profit in 1969. Of the team's $4 million capitalization, $3 million was in loans by shareholders to the company and the other $1 million in shares. After the projection, the club paid $2 million to the shareholders. Later, when ownership realized the projection was off and they would lose money, they took out the loan to put the money back in.

The Milwaukee Brewers Baseball Club, Inc. cleaned up all of Seattle's money issues by mid–April and became 100 percent Brewers on the ledger. The Brewers made their final $500,000 payment on the $10.8 million purchase on April 13 and complied with their contract.

Richard Saunders, the receiver appointed by the federal bankruptcy court, still needed to pay off the creditors. The process could take up to fourth months to finalize. The Bank of California had already been paid $3,592,361, and concessionaire Sportservice, Inc. received $2.044 million.

For all intents and purposes, April was one long road trip for the Brewers, as they had only four home games on their schedule. In the hustle of relocating the franchise, there wasn't enough time for major league baseball to realign divisions. Milwaukee was dropped into the American League West in Seattle's former spot, and this put the team at a bit of a geographical disadvantage.

Milwaukee inherited Seattle's planned schedule for 1970, which meant a lot of long trips to the West Coast followed by short bursts back to the Midwest and the East Coast. Occasionally a scheduled doubleheader would be followed by a flight to one of the coasts and another game the following day.

Milkes continued following the same path he had carved out in Seattle, working the phones to come up with transactions to improve his ballclub. His frantic pace led to a hospital stay in early August when he entered Milwaukee Lutheran Hospital for a complete checkup. Milkes was ordered to stay for nearly a week after being reported in a state of exhaustion.

Despite Milkes' efforts, the Brewers quickly fell to the bottom of the standings. The Brewers front office faced issues the Milwaukee Braves didn't experience when they moved from Boston. The Brewers were a second-year expansion team in search of a new identity in a new city. The front office went to work on building a new image through promotions, ranging from typical baseball fare to completely unorthodox gambles.

The first promotion fell on the oddball end of the spectrum. The Brewers partnered with a local radio station to bring in a witch practitioner named Witch Barbara to cast a winning spell over the team. The idea came about after a broadcaster from the radio station had talked to a Los Angeles woman named Witch Louise about possible pennant contender spells.

Witch Louise touted herself as an empowered protector of toads and demons, along with being a sixth-generation descendent of the occult powers of witchcraft. She explained that the spell would only be effective if it was cast just before the first night of the full moon.

Just before sunrise on April 22, a group of roughly 1,500 fans and Witch Barbara gathered around home plate on a giant cloth. They lit candles and chanted: "We offer this flame to the god of Venus as a gift to the cosmos and so to the wind.... The Brewers are the cosmos, the Brewers are the wind, the Brewers are all powerful. The Brewers will win the pennant."[15]

While nothing is publicly documented about Witch Louise casting pennant-winning spells on California teams that season, if she did, the magic didn't work there either. None of the five California baseball teams won the pennant in 1970.

The long April road trip not only allowed for spell casting, it also gave Selig time to bring in more staff for ticket sales. He also put his head together with Milkes and others to come up with promotions for game days rather than just allowing witches to chant in an empty stadium. Standard promotions for cap, helmet, and bat giveaways were planned, plus player autograph sessions, an old-timers game, and a Banner Night to celebrate the team.

The Brewers held an organizational meeting in early May and named five directors and five officers. Bud Selig, Edmund Fitzgerald, Everitt Smith, Roswell Stearns, and Carlton P. Wilson were elected to the board. All were part-owners, save for Wilson.

Selig was elected president, Milkes and Judge Robert Cannon vice presidents, Dick Cutler secretary-treasurer, and Robert Schoenbachler controller and assistant secretary-treasurer. Milkes received a vote of confidence when he received a fresh five-year contract from team owners.

Within a few weeks of the organizational announcements, rumors circulated that former Chicago White Sox owner Arthur Allyn would buy a stake in the Brewers. Selig shut down the rumors by insisting the group was all sold out and needed no more investors, even though they still thought highly of Allyn.[16]

The new Brewers front office worked out a return of the Braves for an exhibition game on May 14. This, of course, also marked the return of Henry Aaron to Milwaukee, so Selig and the others planned a special pre-game ceremony to honor the legend. At 36 years old, Aaron was only five hits away from the 3,000-hit mark and one of four players remaining from the 1965 team who left for Atlanta. His brother, Tommy Aaron, Phil Niekro, and Rico Carty were the others. Carty was a late-comer to the Braves, arriving in 1963.

Hank Allen had just been acquired by the Brewers from the Washington Senators. Allen decided to wear uniform No. 44 upon his arrival—the same number worn by Aaron in his years with the Braves. When Aaron returned to Milwaukee to play for the Brewers in 1975–1976, he again wore No. 44. Besides Allen and Aaron, only Gorman Thomas used No. 44 (1973–1974) before the number was officially retired after the 1976 season.

A chilly, 45-degree night with occasional showers played a part in keeping attendance to 25,899 fans. Another factor was lackluster play. By the time the Brewers took up residence for their first true home stand in early May, they carried a 5–19 record. Earl Gillespie, former broadcast voice of the Braves, served as the master of ceremonies for the pre-game festivities. Hank Aaron received a two-minute standing ovation during the emotional ceremony.

Fans cheered loudly during the game for Aaron and Brewers outfielder Danny Walton, who had emerged as an offensive star with backers in an enthusiastic bleacher fan club called the Brew Crew. The fan club unknowingly selected a name for their group that would go on to become a well-known nickname for the entire team.

But the night wasn't filled with just cheers, such as "Go Danny, Go!" from the Brew Crew. The crowd used the rare opportunity to boo hated Braves board chairman Bill Bartholomay. Bartholomay noted the impressive turnout and appeared happy to have a chance to cure what he called a self-inflicted wound. He added, "There's no way you can make me popular in Milwaukee, but the important thing is Henry tonight, and it's wonderful. I think this is an amazing crowd for this kind of night, a real tribute to baseball."[17]

What was called a "grudge exhibition" and "two eras of baseball" by local press played out as a stellar performance by Brewers pitcher Skip Lockwood.[18] He scattered six hits while striking out Aaron, and drove in the winning run for a 1–0, complete-game victory.

The team went back to drawing small crowds at home. It would be a month until County Stadium saw a crowd the size of the Braves exhibition, and that may have been bolstered by a softball game between the Lake Geneva Playboy Club bunnies and local media personalities. Poor weather, lingering Braves bitterness, kids being in school, and the constant player shuffle were all touted as reasons for the lack of early interest.

Player transactions were commonplace for the new Milwaukee club. The attempt to rebuild the team led to 45 players making at least one game appearance in 1970—and a few others who joined the team in September but never saw action. Milkes kept the roster hopping, although it wasn't quite to the level of the 1969 Seattle Pilots team which had 53 players appear overall.

The front office decided to hold a second "opening day" on Monday, June 22, with an organized "Welcome to Milwaukee" celebration the night before at Mitchell Field. The second home opener idea came about as a way to introduce the new player arrivals, since much of the roster had already turned over.

Over 1,000 fans came out to wave banners and cheer as each player was introduced when he moved from the airport gate to the concourse. Fan clubs such as the Brewers Bums and Brew Crew led the cheering as a Dixieland band played for the attendees. The crowd size paled in comparison to when the team arrived from Seattle, but it was a reasonably effective springboard for the second home opener against the Minnesota Twins.

Appropriately enough, the Brewers sent Wisconsin native Gene Brabender to the hill, but he lasted just over four innings and took his ninth loss of the season. A little over 18,000 fans came out for the game—which was good considering the Brewers were in last place with a 21–43 record—but still not what Selig and Milkes hoped for. They needed either several small promotions to bring fans out to County Stadium, or at least one big promotion to grab attention.

Milkes had an idea for a promotion that wound up leaving a lasting impact on the team and city. He had the wild notion of hoisting a 24×8 trailer onto the County Stadium scoreboard in right-center field, with 69-year-old Milt Mason as a resident, under the promotional name Bernie Brewer. Milkes confessed the need to have something that would create curiosity.

Bernie was to remain atop the scoreboard until the Brewers either drew a capacity crowd or the season ended. The trailer and the few items inside cost the Brewers roughly $7,000, but that was the extent of the cost as Mason declined a salary. He insisted he wasn't interested in the money and was just happy to do Milkes a favor.

Mason said, "I told Mr. Milkes that I love this game so much that I'd do just about anything to help our team, and if being up on the scoreboard will help focus attention on the Brewers, then I'm all for it."[19]

Milkes had known Mason since 1961, during his stint as Assistant GM of the Angels. Mason was a retired aviation engineer and joined the team as a spring training locker room guard. He also performed a lot of odd jobs for the team and then followed Milkes to Seattle and Milwaukee.

Mason and the trailer were placed atop the scoreboard on Monday, July 6. The trailer had some modern conveniences such as a gas stove, refrigerator, exercise bike, two telephones, and a 21-inch color television. Meals were delivered to Mason via a dumbwaiter, compliments of various Milwaukee restaurants.

The Brewers also gave Mason access to the public address system so he could fire up the County Stadium fans, and he had a pistol to fire into the sky after home runs. He'd also hold up signs calling for the Brewers to hit or steal, and for opposing teams to strike out. Mason paced outside the trailer during ballgames, and his pacing and working the crowd became part of future Bernie Brewer characters.

Mason made the best of his situation and became a great fit for the Bernie persona. He wore authentic German clothing including suspenders, lederhosen, a Tyrolean hat, and socks that went high up his legs. Mason wasn't the only one around County Stadium wearing lederhosen, as the grounds crew also wore this garment.

Besides his distinctive outfit, Mason also became known for his love of beer. He jokingly divulged that he didn't drink beer except on warm days—otherwise he detested it![20] One thing Mason apparently didn't do was bathe. It was reported that he "ripened" as summer dragged on and he remained in his perch.[21]

The Brewers won Mason's first game in his new digs, beating the Chicago White Sox, 3–1. Only 11,363 were in attendance, but team officials had high hopes that Mason's stunt meant droves of curious fans would come out to the ballpark. Some thought Mason would be on top of the trailer for a week, tops. But they were quite wrong with such a conservative estimate.

Mason spent the All-Star break in the trailer while every Brewers player took time off, save for Tommy Harper, the lone representative at Cincinnati's Riverfront Stadium. The Brewers clearly needed a break after playing to a 32–57 record, 25.5 games out of first place.

The Bernie Brewer stunt helped the team draw weekend crowds consistently over 20,000. On August 2, the team surpassed the entire 1969 Seattle Pilots season attendance mark. With 22 remaining home dates, Selig was elated. Selig said he felt the bitterness over the Braves was long gone, and the new breed of fan seemed to be predominantly younger and very enthusiastic. "Things have been hectic—almost hysterical—around here the last three months," Selig noted. "This should be an experience a man lives thru only once. Not only did we have only a week's notice to sell season tickets, but early in the season the weather was worse than horrendous. During a three-game series with the Yankees, it was 38 degrees and raining."²²

While Selig remained optimistic over attendance marks and fan engagement, the team did little to help matters. As for Bernie Brewer, the only thing that was going to get him down from the scoreboard was a crowd of more than 40,000 fans. The original, capacity-crowd target had been dropped to something that seemed a bit more attainable.

The Brewers came home for an eight-game stretch that would take them through mid–August. Selig and Milkes had pushed many other promotions so far—but perhaps the only visual that could rival Bernie Brewer was a cow-milking contest before a game between the Brewers and California Angels.

Brabender went up against Eddie Fisher in a battle between a former farm boy and a knuckleball relief pitcher. They milked cows named Moochie Marie and Myra, with the winner of the contest determined by most milk by weight in three minutes. Fisher ended up winning with ten pounds of milk to Brabender's six pounds.

The peculiar promotion was a polar opposite of the more subdued "Wisconsin Backs the Brewers Night" that also included Brabender. Over 100 leaders representing 29 Wisconsin communities were special guests of the Metropolitan Chamber of Commerce and the Brewers. They toured the Joseph Schlitz Brewing Company and attended a Brewers game, where they mingled with players and team executives. The objective of the promotion was to send happy leaders back to their communities to extol the virtues of Milwaukee.

Milkes often maintained that baseball franchises needed to make an extra effort beyond just having games to get people out to the ballpark. His stated goal was to make attending a game fun at all times, and he drew from his minor league promotional experience in setting up Milwaukee County Stadium promotions. He asserted that the team would be promoting just as hard if they were contending.²³

A planned Bat Day promotion on August 16 was targeted as a possible game that could pull in enough fans to bring Mason down to earth. It was the most expensive promotion all season, as the bats cost a dollar apiece. Most promotional items cost .50–.80 each, but the team paid more for the bats due to an overall hope that interested youngsters could talk their parents into attending the games.

According to other teams, Bat Day was always the best promotion to attract people to the ballpark. The advance ticket sales amounted to just over 15,000 two days before the game. Excitement continued to build as

Paul Trione, (*left*), the city manager for Two Rivers, and Bob Humphrey (*right*), the executive vice-president of the Manitowoc–Two Rivers Chamber of Commerce, stand with Brewers pitcher Gene Brabender on Wisconsin Backs the Brewers Night in 1971. The promotion, aimed at generating buzz about Milwaukee's new team, brought 100 local leaders to County Stadium for a game and a tour of Schlitz Brewing (courtesy Wentorf Photo Collection, Lester Public Library, Two Rivers, Wisconsin).

team officials kept pushing the game in the local media, but pessimists were still claiming that Mason had better get a heater in his trailer for the upcoming winter.

Mason stayed atop the scoreboard for 40 days until 44,387 fans attended Bat Day. A total of 25,054 children under 14 years of age received a free, regulation Little League bat. It was the last time the Brewers would see single-game attendance that high at home for the remainder of the season. It was also the last time fans would see the following on the Fan-a-Gram:

"Where's Bernie Brewer! Can You Help Find Him!"
"What Will Bernie Brewer Do If He Sees a Lot of People!"

The Fan-a-Gram was not equipped with question marks, so exclamation points were used liberally. The Brewers also used exclamation points that

Seven. One Million or Bust

day in treating their fans to an exciting game, winning in comeback fashion, 4–3, over the Cleveland Indians.

Mason's 80-foot descent from the trailer was a joyous sight for the fans, but not much fun for the senior citizen. He descended from the trailer by sliding down on a rope and badly burned his hands. Mason spent a couple of days in Milwaukee Lutheran Hospital for observation and had a complete physical checkup. He might have ended up with a different end result—his first choice of jumping into a fireman's net got nixed.

Through sweltering heat and playful threats of shutting off his water supply unless a record crowd came to the ballpark, Bernie Brewer made his mark. But it wasn't the last time the Milwaukee Brewers would see Milt Mason or Bernie Brewer. Mason helped the team in spring training at Tempe in 1972, mainly performing clubhouse duties. He had also spent a couple of months with the team during the 1971 regular season.

In 1973, Bernie Brewer became the team's mascot as a tribute to Milt Mason. The new Bernie was depicted as a funny guy with a huge mustache, although he would go through some revisions over the years. Bernie had a beer-barrel chalet in the early 1980s before it was replaced by a sound tower. This change put Bernie into "retirement" from 1985 through 1992, but fans voted for his return, and he was back for good in 1993.

Mason was officially recognized as the original Bernie Brewer before his death from cancer on June 12, 1973, in San Diego. Mason had many different life experiences, including riding the wings of a stunt plane in the 1920s, yet he regarded his time as Bernie Brewer as a personal highlight.[24] "That whole period of time was my biggest thrill," he said. "I'll never forget those days."[25]

After the Bernie Brewer promotion ended at Milwaukee County Stadium, attendance resembled the early-season totals. Kids went back to school. The Green Bay Packers took the field for their 50th season but weren't expected to do well. Yet some Brewers fans turned their full attention to football, as is often the case in Wisconsin during September.

No matter the fans' allegiance, general news of the Packers and Brewers was eclipsed by the passing of former coach Vince Lombardi on September 3. Sorrow and personal loss rippled through the football community, especially in Wisconsin, where he revitalized the Packers franchise. The Packers were still a huge draw at County Stadium. On October 4, nearly 48,000 turned out to see the team take on the Minnesota Vikings.

Lost in the news at the time of Lombardi's passing was Milkes sharing a few possible storylines to follow in the baseball season's final month. He pointed out the possibility of a fourth-place finish for the Brewers in the

American League West and noted that the Brewers could be spoilers in the pennant race between the Minnesota Twins, California Angels, and Oakland Athletics.[26]

Milkes commented about reaching the million mark in attendance and what that meant not only financially, but also in comparison to what the other recent expansion clubs might draw.[27] A group of Milwaukee businessmen led by Fred Siekert and Alderman Robert Ertl launched a drive to help in the final attendance push.

Attendance (or more appropriately, a lack thereof) at County Stadium became a side story for any local media covering the Brewers. Countdowns were listed in newspapers showing the number of home games remaining on the season and what the average needed to be if the team had any hopes of reaching the magic million mark.

Even a 15–13 record in September and a visit from Commissioner Bowie Kuhn didn't help boost attendance. Kuhn mingled with the Brew Crew in the bleachers while the Brewers played a father/son game. Time eventually ran out on the season, and the Brewers ended with an attendance mark of 934,820 in 80 dates at home, finishing 16th out of 24 major league teams overall. "It was a good way to bring down the curtain," Milkes commented. "I guess I'm just a sentimental slob."[28]

Selig had good reason to be happy for reasons other than the final-month surge by the team and fan attendance. When all was said and done, the franchise reportedly showed a positive balance and appeared to be in Milwaukee to stay.

Bob Woessner of the *Green Bay Press-Gazette* interviewed Selig as the season wound down, and the two discussed everything from the Braves leaving Milwaukee to promotions. Selig pointed out the willingness of the Braves to give themselves away with discount tickets to groups, thereby cheapening the product. He assured Woessner the same mistakes would not be made by Brewers ownership.

Selig's group had two goals that he mentioned—respectability and at least a million people in the stands each year. Respectability was hard to define, but Selig mentioned that a fourth-place finish suited him in 1970. Beyond those goals, Selig felt there were many intangibles a major league team brought to Milwaukee. Selig said, "For a city, you recognize how important a ball team is when you don't have one. A team provides a spirit, it gives the city good advertising and public relations, the city's name goes around the county all the time."[29]

With one full season in the books, the Milwaukee Brewers front office could take a collective breath before planning for the future. As with any team, transactions are commonplace immediately following a season. Milkes started out slowly with a few expected moves after the season, but would soon leave his position as general manager. His successor and the person Milkes was often compared to—Frank Lane—would pretty much turn over the entire roster in less than a year.

Selig gave Milkes a vote of confidence in November, saying he did a remarkable job in sculpting a club that finished in a fourth-place tie with the Kansas City Royals.[30] With Selig's support along with the five-year contract Milkes signed back in May, his job appeared to be safe for the time being, but Milkes wasn't as secure as he was led to believe.

The franchise moved forward and took care of details that established clubs do routinely each year. The team could advertise season-ticket sales for the first time, having 158 days to sell tickets rather than just a week. The team set a goal to sell 6,000 season tickets and draw one million and one fans for the 1971 campaign. Selig announced a new club slogan—"One million and one in '71."

A total of five special promotions were scheduled for the upcoming season, all geared toward fans 14-and-under—caps, batting gloves, batting helmets, bats, and loose-leaf notebooks. The three main promotions in 1970 helped bring a total of 103,165 fans to County Stadium, so the Brewers again expected a high turnout for Bat Day, the most popular event of all.

The team held a luncheon for media at the Schroeder Hotel in early November, hosted by Selig and Milkes. Selig noted that an improved schedule with more weekend home dates than the previous year could boost attendance.[31] Players Dave Baldwin and Mike Hershberger also attended the luncheon, and this event led to additional winter off-season dinners to promote the team. Other players, including Phil Roof, Ted Kubiak, Lew Krausse, and Ken Sanders, pledged to help promote season-ticket sales.

The Wisconsin State Chamber of Commerce named Selig the Wisconsin Sport Figure of the Year and inducted him into the newly-established Hall of Fame on November 24. Selig received the honor for remaining dedicated to bringing baseball back to Milwaukee.[32] The main consideration for the award was the person's contribution to the advancement of sport in Wisconsin.

Milkes remained with the team until just prior to Christmas before stepping down. He explained that due to "personal and business reasons, there was a pressing and immediate need for me to spend more time in the Los Angeles region."[33]

Selig said he would temporarily share the GM duties with Bobby Mattick, director of player procurement and development; Dave Bristol, field manager; and Tommy Ferguson, traveling secretary. A special type of person would be hired as GM, according to Selig, as he immediately took himself out of the running for the position.[34] Rumors swirled that Selig had been considering selling his auto dealership to devote himself full-time to baseball, but he wound up keeping Knipple-Selig Company and split his time.

When asked if Milkes jumped or was pushed from the GM position, Selig stated that the change had been made to the mutual benefit of both parties.[35] Milkes didn't disagree with Selig's comments and took the position of special assignment scout in California.

Milkes officially left the Brewers organization by early 1971, but he insisted there were no hard feelings and he didn't leave due to poor health. He moved to Las Vegas, where he attempted to establish residency for his fourth divorce. Milkes said his doctor told him the amount of stress he had been under "would have killed any other man."[36]

Milkes' resignation didn't stay in the news for long. As the year ended, two panels of sports writers and broadcasters with the *Associated Press* and *United Press International* named the return of baseball to Milwaukee as the top Wisconsin sports story of 1970. Both panels placed Vince Lombardi's death as the No. 2 story of the year.[37]

The good press followed the Brewers into 1971 as they sent a large delegation of players and officials on a week-long goodwill tour. The route took the group to major Wisconsin cities for dinners and autograph sessions to help fans become better acquainted with the team. Selig appeared at a few of the tour stops, including Madison, where he named Baltimore as the type of organization he would like Milwaukee to emulate—but he didn't want to wait 12 years to raise a pennant as the Orioles had after they moved from St. Louis.[38]

Selig kept working in the background to hire a new GM, and by the end of the month announced that Frank "Trader" Lane would assume the role. Lane lived up to his "Trader" nickname as he reeled off three trades in his first week on the job on the way to orchestrating 20 major trades involving 53 uniform changes by the end of October. Lane didn't believe in standing pat with a team that finished in the lower half of the division.

Lane was the oldest person to hold his position in the big leagues, at age 74. His age starkly contrasted with Selig, the youngest club president at age 36. Selig announced that Lane would be appointed as vice president of operations rather than general manager. Selig said, "The old concept of a general manager was very practical in its day, but it's now probably outmoded for a major league club. We needed a concept that could be adaptable to today's needs."[39]

Both Selig and Lane agreed that Lane's age would not affect the job he needed to do in turning an expansion club into a contender. Lane joked, "There's no truth to the rumor I was a colonel in the confederate army. I know I should be a good ad for the senior citizens. If you maintain interest you don't get old."[40]

One roster addition that Lane made paid off in big dividends a decade later, when Harvey Kuenn led the Brewers to the World Series as manager. Lane hired the 40-year-old Kuenn before spring training as a special batting instructor and placed him on the active roster. Lane activated Kuenn on September 3 with the idea of increasing his pension benefits, but the trade-off meant that Kuenn wouldn't be eligible to be voted into the Hall of Fame for another five years. Lane mentioned the possibility of having Kuenn pinch-hit, but it never happened.

Kuenn and Lane knew each other for many years, so it was not surprising to see Lane make such an unorthodox move. When Lane was GM of the Cleveland Indians in 1960, he pulled off one of the most controversial trades in history when he dealt popular slugger Rocky Colavito for the American League batting champion, Kuenn. Fan reaction was bitter in Cleveland, but Lane kept moving forward, caring to deal in talent rather than sentiment.

With his front office taking shape for the season, Selig accepted election to his first position within major league baseball's ownership. He would go on to work on several committees in the 1970s that studied topics such as expansion and interleague play.

Eight

A Fun Place for Fans

Bud Selig's first work with other owners happened when he was named to the ten-man board of directors of MLB Promotion Corporation. It would give Selig the opportunity to team up with former Milwaukee Braves GM John McHale and Braves owner Bill Bartholomay.

As the Brewers opened their second season, team officials exuded what can best be described as optimism tempered by reality. Selig felt the team had moved ahead of the other recent expansion clubs, but cautioned about the ability to produce an instant pennant. Frank Lane believed the team had improved and that fans would like what they saw on the field.[1]

After the season started, Selig moved into the background and let Lane and Dave Bristol run the team. He resurfaced in the press in late May to authorize Lane spending up to $250,000 on young talent in the June draft.[2] Lane agreed with Selig and Vice President Edmund Fitzgerald about sacrificing the future by trading away youngsters, even though he believed he could get four veteran players for previous No. 1 draftee Darrell Porter.[3]

Lane preferred to draft position players first and worry about pitching later. He felt that paying high prices for a couple of pitchers could be a risky proposition, so he tended to pick up several hurlers for less money. The most notable selection in Lane's draft turned out to be catcher/outfielder Charlie Moore in the fifth round. His path to the majors was a fast one as he made the team in 1973 and stuck around as a key component when the team became a contender later in the decade.

Many of the trade and draft announcements were mere blips on the radar as fans tuned out. One such announcement came as a single paragraph in the Milwaukee sports pages on July 20, 1971. Former Milwaukee Braves catcher Bob Uecker joined the Brewers as a full-time scout and public relations worker. Selig said Uecker's speaking talents would make him an ideal representative for the Brewers and for baseball.[4]

After his 13-year playing career ended, Uecker appeared on several network television shows, including "The Tonight Show" with Johnny Carson, where he would go on to make over 100 appearances. Uecker had also worked as a public speaker and comedian, was employed by the Atlanta Braves as a PR representative, and did some game broadcasting.

Uecker's early days as a Brewers employee often were used as joke material for both Uecker and Bud Selig. "Worst scout I ever had," Selig has often joked.[5] Uecker said he wrote "fringe major leaguer" on every report, so in case any of the players ever made it to the major leagues, he wouldn't be asked how he missed seeing how good the player was going to be.[6]

But perhaps the most infamous story of Uecker's brief scouting career involved a report he turned in with food stains. "We didn't have a scout in the Northern League," Uecker revealed. "Frank Lane tells Bud, let's send him there. I didn't have a stopwatch or anything. It was a Class C league, and I didn't even know how to grade the players."[7]

Uecker said that he had to make the reports out in triplicate, but he accidentally dropped food particles and gravy on the reports while at dinner with a couple of scouts. He wiped off the reports because he didn't want to do them all over again.

The reports arrived back at Lane's office, and Uecker said Lane told Selig: "Look at the crap this guy is sending back. There are food stains. Gravy stains. What the hell?"[8]

"Buddy's never forgotten that. He uses that all the time," Uecker said. "One of the players that I got gravy on his report, we later on drafted him. His name is Bob Galasso, he's a pitcher. So, the report was all right, and the gravy and everything was all right too."[9]

Uecker was added to the broadcast booth behind lead voice Merle Harmon and his partner, Tom Collins. Later he worked his way up to being Harmon's partner, and when Harmon left he took over as the voice of the Brewers.

Lane continued to garner the most headlines as summer dragged on—at least until Brewers vice president Robert Cannon suggested a radical idea. Cannon said he spoke for himself and not the ball club when he suggested that northern teams play about five of their early-season games in the south.[10] He had suggested the idea about seven or eight years before to Commissioner Ford Frick, but it never gained any traction.

The Cleveland Indians had been rumored to play as many as 30 "home" games in New Orleans' planned domed stadium in 1974. Cannon listed other southern cities such as Miami and Dallas as good possibilities for relocated games. He hadn't formally suggested such a move for the Brewers and said it was up to Selig. Cannon's idea met a quick end as Selig said there would be no possibility of the Brewers playing elsewhere. An informal survey of team owners also had Selig listed as opposing the Indians playing games in New Orleans.

Selig had more pressing matters with his franchise as September rolled around. He refused to confirm a report that the Brewers would suffer a $1.3 million loss on the season. Selig reminded the press that operating an expansion club was a costly proposition with no chance of making money in the first five years.[11]

It had been a trying year at County Stadium, and not even a ten-cent beer promotion in June could produce a sellout. Many of the 27,472 in attendance held drinking contests and showered one another with beer and empty cups. Fights broke out, and the police struggled to keep order on what turned out to be the wildest night of the season.

It seemed fitting that most of the action in 1971 happened within the front office and in the County Stadium stands. The team won just four more games than the previous season and finished 69–92, last in the American League West. A disappointing total of 731,531 fans came through the gates, and the "One million and one in '71" goal went by the wayside.

Milwaukee replaced the Washington Senators in the American League Eastern Division after the 1971 season. Club owners and representatives met to discuss the matter during the World Series after Washington had been approved for a move to Texas. The action wasn't unanimous, as the Chicago White Sox also desired a move to the East, where they could renew old rivalries with the New York Yankees and Boston Red Sox.[12]

Chicago also took issue with playing a large slate of West Coast games which couldn't be shown on TV back home and didn't make the newspapers the following morning. Anyone hoping for a geographical realignment could point to the White Sox having to play on the West Coast as a reason to make such a change.

The West didn't want to lose the White Sox, as the division would be already picking up a poor team in the Senators/Rangers. Chicago had voted against the Senators' move and thought they may have been blocked from moving as punishment.[13] The Brewers also had an application in to move to the East, but withdrew, leaving only the White Sox. But most clubs, including Milwaukee, abstained, and the White Sox did not receive the required seven votes to switch divisions.

Eight. A Fun Place for Fans

Baltimore proposed Milwaukee for the East later in the World Series, and the idea turned into reality. East clubs welcomed the expansion Brewers with open arms as they were a weaker club than the White Sox. White Sox owner John Allyn felt something had gone on behind the scenes because league president Joe Cronin had felt that the Sox move would go through. Allen also thought that Milwaukee would vote for the White Sox to move rather than abstaining.[14]

Cronin said the complexities of scheduling Milwaukee with the other East teams made the meeting last for two days.[15] The only owners left on the second day were Selig and Calvin Griffith of the Minnesota Twins. A subsequent meeting was required to finish ironing out the schedule. The Brewers would remain in the Eastern Division until the conclusion of the 1993 campaign.

Moving to the East meant the Brewers would play 18 games each against Baltimore, Boston, Cleveland, Detroit, and New York. The number of games against teams in the West would decrease to 12 each, and Selig expressed disappointment in losing six dates against the White Sox.[16]

Lane finished his roster makeover around the time of the team's move to the East. He made arguably the biggest trade in the young team's history when he sent four players to the Boston Red Sox, including popular speedster Tommy Harper and starting pitcher Marty Pattin. In return, he received six players, with slugger George "Boomer" Scott at the top of the list. Lane felt that three of the players could be inserted into the starting lineup immediately.[17]

A *Milwaukee Journal* headline on October 21, 1971, proclaimed "Brewers Trade Last Original." Left-handed pitcher John Morris was the last remaining member of the roster from Opening Day in 1970 until being traded to the San Francisco Giants. He had the distinction of being the only other pitcher besides Ken Sanders to earn a save for the 1971 Brewers.

The front office also went through a change when the team lost Bobby Mattick, director of scouting and player development, to resignation. Mattick abruptly left the team with two years on his contract, and Selig announced a settlement had been reached.[18] Mattick had been a scout with a half-dozen major league teams and made the move to Milwaukee from Seattle.

Mattick was considered a top scout and had helped sign Curt Flood, Frank Robinson, Rusty Staub, Vada Pinson, and Tommy Harper. He signed three of the Brewers' top prospects, catcher Darrell Porter and pitchers Jim Slaton and Bill Parsons.

Selig tapped former Braves pitcher Jim Wilson to replace Mattick. Wilson had a long background in baseball, having thrown the first no-hit, no-run game in Milwaukee's major league history in 1954. He also had connections to Seattle, having played for the Rainiers in 1950. His minor league travels with teams in Louisville and Toledo had brought him as a visitor to Milwaukee's Borchert Field. "That park had to be one of a kind," Wilson recalled. "The stands ran right along the foul lines. And I shudder every time I think of those short distances to the fences."[19]

After Wilson retired as a player in 1958, he went into scouting for Baltimore and Houston, and his resume included signing Jim Palmer and Dave McNally. He admitted being unfamiliar with Milwaukee's players, apart from scouting Darrell Porter in high school.

Wilson's first big move in the role involved scheduling and running an unprecedented, three-day organizational meeting at County Stadium in November. The gathering brought together all of Milwaukee's minor league managers, 13 scouts, and the team's front office, including Selig. He stressed to the media how crucial the appointment was to the future of the team, as success started with a winning executive lineup.

As Selig and Wilson prepared for the meeting, the *Chicago Tribune* published a front-page story about concessions company Emprise (also known as Sportservice) having financial interests in 39 states and nearly every major sporting event.[20] Some form of Emprise could be found in airports, bowling alleys, restaurants, and even vending machines.

Emprise offered up millions of dollars in the form of low-interest loans to baseball team owners and other sports entities. The article named the Milwaukee Brewers, Chicago White Sox, Baltimore Orioles, Detroit Tigers, Kansas City Royals, and Montreal Expos as franchises which were recent borrowers from Emprise. Milwaukee (when the franchise was located in Seattle) and Montreal took out loans in 1969 as part of baseball's expansion and remained as the only teams with unpaid loans.

John McHale, Expos general manager, testified that a 25-year contract had been signed making Emprise the team's exclusive concessionaire.[21] The loan went hand in hand with the contract, and a first payment with 3.5 percent interest would not be due until 1972. The Arkansas Racing Commission had been examining a state dog track that Emprise had stock interests in, and called McHale to speak.

McHale made it sound as though the deal with Emprise was too good to pass up because, although the money could have been borrowed from a bank, Emprise did not require any collateral.[22] Yet the deal was essentially a second mortgage with Emprise as a lienholder.

Eight. A Fun Place for Fans

Selig didn't offer much of a comment for the article other than to say the deal Milwaukee had with Emprise was identical to Montreal's.[23] Within a few days, Selig elaborated to the *Milwaukee Journal* and said reports the loan had ballooned to $3 million were incorrect, although the loan had increased slightly after Milwaukee moved the team from Seattle.[24] Emprise did have a clause in their loans allowing them to move with a franchise to a new city and continue with exclusive concession rights.

The loan was not unique in the sports world as far as Selig was concerned. Jeremy Jacobs, president of Emprise, echoed Selig's thoughts.[25] However, other sports operators didn't feel the same way. The New Mexico Racing Commission passed a resolution prohibiting a concessionaire from owning more than five percent of a race track, and the contract could be no longer than five years. Despite changes in other venues with contracts, the Milwaukee Brewers still maintain a relationship with Emprise (now known as Delaware North Sportservice).

Selig and the Brewers did not disclose any further details about the Emprise loan, nor did they speak publicly about the results of the three-day organizational meeting. When the annual winter tour and Baseball Writers' Dinner happened in January, the team looked forward to the coming season with excitement due to the huge trade with Boston the previous October.[26]

Old wounds were reopened at the Writers' Dinner when Selig and Toastmaster Lloyd Larson both called out the White Sox for what they felt was a boycott of the event. The White Sox did not send any representatives, as they had three tables at an annual dinner in Chicago where several of their personnel were to be honored.

Selig and Larson took the absence as a snub over Milwaukee's upcoming move to the American League East.[27] White Sox owner John Allyn said he had no resentment, and his team might be in a good divisional race in the coming years.[28] The evening wound up being a far cry from the previous year when White Sox owner John Allyn, manager Chuck Tanner, and general manager Stu Holcomb had all been honored. The next day Allyn said, "We wouldn't be that small to boycott the Milwaukee dinner. I'm surprised they would make such comments."[29]

Selig put his hands on the shoulders of Baltimore general manager Frank Cashen at the Writers' Dinner and talked about finding out who your friends are in baseball.[30] Reporters took note of the new friendship and also noticed when Selig stated that Joe Reichler (publicity director for Bowie Kuhn) was the only guy in baseball who would talk to the Brewers contingent when they were wrangling for a team.[31] As Selig handed Reichler a plaque of appreciation, writers noted the long-running (but since forgotten) relationship between the Brewers and Arthur and John Allyn.[32]

Topics on the winter tour covered the current state of the team rather than the feud with the White Sox. Selig talked about operating costs per year and noted that the franchise paid out more than $2 million in salaries. Landing an affiliate radio station in Madison was high on Selig's list to improve coverage of the team. He defended baseball's draft as a way to improve the team drastically and expressed optimism for the future.[33]

Selig found another way to bridge the divide between Madison and Milwaukee when he jointly announced, with University of Wisconsin athletic director Elroy Hirsch, a special game late in spring training.[34] The UW baseball team would play its first-ever baseball game against a major league team in Tempe against the Brewers. The UW already had a spring schedule in Arizona against various universities, and the game helped fill an open date for both teams.

The teams never played the game as major league players went on strike from April 1 to April 13. The first player walkout ended when an agreement was reached to add salary arbitration to the Collective Bargaining Agreement and a $500,000 uptick in pension fund payments. Most teams lost between six and nine games due to the strike, with the Brewers at six—two of which were home games.

A debate raged over the role of Commissioner Bowie Kuhn in settling the strike and the fact that he didn't prevent it from happening in the first place.[35] An anonymous owner believed Kuhn stood apart and risked diminishing the value of the commissioner's office.[36] Dick Moss, counsel for the Players' Association, thought Kuhn played a proper role but for all the wrong reasons—mainly because team owners told him to keep out of the dispute.[37]

On the opposite side, Los Angeles Dodgers owner Walter O'Malley gave Kuhn a lot of credit for putting pressure on the owners and working tirelessly.[38] Selig agreed and said, "I have to chastise those who said Mr. Kuhn was inactive. Nothing could be further from the truth. I have talked to him over the phone every day, and at any hour, for almost two weeks straight."[39] As for Kuhn, he believed timing was critical in making the settlement happen, and that he acted decisively.[40]

The strike left a bitter taste in the mouths of baseball fans, and they voiced their displeasure by staying silent—simply by not attending games. Opening Day attendance dropped nearly 14,000 from 1971 when averaged across all MLB clubs. A long-term drop could have substantial impact on a newer expansion club like Milwaukee. It didn't help matters when the

Eight. A Fun Place for Fans 131

Brewers started out slowly and slumped by late May to the American League's worst record at 10–21.

Few noticed when Selig and Lane made a managerial change on May 28. Selig delivered the news to Dave Bristol that he was being fired but denied that Lane had put pressure on him to make the move.[41] Lane did say that Bristol was one of the hardest workers he had ever seen in his life, but a change was needed due to the prolonged slump.[42] The franchise continued paying Bristol his $60,000-a-year salary.

It was that salary and Bristol's faith in the new players assembled by Lane that made him reject an offer from Cleveland in the off-season. Gabe Paul of the Indians offered Bristol their manager job, but Bristol decided to stay in Milwaukee as he believed the team didn't need to succeed right away.[43] Bristol needed time to help the revitalized team adjust to one another before results showed in the standings, but he clearly ran out of time.

Bristol was immediately replaced by Evansville farm club manager and former Milwaukee Braves catcher Del Crandall. The move to promote Crandall also helped keep the Atlanta Braves at bay, since they were looking at Crandall as a possible coach. Crandall commented, "If I have any conviction about managing, it is that baseball should be fun; fun for the players and fun for the fans."[44]

The Brewers played to a 54–70 record under Crandall and ended at 65–91 for the season. Between the strike, unfamiliarity with the new AL East rivals, and general unfamiliarity with the Brewers players, fans stayed away in droves. The Brewers drew an AL-worst 600,440 fans, and rumors swirled about the financial viability of the franchise. Late in the decade, when the tide turned for the team, both financially and on the field, Selig recalled the biggest issue being familiarity with the players.

Selig said, "We took a marketing survey that year we had drawn 600,000 people, the fewest in the major leagues, and found that only 25 percent of the fans could name one of our players."[45]

Club officials had no regrets regarding the move from the West to East division, and Selig said they would make the move all over again if asked.[46] The East clubs were outdrawing the West, even in a year when attendance was down across baseball.

The exciting 1972 World Series between the Cincinnati Reds and Oakland A's helped bring fans back to baseball for the coming season. In Milwaukee, the tide toward increased attendance and fan engagement came in the off-season. George Scott was identified by Selig as the team leader and the player they wanted to build around.[47] Scott had spent the early part of the season slumping and admitted having a miserable time playing under Del Crandall early on, but they developed a mutual respect.[48]

The Brewers front office went through a shakeup when Selig announced that Lane would move into a vice president and special assignment scout role. Selig insisted Lane still was an important part of the team's plans going forward.[49] Lane expressed being free to travel whenever the need arose to help the entire franchise, rather than always traveling with the big league club.[50]

Scouting and player development director Jim Wilson succeeded Lane. Wilson threw the first no-hitter in Milwaukee's major league history. When his playing career ended in 1958, he went into scouting and eventually made his way back to Milwaukee as head of scouting.

Wilson questioned how to replace a legend in Lane, but he didn't waste time in grabbing headlines about a month into the job.[51] Wilson worked out a deal to land third baseman Don Money in a seven-player trade with the Philadelphia Phillies. Otherwise, Wilson agreed with Selig that the team should continue to draft and develop players.[52]

The Brewers also made headlines for a game that would not be played for another three years with the announcement that Milwaukee would host the 1975 All-Star Game. Commissioner Bowie Kuhn announced locations for the three upcoming All-Star Games at the 1972 winter meetings in Honolulu, Hawaii. In 1973, the game would be held in Kansas City, in 1974 in Pittsburgh, and in 1975 in Milwaukee.[53] Kuhn described baseball's team owners as being very enthusiastic to return the All-Star Game to Milwaukee.[54]

This was the first of two times in Brewers franchise history that the team would host the ASG, and the second time the game was played at Milwaukee County Stadium. The first time was in 1955, when the Braves were hosts. This gave County Stadium the distinction of being one of three ballparks to host the ASG with two different franchises. The others were Shibe Park in Philadelphia and Sportsman's Park in St. Louis. Selig said, "This is a great accomplishment for our franchise. The 1975 All-Star Game will continue to build a kind of excitement we've been working for since we brought baseball back to Milwaukee."[55]

Selig also noted that some improvements to the 20+-year-old County Stadium were on the way, including triple the lighting capacity and improvements to the press box. Speakers would be installed at concession stands and outside the stadium that would carry radio broadcasts of the games. The scoreboard received some modernization, including the addition of a quick message board. A message board was also installed on the exterior of the stadium, along with a large Milwaukee Brewers identification sign.

The County Board allocated $750,000 to expand seating to over 50,000, but this was contingent on getting a commitment from the Green Bay Packers to continue playing home games at County Stadium (which they did until 1994). The existing seats in the lower boxes were changed over to colorful plastic seats.

As the team prepared to head off to spring training in February 1973, Selig announced plans to make County Stadium a fun place for fans without detracting from the games.[56] The return of Bernie Brewer led off the list of festive enhancements, and he would be joined by a female companion named Bonnie Brewer.

Donna Bozmoski played the first Bonnie with an outfit consisting of a skirt, lederhosen, and a gold blouse. Part of Bonnie's shtick involved interacting with the opposing team's third base coach after she swept off the bases during the seventh inning stretch. The lucky coach generally received a kiss on the cheek and a playful swat on his rear end from Bonnie's broom. Bonnie lasted for about five years and disappeared into Brewers lore until returning for one appearance during the final home game of 2000.

Bavarian costumes were ordered for the grounds crew and a new strolling group of wandering fun-makers that toured the grandstand on Friday nights, Sundays, and holidays. Colorful costumes and seats weren't the only items brightening County Stadium. Both dugouts received a makeover, and the infield tarpaulin became blue and gold to match the team colors. AL team pennants were installed on the stadium roof to enhance the festive atmosphere.

New sounds came from a Dixieland band in the stands and lifelong Milwaukeean Frank Charles on a Hammond organ. Charles had been playing in a supper club lounge and local hotel besides teaching a band program at a local high school for a few years. He took the new opportunity and ran with it, starting the "Go Brewers Go" chant and playing walk-up music for hitters, such as the theme from *The Godfather* for Bob Coluccio. Charles became a staple of Brewers home games until he retired in 1986, and recordings of his playing were used until 2002.

The front office made plans for an old-timer's game in June to celebrate the 20th anniversary of Milwaukee's first major league game in half a century. The celebration would reunite many Milwaukee Braves and St. Louis Cardinals who had appeared in the Braves home opener in 1953. Even though this was yet another nod to Milwaukee's baseball past, the

Brewers were clearly concerned about their current image and continued to take well-thought-out steps to increase attendance at County Stadium.

A new delegation called the Milwaukee Brewer Ambassadors started stumping across the state of Wisconsin to boost ticket sales, with a goal of selling 3,000 to 3,500 season tickets. The upcoming season was viewed as make or break, and the Brewers realized the key to financial success hinged on getting fans from outside the Milwaukee metro area to attend games. The farm system alone cost roughly $1.25 million to operate, and according to Selig, the team needed a million fans to attend games just to break even.[57]

Selig was joined on a whirlwind, 12-city tour by general manager Jim Wilson, batting coach Harvey Kuenn, broadcaster and former Braves player Johnny Logan, ticket director Dick Hackett, public relations director Art Keefe, and former Wisconsin governor Warren Knowles.

Milwaukee County Stadium, 1973. A new festive atmosphere helped push attendance past 1,000,000 fans for the first time, despite the team's finishing fifth in the six-team AL East (National Baseball Hall of Fame Library, Cooperstown, New York).

Many of the stops on the late-winter tour were organized by local Brewers booster clubs that held the events by invite only. Selig said in some cases on previous winter tour stops, the contingent outnumbered the attendees, which said a lot about the lack of interest in the club.[58] The new, narrowed focus helped the Brewers group pitch ticket sales to those who were most interested. Keefe said the team's market research showed that people didn't necessarily dislike the Braves or the Brewers, but they disliked baseball in general for leaving Wisconsin.[59]

The group expressed embarrassment over finishing last out of 24 teams in attendance in 1972 but insisted the product was getting better.[60] Wilson called manager Del Crandall the key to success, and he ran down a probable lineup that on paper looked to be the best in the team's young history. While some of the players were talking about having a chance to win the pennant, Wilson didn't believe the team could win the flag, but they would surprise a few people.[61]

Wilson used the tour as an opportunity to tout the improvements in Milwaukee's farm system, and he previewed three young players moving up to the big leagues—catcher Darrell Porter, second baseman Pedro Garcia, and outfielder Gorman Thomas.[62] Wilson was especially high on Thomas and called him probably as exciting as Hank Aaron.[63]

The tour stops also afforded Wilson an opportunity to answer critics of his trade that brought infielder Don Money to Milwaukee. Wilson felt the controversy was unwarranted mainly because people didn't know what Money's attributes were as a leader and gap-filler at third base.[64]

At the Madison tour stop, Selig discussed how difficult it was for an expansion team to reach parity, especially when the team had been bankrupt and wasted a year and a half of player development. He noted that the Brewers had finally reached a turning point in being able to rely on their farm system to turn out talented players. Selig said, "When I think of the team that took the field on April 7, 1970, and think of the team we've got now, it's amazing."[65]

Selig also stressed the team ownership being local, civic-minded people, just as he had before Milwaukee regained their major league status.[66] Unfortunately, just as in those days, there was an identity crisis with the team. Two times, speakers accidentally called the current team the Milwaukee Braves.[67]

The new-look Brewers spent spring training at their new location in Sun City, Arizona. The organization was successful in lifting the 30-year lease for Diablo Stadium in Tempe that the Seattle Pilots set up. Milwaukee took on the long-term contract when they bought the Pilots from Seattle, but paid off the $400,000 obligation to the bank.

Changes were coming to the American League on a much larger scale than the Brewers' spring training facility move. The AL had been pushing for interleague play for at least a decade and added the use of a designated hitter for pitchers to their list of wants. Team owners held a meeting led by American League President Joe Cronin the previous December and voted to exert every effort to make their ideas a reality by the 1973 season.

AL owners had grown tired of having their proposals rejected by NL owners and requested a joint hearing between the two leagues with Commissioner Bowie Kuhn acting as arbitrator and a tie-breaking vote. The AL also wanted to pass the use of a designated pinch-runner for anyone in the lineup. Kuhn had previously expressed favor for the designated hitter, but it was unclear at first where he stood on the other two proposals.[68]

The AL didn't push for widespread interleague play and outlined a plan for two three-game series where natural geographic rivals would meet. The AL hoped the interleague matchups would boost attendance in their ballparks, as they were outdrawn by the NL by an approximate rate of 3–2. Some owners in both leagues were concerned about what games might be taken off their schedules at the expense of playing a geographical rival.[69]

AL owners took two votes at the winter meetings in Honolulu, Hawaii, and both times were in favor of the designated hitter. The Playing Rules Committee rejected both votes and would not give approval for a rule change. Cronin and the owners then asked Kuhn for a joint hearing with the NL.[70] Kuhn scheduled the meeting for Chicago in mid–January.

Cronin said the two largest proponents of the AL's proposals were Selig and Mike Burke, president of the New York Yankees.[71] In fact, it was Burke and Selig who pushed for the initial meetings of AL owners. They and the other AL owners received approval at the January meeting for the designated hitter, but initially on a test basis for three years. The other AL proposals had already been voted down by the NL at their league meeting and were not offered at the joint session.

After interleague play was shot down, Selig received appointment to a committee that would study the issue and report to owners later in the season. Selig represented the AL owners, and Frank Dale of Cincinnati represented the NL. A separate committee was formed to study the format of the Playing Rules Committee, as some owners scoffed at having minor league members voting on major league rules.

Selig could add his new committee work to a list of community involvement, which included serving on the Milwaukee Jewish Federation Board of Directors, as a trustee on the board of Mount Sinai Medical Center, and as chairman of the Civic Division in the annual Welfare Fund campaigns.

The Brewers front office geared up for what potentially could be their best season yet, but the schedule started off with a thud. After two games in Baltimore followed by a rainout and a scheduled off-day, the Brewers prepared for their home opener against Boston.

Weather reports for the County Stadium opener against Boston were questionable, with eight inches of snow predicted. Selig said the team would wait until Tuesday morning before deciding if the team could play that afternoon.[72] By the next morning, when the storm dumped 13.8 inches of snow on the city, the only answer was to postpone the game. The Red Sox were unable to make it to town anyway because the Milwaukee airport was closed.

Officials fielded a team—but it was a roster full of workers to clear the snow off the tarp on the infield. Worries about damage to the field prevented the use of machines to clear the snow. Workers filled wheelbarrows and carted the snow away, but left the outfield to melt on its own. At any given time, there were 200 people helping, but they were coming and going due to the hard work. Even a helicopter that cost $90 an hour helped as a hair dryer for the field.

The team of grounds crew and volunteers put in 32 hours of work in two days, ending with a sweep of the seating areas. An additional two inches of snow in mid-week made for extra work, and unfortunately some snow remained in portions of the stands. Temperatures in the 40s helped melt the snow depth outside of the stadium to less than six inches by the first pitch of the new home opener.

The Brewers used the unexpected time off to stage workouts at the UW-Milwaukee fieldhouse as the break wound up lasting six days. When the team finally opened the season, just 13,883 fans were on hand. The low attendance was a sign of things to come—at least for the first month of the season. Team ownership and personnel again had reason to be concerned as poor spring weather and lackluster play in May kept attendance low, with just one crowd in the first two months exceeding 20,000 fans.

Selig started a presentation in Madison in April much like the team's season started—focusing on the negative. The state meeting of the Wisconsin Associated Press sportswriters gave him an opportunity to voice concerns about how the Brewers were portrayed by the press. He wasn't happy with the vote by AP sportswriters that put the firing of Dave Bristol and hiring of Del Crandall into the No. 7 for top Wisconsin sports stories of 1972.[73]

Selig turned things around with the latter half of his speech and voiced the positives of the team and farm system. His enthusiasm was captured by reporters and gave them fodder for articles as the season got into full swing.[74] The competitive play of the team and leadership of Wilson and Crandall took it from there, as reporters took a renewed interest in covering their state team.

Optimism rippled through the front office in June as temperatures warmed, school let out, and the team caught fire. A steady stream of fans regularly came to visit County Stadium and offered largely positive comments on the improved game experience.[75] The team posted the first ten-game winning streak in franchise history and won 15 of 16 games, 11 of them on the road.

Baseball at County Stadium finally had become more than just a sideshow to popular promotions like Helmet Day, Family Day (with discounted tickets), or 10 Cent Beer Night. The total attendance hit 341,053 a third of the way through the home schedule, which naturally gave everyone hope that 1,000,000 fans would see Brewers baseball that season.

While the focus in 1973 had been on the invigorated team and stadium offerings, off the field the Brewers made their biggest draft choice in history. On June 5, they selected 17-year-old infielder Robin Yount with the third pick of the first round. The youngster was from William Howard Taft High in Woodland Hills, California. He had attracted scouts from every major league team during his junior and senior years. In fact, some teams sent more than one scout at a time to have a look at the boy wonder.

In mid–August, Del Crandall was awarded with a new one-year contract to continue managing the team through 1974. The Brewers had led the division or been in a tie for first place 17 times. The turnstiles had been kind as 917,979 had passed through on the way to watch the team in action. Selig marked progress in all phases of the operation, more so than even the most optimistic predictions prior to the season.[76]

National League owners met behind closed doors at the same time Crandall received his contract. Discussions revolved around interleague play and the designated hitter rule. Selig, NL President Chub Feeney, AL President Joe Cronin, and Cincinnati Reds president Bob Howsam had finished their interleague proposal, but Feeney mentioned that the four were unable to come to a unanimous agreement.[77]

Selig presented the committee's ideas to the owners, which he later

Eight. A Fun Place for Fans

said was a lengthy report.[78] The committee had looked at several formats, which included a range of a minimum of four interleague games to a maximum of 18 per club. When it was put to a vote, Selig wasn't surprised that interleague play was turned down.[79] Commissioner Bowie Kuhn would not cast a vote to break the tie, despite a challenge by the NL of his legal powers to avoid settling the impasse. Kuhn had previously spoken about favoring limited interleague play.

Back in Milwaukee, the club readied for the moment everyone had been waiting for—the coveted 1,000,000 attendance mark. They became millionaires on Saturday, September 1, against the Boston Red Sox. The 5–0 loss against former Brewer Marty Pattin didn't put a damper on the festivities as the team and local merchants gave presents to fans, appropriately including beer.

The top prize was a new car won in a drawing of ticket stubs. Choice steaks, an outboard motor, and a power lawn mower also were given away. All fans in attendance received "Thanks a Million" buttons with thanks from Selig and the rest of the organization.

It had been since 1961 that Milwaukee baseball attracted over a million fans to the ballpark, when the Braves drew 1,101,414. The Brewers couldn't help but note that the current Atlanta Braves team had drawn just 658,701 fans so far.

Milwaukee was in good shape to go over the 1,100,000 mark, as they had 11 home dates remaining. They ended just short at 1,093,158, as most of the September games attracted under 10,000. Just 4,804 saw the second-to-last home game that featured two franchise milestones. Jim Colborn became the first Brewers pitcher to win 20 games in a season, and George "Boomer" Scott hit the 100 runs batted in mark for the first time in team history.

The excitement over an improved 74–88 team and attendance record carried over to the mid–October baseball owners meetings held in Milwaukee. Selig's interleague committee again presented recommendations to owners, but NL officials were quick to shoot down the proposal. Two franchises were also under discussion—a possible move of the San Diego Padres to Washington and a pitch from Seattle for a new club.

As the off-season took hold, the Brewers went to work, negotiating salaries with several players who turned in good years. At the top of the list was George Scott, looking to become Milwaukee's first $100,000-a-year player. Warren Spahn had earned $85,000 a year at the end of his Braves days, and Hank Aaron didn't ink a six-figure deal until the team moved to Atlanta. Scott ultimately demanded a two-year contract at

$140,000 a year, saying that if he didn't think he was worth it, he wouldn't ask for it.[80]

GM Jim Wilson announced Scott's new one-year deal for $100,000 just before Christmas, making the big slugger one of eight AL players with a six-figure salary.[81] The record deal was a far cry from Tommy Harper leading the team in salary in 1971 with a mere $40,000. Scott's contract made the Brewers' total payroll nearly double the previous year's, but Selig saw the increased salaries as a good thing—a testimonial to how far the franchise had come and what the future might hold.[82]

Selig also spoke about the team's tremendously improved roster as the year wound down. He looked back to the first two years of the franchise and the criticisms the front office received for the overwhelming number of trades. Credit in Selig's opinion went to Frank Lane for taking action and dealing quality for quantity.[83]

Selig said, "He [Lane] saw that the roster included a lot of has-beens and never-will-bes and proceeded with a series of moves that lopped off the dead weight and got younger players into the organization that filled two or three positions instead of just one."[84]

Lane appeared in the news six months later in connection to Milwaukee. He and Selig disagreed publicly about the team's 1973 profit levels.[85] Lane said that Selig told him privately the team made between $800,000 and $900,000.[86] Selig claimed Lane's financial terminology was imprecise, and the figure was the gross margin on operations. After deducting capital expenditures, player development costs, and financial expenses, the profit margin landed in the $80,000 range, according to Selig.[87]

Nine

Prospects and All-Stars

Even if Bud Selig and Frank Lane disagreed about team profits, the Milwaukee Brewers were indeed profitable. The front office gained more knowledge about what type of team they needed to field and promotions that would bring fans to County Stadium in 1974.

As the team's delegation made their annual winter trek, the group agreed that greatness was in the future—the only question is when it would happen.[1] General Manager Jim Wilson thought the team did a good job of turning winter optimism into results on the field and would be heading to spring training with a positive attitude.[2]

Selig reveled in the fact that the team had the largest percent attendance increase in the major leagues, making the heartache of the year before worth going through. Being steadfast in the franchise's player development philosophy despite a gloomy outlook took courage, according to Selig, but was beginning to pay off.[3]

Selig went into the background a bit with his team poised for good things. He backed away from doing more work on the interleague committee, as he wasn't happy about giving up a year creating multiple interleague scenarios that went nowhere.[4] Instead, Selig spent time on the AL Long-Range Planning Committee with fellow owners Ewing Kauffman of Kansas City and John Feltzer of Detroit. California GM Harry Dalton rounded out the committee, which studied such things as spring training length and expenses.

Dalton laid out plans for his club to test a later report date for players, shorter exhibition game schedule, and two-day delay of the season opener in 1975. A cost savings from the new initiatives was estimated to be $30,000 to $35,000. If everything worked, Dalton thought he could push for a shorter regular season schedule—back to 154 games or even 152.[5] None of the ideas took hold, but the committee gave Selig and Dalton a chance to work together, which laid the foundation for Dalton being hired as Milwaukee's GM in late 1977.

Milwaukee needed a new GM in 1974 as well after an unexpected move by Wilson. In early August, he announced he would be stepping down to head up a new Central Scouting Bureau, effective September 1.[6] The new group would provide recommendations to their members based on scouting reports. Seventeen of the 24 teams joined immediately, with the hopes of getting a better bang for their scouting budgets.

Wilson worked on a committee with fellow baseball executives who studied the possibility of establishing a scouting bureau. The top job had been offered to him, but he initially turned it down. Joe Brown of Pittsburgh led the committee and spoke to Selig during the All-Star break about getting Wilson to reconsider.[7] Selig gave Wilson his blessing to take the job, calling it a team sacrifice for the best interests of baseball.[8]

It was a tremendous opportunity for Wilson to have a wide impact on the game. Participating teams were expected to have information on at least 600 players prior to the June 1974, draft, when in the past they may have had reports on 250 players. On a personal level, Wilson saw his new role as a way to pay baseball back for all the good things he had gotten out of it.[9]

The Brewers soldiered on without a GM until scouting director Jim Baumer took over in late November. Like Wilson, Baumer had a long background in baseball, first as a player and then a scout, starting in the Houston organization. Baumer had the odd distinction of playing briefly in the majors in 1949 before spending the entire 1950s in the minors and coming back up in 1961. Baumer brought even more youthful energy to the GM position, being nine years younger than Wilson at 43 years old.

While the franchise gained energy in the front office, they worked to decrease energy consumption. Commissioner Bowie Kuhn and federal energy office chief William Simon proposed that teams meet a 25 percent energy savings mark in the coming season. The Brewers put together a plan to exceed Kuhn's and Simon's suggestion by saving 42.28 percent in energy.

One of the most significant measures was reducing the team's charter flights from 35 to nine. This move would bring a 68 percent savings in fuel consumption. Changes in lighting practices at County Stadium would also bring a savings of 100,000 kilowatt hours. Stadium lights would not be turned on until 15 minutes before night games, which paired with a practice already in effect of turning out exterior stadium lighting.

Leading up to the season opener, the front office again worked to shed labels placed on the team in previous seasons. Umpire Jim Honochick allegedly called the Brewers "ragamuffins" during a game argument in 1971, and the term occasionally was used in articles regarding the team long after the fact. The Brewers were also called "orphans" and "expansion babies" even though they had become a much stronger team.[10]

Stories about the Brewers believing they were as good as any team in the American League East quickly faded into the background. The baseball spotlight turned toward Hank Aaron's quest to break Babe Ruth's record of 714 career home runs. One of the many congratulatory telegrams Aaron received came from Selig, who spoke for his fans in Wisconsin in a salute on the special occasion.[11] Selig also mentioned the upcoming homecoming for Aaron in Milwaukee for an exhibition game between the Braves and Brewers.[12]

The exhibition on May 6 figured to be the last time the current and former County Stadium teams would meet, as Aaron hinted toward retiring after the season.[13] It seemed to be customary that the game had a bitter wind chill, and since Aaron was involved, there had to be a ceremony commemorating the event.

Aaron received a plaque for hitting 185 of his record home runs in County Stadium and gave a speech prior to the game thanking fans for their patience with him.[14] Aaron didn't hit a homer that night and was replaced by a pinch-runner in the fourth inning. The 21,153 frozen fans assumed it was the last they would see of Aaron in County Stadium—a place where he could not recall ever being booed.[15]

As much as Aaron symbolized Milwaukee's baseball past, shortstop Robin Yount symbolized potential for the future. The philosophy of quality farm development and certain young players like Yount not being for sale at any price still rang loud and true in the team's front office. Yount had played just 64 games in the minors, but he had obvious talent that needed to be refined.

Yount went hitless in his first four games but went on to hit a game-winning home run in his sixth game. He played in 107 games in 1974 and hit .250 with three home runs and 26 runs batted in. Defense was an issue for Yount early in his career. He committed 19 errors for a .962 fielding percentage.

Yount and other young players on the roster were learning lessons that would pay off later. Other youngsters included catchers Darrell Porter and Charlie Moore, outfielders Sixto Lezcano and Gorman Thomas, and pitchers Bill Castro and Jim Slaton. All were products of the Seattle Pilots and Milwaukee Brewers early drafts and free agent signings.

The Brewers continued to stockpile for the future by drafting pitchers Jerry Augustine and Bryan "Moose" Haas along with infielder Jim Gantner. Augustine and Gantner were both Wisconsin natives, hailing from Kewaunee and Fond du Lac respectively. Haas' father gave him the "Moose" nickname upon birth, thinking he'd be big. While 6–0 and 180 pounds wasn't big, the nickname stuck, and Haas was rarely, if ever, called Bryan.

But it was the return of Aaron to Milwaukee that helped link the past to the present. The last tie to the 1970 team still on the Brewers roster was outfielder Dave May, and it's hard to imagine a more fitting trade scenario script for his departure. May was traded with minor league pitcher Roger Alexander to Atlanta for home run king Hank Aaron on November 2, 1974.

Selig spent two months diligently trying to bring Aaron back to Milwaukee when it became clear the Atlanta Braves wanted him only for a figurehead front office job. Aaron had been hoping to find a home with an American League club to continue playing as a designated hitter, and Braves owner William Bartholomay was "happy to give Hank this opportunity in accordance with his wish to become a designated hitter with the Brewers."[16]

Aaron provided Brewers fans with an opportunity to see him return to the city where he hit more than half of his career home runs—398 with the Milwaukee Braves—over a 12-year stint. Stacks of mail and phone calls flooded the Brewers ticket office, inquiring about season tickets when the news broke. AL president Lee MacPhail expected a ticket sale boost in other cities where Aaron had never played.[17] MacPhail also saw the work of himself and others who worked to get the DH rule through finally paying off.

Selig was understandably elated to bring "unquestionably the greatest player of our generation" and his friend back to Milwaukee. "Henry is coming home," Selig proclaimed.[18]

Two weeks later, the Brewers held what turned out to be one of the largest news conferences ever in Milwaukee. Aaron had returned from Japan, where he won a home run contest, and the time was right to announce his return to the city where he first found stardom. At the news conference, Aaron said, "I want to end my career here. My main challenge is to come back and bring a championship to this city that I love so dearly."[19]

Aaron admitted he was nowhere near the same player in his prime and dealt with knee issues, but he was still a great guy to have around the clubhouse. If Aaron could help teach the other players a few tricks, it was a bonus to the club. He wouldn't play if his productivity continued to decline, thinking that he'd rather retire a year too early than a year too late.

Aaron prepared to play for former teammate turned manager Del Crandall, who didn't think Aaron was the type of player who needed to be managed.[20] Aaron said he'd do whatever Crandall asked of him, including mentoring the young players. "Over here at least I know I'll get an opportunity to help the kids," Aaron said. "That's all I was really looking for in Atlanta."[21]

Infielder Don Money was understandably excited to be on the same team as the legendary Hank Aaron. At their first spring training together in 1975, Money told reporters, "I'm 27, this is my seventh year in the big leagues, and I feel just like the kids do."[22]

Money pointed out that Robin Yount wasn't even born yet when Aaron started playing in the big leagues (Yount was actually a little over a year old). He said, "Two years ago Yount was in high school. Aaron was one of his idols, and now he's playing on the same team as him."[23]

The Brewers attempted to sign more veterans to mix in with Aaron as the off-season went on, most notably 20-game winner Catfish Hunter. After Hunter was declared a free agent due to a contract violation in Oakland, the Brewers faced off in a bidding war with several other teams for his services. Selig believed the Brewers were one of the final eight teams with a shot to sign Hunter after they made a second and final offer.[24]

Hunter signed with the New York Yankees, but reportedly told Selig he liked the city of Milwaukee and thought the idea of playing on the same team as Aaron was intriguing.[25] Selig declined to put a dollar amount on the offer to Hunter, instead saying it was something the franchise could live with.[26] The Brewers were still a couple of years away from signing any big-name free agents with a high price tag.

Dollar signs didn't matter to Aaron when he spoke at the annual Milwaukee Baseball Writers' awards dinner in early 1975. He told the capacity crowd that he had not been out to go to the highest bidder and had told his attorney that he'd play for no club other than the Brewers. Aaron signed autographs for fans at the event and told reporters how good he felt over the reception he had been receiving in Milwaukee.[27]

Milton Richman, sports editor of *United Press International*, wrote a column shortly after the dinner about Aaron finally feeling wanted. Richman pointed out that Aaron had basically been a designated hitter in Atlanta as he chased Bath Ruth's home run record because nobody cared about what he did in the field or on the bases.[28]

In Milwaukee, Aaron had a job in perpetuity if he liked, according to Selig. The press and fans liked to speculate over Aaron becoming the manager or general manager, but Selig clearly saw him as working in player development and scouting.[29] Either way, Aaron felt coveted by the team and community. Aaron said, "For the first time in my life I feel wanted. You know what that means! I'll tell you what it means. It makes a helluva difference. Sometimes it makes all the difference in the world."[30]

The response to Aaron's return continued through the chilly Wisconsin spring right up to Opening Day. Demand for tickets soared beyond previous seasons, and team staff prepared for their biggest opener in history. The 48,160 who packed County Stadium that day made history as the single-game attendance record for a Brewers game and came close to the Braves' record of 50,024. Even when the Braves routinely drew 2 million fans a season, Opening Day never drew more than 45,000 fans.

As of Opening Day, season-ticket sales had risen 20 percent over the previous year at 3,000 total. Group sales for nights and promotional giveaway dates also saw an increase. The front office expected at least 1.2 million to come through the gates that season, and that prediction proved to be spot on (1,213,357).

Aaron enjoyed the warm welcome when he hit the County Stadium field wearing a Brewers uniform. "I guess they want to be part of history," he said. "It makes me feel good to see that as much of a problem we have here in America, the fans can bring their kids out to something as wholesome as a ball game."[31]

The record crowd sat through a windy, 40-degree, pre-game ceremony that led up to Aaron's introduction and speech. As expected, Aaron and Selig received the most cheers, while state politicians and Commissioner Bowie Kuhn were booed.[32] The announcement of an additional ten-minute delay to allow more fans to get from the parking lot to their seats also received boos.

Aaron went on to play in 137 games in 1975, but he hit just .234 with 12 home runs. His totals were lower in 1976, with just 85 games and a .229 average with ten homers. Aaron spent his final two seasons primarily as a designated hitter and appeared in left field for only four games (23 innings).

Along the way, Aaron broke Babe Ruth's career record for runs batted in. On May 1, 1975, the Brewers routed the Detroit Tigers, 17–3, behind Yount's three run homer and four RBIs. Aaron moved past Ruth in the blowout and deflected praise after the game, instead choosing to turn the attention toward Yount. Yount was leading the team to that point in batting average, homers, runs batted in, runs, and hits. He had been named American League "Player of the Month" for April. Aaron said, "That Robin Yount! This kid is for real. He has tremendous talent and he wants to play. Bud Selig, the rest of the owners were always talking about him this winter. You can see why."[33]

When a reporter suggested that Yount had been upstaging Aaron, "The Kid" made sure to correct him. "Henry's still the man, always will be. He's really helped me a lot," Yount said. "Like, we talked in spring training. He told me about certain pitches in certain situations."[34]

Yount played in 147 games, raising his batting average to .267 from the prior season's .250 and increasing his stolen bases, home runs, and runs batted in. Unfortunately, his defense went even further south, and he wound up with a league-leading 44 errors and a .939 fielding percentage. Still, fans were excited to see Yount and Aaron, so they continued to turn out in record numbers. One game that packed in the fans even attracted national interest—the 46th All-Star Game on July 15.

The ASG wound up being sold out virtually overnight, with demand way exceeding available seats, according to Brewers officials. A standing room only crowd of 51,480 was announced on game day.

The Brewers had six players on the ASG ballot that year—first baseman George Scott, shortstop Robin Yount, third baseman Don Money, catcher Darrell Porter, and outfielders Johnny Briggs and Hank Aaron. However, just two Brewers were selected for the AL team—Scott and Aaron. It was Aaron's final ASG appearance.

Aaron did come full circle with his final ASG, as his first appearance in 1955 also happened in County Stadium. In that game, he collected two singles and drove in a run to help the NL to a 6–5 victory. In 1975 at age 41, he was the only player still active from the 1955 game. He tied Willie Mays and Stan Musial with 24 ASG appearances.

Milwaukee manager Del Crandall was named to the AL coaching staff, along with Billy Martin. They joined manager Alvin Dark. The NL was led by manager Walter Alston, with Red Schoendienst and Danny Murtaugh as coaches.

Secretary of State Henry Kissinger threw out the first pitch to Rod Carew, and country artist Glen Campbell sang the National Anthem. Kissinger gave a foreign policy "grass roots" address to 1,050 attendees at the Milwaukee's Plaza hotel on the eve before the game.[35] He had also given similar speeches in Atlanta, Kansas City, and St. Louis in recent weeks. Articles about Kissinger and his wife Nancy appeared in several Wisconsin newspapers during the All-Star break.[36]

The weather had been anything but summerlike in the weeks prior to the game, and June felt particularly chilly. But a warming trend put the temps in the mid–80s under partly cloudy skies as the game started.

NBC broadcast the game to an estimated 50 million viewers, with Joe Garagiola, Tony Kubek, and Curt Gowdy sharing the announcing duties. Gowdy admitted that the ASG was the most difficult game to announce due to the combination of 50 different personalities on the teams and the play-by-play action. The announcing team prepped by going over the season's stats and other information with NBC statistician Allan Roth.

The Cincinnati Reds and Los Angeles Dodgers populated most of the starting lineup for the NL in a near-repeat of the previous year's lineup. Johnny Bench of the Reds led all NL players with 2,930,147 votes. Rod Carew led the AL with 3,165,614 votes.

Vida Blue got the start for the AL against Jerry Reuss of the NL. Blue was followed by Steve Busby, Jim Kaat, Catfish Hunter, and Goose Gossage. Reuss was followed by Don Sutton, Tom Seaver, Jon Matlack, and Randy Jones. The NL won, 6–3, but it was a 3–3 game until the Senior Circuit pulled away in the ninth inning. Matlack got the win, and Hunter took the loss.

Aaron and Scott did see action in the game, despite Aaron nursing a shoulder injury and listed as questionable to play. Scott struck out in his two trips to the plate, and Aaron lined out in a pinch-hit at-bat.

As for the Brewers, they came into the All-Star Break just 4½ games back of the AL East-leading Boston Red Sox. Most of the players were realistic about the uphill battle of contending in the second half against a division that featured superior hitting and pitching. Aaron spent the latter part of the season listening to rumors that he would be replacing Crandall as manager. Even the idea of Aaron being player-manager was floated at the slugger by reporters.

Besides the ASG, highlights on the field were few and far between for the foundering Brewers. Scott finished the season with 36 homers to earn a tie for the AL title with Reggie Jackson, and he led the league with 109 RBI. Scott said he loved his "taters"—a personal nickname for home runs.[37]

The Brewers collapsed and finished in fifth place with a 68–94 record. Crandall lost his job with one game remaining in the season, and hitting coach Harvey Kuenn took his spot for the final game. Like Aaron, Kuenn also appeared to be a solid internal candidate for the manager job.

Instead, the team hired Alex Grammas for the 1976 campaign. Like

Crandall, Grammas was a former big leaguer with coaching experience under his belt. He played as an infielder in the 1950s/'60s and was the Cincinnati Reds' third base coach during their "Big Red Machine" era under manager Sparky Anderson.

Selig was thrilled to land Grammas and admitted he was the only manager they wanted. Selig commented, "There is no question in our mind, we got the best man available. In the years I've been in baseball, never has anybody been recommended by as broad a spectrum of people as Alex Grammas."[38]

While Grammas was highly regarded when he was hired by the Brewers, some players didn't think much of his methods. A lot of finger pointing went back and forth during his tenure. Grammas claimed that some players were copping out as the season wore on.[39] In 1977, infielder Mike Hegan said, "Grammas is a nice guy, but as a manager, he makes a good third base coach."[40]

Grammas was thought to be the leader who could finally get the team to the .500 mark in a season. Milwaukee had finally won more than 70 games—74 in 1973 and 76 in 1974. Del Crandall was given much of the credit for those increased win totals. When Jim Wilson was GM, he said of Crandall, "He had the courage to stick with our plan of using the youngsters on a regular basis."[41]

The press speculated as the off-season dragged on that Grammas would be saddled largely with the same team that finished fifth in 1975.[42] The biggest addition had been the signing of veteran outfielder Vada Pinson, and he didn't even make the team out of spring training. Both Baumer and Grammas agreed in not making a trade for the sake of change, so the team remained largely unchanged.[43]

Selig's triumphs of bringing Aaron back to Milwaukee, hosting the All-Star Game, and hiring Grammas to manage the team were offset by an upheaval on the home front. Selig's wife, Donna, filed papers in Milwaukee County Circuit Court asking for divorce after 18 years of marriage. Donna later testified in court that after Selig became involved in baseball, he divorced her and married baseball.[44] The judge agreed and granted the divorce.

Selig continued moving forward—devoted to his own team and the game itself. He was named to a four-man committee in early 1975 to study relocation and expansion. Donald Grant of the New York Mets chaired the committee, and other members were Ewing Kauffman of the Kansas City Royals and John McHale of the Montreal Expos, familiar to Milwaukeeans during his time as Braves GM. League presidents Chub Feeney and Lee MacPhail were automatically on the committee.

Major league baseball owners had been discussing the pros and cons of expansion for a few years. Commissioner Bowie Kuhn mentioned the possibility of three divisions: East, Central, and West, with a potential for teams in Hawaii, the Philippines, and Japan.[45] A poor U.S. economy made team owners and executives think long and hard about adding more franchises.

McHale believed expansion would be inevitable, but this time it would be intelligent and planned rather than forced, as was the case with previous moves. He mentioned Toronto as being the best city prepared for a new team based on finances and stadium plans, but his committee would deeply study the viability of other cities.[46]

Peter Bavasi, vice president and general manager of the San Diego Padres, told the press about the heavy financial cost to start up a new team and how those franchises operated with inferior players for years. It took the Padres until 1974 to make a profit, but they still had back debt to pay that went back to their first days in 1969. Bavasi also pointed to the increased costs of a franchise in the mid–1970s compared to the previous decade—and these costs had dramatically risen in all sports.[47]

Kuhn and Bavasi agreed that baseball was less affected by the latest economic crunch, and at least 12 clubs were running ahead of the previous year on advanced ticket sales, including Bavasi's Padres.[48] Bavasi said the lower ticket prices in baseball compared to other professional sports meant that fans could still attend games, even in an up-and-down economy.[49]

Still, speculation regarding possible expansion revolved more around a move of a possible existing team to the Seattle market. The San Francisco Giants, Chicago White Sox, and Oakland Athletics were all mentioned as possible candidates to wind up in the seaport city.[50]

In early July, Kuhn said a major league team would be assigned to Seattle, possibly for the 1976 season. He refused to name a specific team but said the San Francisco Bay Area could not continue to support two teams. Kuhn hadn't made a proposal to the teams, but he promised to negotiate until a solution could be agreed upon.[51]

Kuhn visited Seattle and inspected King County's domed stadium, scheduled for completion prior to the upcoming baseball season. He had a lot to consider, as a $32.5 million lawsuit remained in Superior Court challenging the Seattle Pilots' move to Milwaukee. The plaintiffs in the suit accused baseball of antitrust violations, fraud, and breach of contract over the Pilots' move. Plaintiffs agreed to defer a trial until baseball owners reached a decision on whether major league baseball would return to Seattle.

Nine. Prospects and All-Stars

The suit went back on the court schedule for January 12, 1976. Kuhn asked for forbearance from the plaintiffs while baseball sorted out ownership issues.[52] Bill Veeck had been approved to purchase the White Sox, and that meant the team would remain in Chicago. Charley Finley of the A's insisted his team would not move from Oakland. That left San Francisco, and Kuhn continued to maintain that the Bay Area had too much baseball and a team needed to go.[53]

The Giants had lost a reported $3 million over two seasons and received a $500,000 loan from the league. At least a half-dozen groups lined up to purchase the team, with the clear majority lobbying to keep the club in San Francisco. The city also was involved as officials decided to ask for a $7 million indemnification should a purchaser move the team. The league gave the Giants until December 31 to resolve the sale of the club.

In early January, a Honolulu sportscaster erroneously told his listeners that the troubled Giants franchise had been sold and would be moving to Toronto. A group led by Labatt Brewing Company had purchased the team, according to the false report.[54] The group had been pushing to buy the franchise for months and received assurance that their $12,500,000 offer was the best on the table. They would have to wait another week until owners reconvened to discuss the matter.

It didn't take long for owners to vote overwhelmingly in favor (11–1) of a franchise committee's recommendation that franchise problems be solved via expansion. AL President Lee MacPhail said owners were interested in expanding to Seattle, and details would be worked out later.[55]

The National League solved one ownership issue by approving the sale of the Atlanta Braves to millionaire yachtsman Ted Turner. The Giants went on to be purchased by minority owner Bob Lurie after being moved to action by Mayor George Moscone, who won an injunction to block the sale to Labatt Brewing and the subsequent relocation to Toronto.

AL owners resolved over the final weekend in January to put a team in Seattle if three conditions were met. MacPhail called for the lawsuit to be dropped.[56] He also asked for the new franchise to go to a group led by Lester Smith that included entertainer Danny Kaye, and urged that an acceptable lease agreement be worked out.

After a scuffle between the AL and NL over which league would wind up with a Toronto franchise, the team ultimately landed in the AL in the East Division, alongside the Brewers. Labatt Brewing finally got to own a team, as the company became majority owners of the Blue Jays. Toronto and Seattle had a year to prepare for league play in 1977.

The Brewers also had to prepare for 1977 after taking a step backward in 1976 under Grammas despite good individual offensive performances from George Scott (.274 batting average with 18 homers and 77 RBI), Don Money (.267 BA, 12 HR, 67 RBI), and Sixto Lezcano (.285 BA). Jerry Augustine had a low 3.30 earned run average but only managed a 9–13 record. Danny Frisella led the team with just nine saves that season and Ed Rodriguez and Bill Castro were right behind him with eight saves apiece.

Milwaukee finished with a 66–95 record, landing them in sixth place in the American League East division, 32 games behind the front-running New York Yankees. It was the team's seventh consecutive losing season, but it still had some memorable highlights. One came on September 3, when Mike Hegan hit for the first cycle in franchise history.

Hegan faced a tough pitcher in rookie Mark "The Bird" Fidrych during his incredible 19–9 season when he posted a 2.24 earned run average and won the AL "Rookie of the Year" Award. Yet Hegan got to him and took care of getting the double, homer, and triple by the fourth inning. Hegan completed the cycle in the sixth inning with a single off reliever Bill Laxton. His final line was 4-for-5 with six runs batted in. The Brewers scored nine runs (seven earned) off Fidrych on their way to an 11–2 blowout.

Two other special moments that season involved Hank Aaron in what turned out to be his final big league campaign. On Tuesday, July 20, Aaron hit his 755th and final home run in a 6–2 win over the California Angels. It was mid-season, so most likely none of the 10,134 fans in attendance at Milwaukee County Stadium had any idea it was the last time Hammerin' Hank would hit one out of the park.

Milwaukee was struggling to the tune of a 35–49 record and had just dropped a doubleheader to the Angels the day before. Somehow, they managed to pull off an 18–13 record in July and a 15–15 August, but other months like September (8–23) buried the team in the standings.

The Brewers held a 4–1 lead in the bottom of the seventh inning when Aaron came to bat against relief pitcher Dick Drago. He smoked a solo home run to deep left field, close to the foul pole, to extend the team's lead. It was Aaron's only hit that day and followed a home run by George Scott. He had appeared in just 85 games so far in 1976 and carried a .246 batting average with nine homers into the Angels game.

Groundskeeper Richard Arndt retrieved the ball after it deflected off the hands of a fan. Arndt had been sitting in the bleachers with the other groundskeepers and wanted to deliver the ball to Aaron after the game and hopefully get a photo with the future Hall of Famer. He was told that the team was in a meeting, but he should hand the ball over, and it would be given to Aaron later. Arndt kept the ball in hopes of meeting him after the team's upcoming road trip, but was fired later that day for not returning club property.

The termination story was published in the July 23 edition of the *Milwaukee Journal*. Arndt wisely called the *Journal* and gave them the tip. This provided proof that he had possession of the ball—a fact that would come in handy years later. In the article, head groundskeeper Harry Gill stated that employees were not allowed to keep balls, even batting practice balls. Arndt claimed the rule was seldom enforced but became an issue because Aaron had been collecting his recent home run balls. Arndt also said the Brewers wanted him to turn the ball over immediately or not at all. Gill agreed, saying, "How do we know he brings back the same ball? It could be any ball."[57]

After the team returned from their next road trip, Arndt and a friend hung around the players' parking lot at County Stadium after a game. Arndt waited for Aaron to exit the stadium, got his attention, and told him he had home run ball #755. He asked Aaron to sign the ball, but Aaron refused and told Arndt that he should have given the ball back to the Brewers in the first place.[58]

Arndt placed the ball in a safe deposit box at his bank for the next 23 years because he knew the ball was important. He relocated to Albuquerque, NM, and became a social worker. Over the years, he turned down offers from collectors to purchase the ball and even a few offers from Aaron himself. Aaron stated that his final home run ball meant a lot because 755 was the all-time home run record, not 715 (the number of homers he hit to break Babe Ruth's original record).

In 1994, Arndt took the ball to a Phoenix card show and got Aaron to sign the ball. Aaron had no idea he was signing his final home run ball and later claimed he was duped into doing so. A couple of years later, Aaron stated that he held the ball in his possession—not Arndt—but later retracted his story.[59]

Arndt picked up an agent named Tim Sullivan to represent him in any selling negotiations. He held out hope that either Aaron or the Baseball Hall of Fame would eventually receive the ball.[60] Sullivan had a deal worked out with the Brewers for Arndt to "donate" the ball when Miller Park opened in 2001. In exchange, the Brewers would give him cash, signed items by Aaron, and a few other unique items. Arndt asked for an hour of time with Wade Boggs, and the Brewers decided to pull their offer.

In 1999, Arndt decided to place the ball into a Guernsey auction that also featured Mickey Mantle's 500th home run ball and Mark McGwire's 70th home run ball from 1998. The Aaron ball was pulled from the auction when bidding for it dropped off at $800,000—a far cry from the $3.1 million that McGwire's ball fetched. Arndt eventually sold the ball to a Connecticut portfolio manager for a reported $655,000. Arndt donated $162,500 to Aaron's "Chasing the Dream" foundation, saying he believed the donation was the right thing to do.[61]

In a 2007 interview, Arndt said, "Uncle Sam got a good chunk, the state of New Mexico got a good chunk, I gave some to our church and my wife, and I gave some money to our children. We were able to do some good things with it." He added, "I'm sure everybody would have handled this much more diplomatically had it been September 30 instead of July 20, but everybody assumed he would hit more home runs. Nobody thought that would be his last home run."[62]

Also in 2007, a group of engineers and students from UW–Milwaukee worked to calculate the exact spot where Aaron's final homer landed so the Brewers could mark the location with a commemorative plaque. County Stadium was long gone, having been replaced by Miller Park—but not in the same spot. The former County Stadium grandstand was now part of Parking Lot 1 close to Helfaer Field. The engineers used a combination of aerial photos of both Miller Park and County Stadium, plus they studied the film of Aaron's homer frame by frame to determine the exact landing position.

Team officials decided to place the marker where

Hank Aaron in his final season, 1976. Just over a year earlier, the Brewers had brought him back to Milwaukee, where he had begun his major league career with the Braves. "For the first time in my life I feel wanted," he said of the reunion (National Baseball Hall of Fame Library, Cooperstown, New York).

Nine. Prospects and All-Stars

the ball was touched by the fan, rather than where it eventually wound up. The thinking was that the marker should denote where the flight of the ball officially ended. It was announced that the coordinates were N 43 degrees 1.821 minutes/W 87 degrees 58.347 minutes, and the ball traveled 363 feet.[63]

On June 7, 2007, the plaque was unveiled and dedicated with Aaron in attendance. He said, "The city of Milwaukee and its fans have provided countless memories, and I am fortunate to have played 14 professional seasons in this city. My wife Billye and I truly enjoy coming back to visit Milwaukee. This is a very meaningful gesture on behalf of the Brewers organization."[64]

After his final career homer, Aaron appeared in just 23 more games. One of his final games was "Salute to Hank Aaron Night" in September. Aaron went 0-for-5 as the Brewers fell to the New York Yankees, 5–3, in 11 innings. The most emotional moments in the hour-long, pre-game ceremony came when fans gave Aaron three standing ovations. Each ovation lasted more than two minutes. Aaron also received standing ovations every time he came up to bat.

Former Milwaukee Braves radio voice Earl Gillespie was the Master of Ceremonies for the evening. Presentations were made by the likes of Commissioner Bowie Kuhn, American League President Lee MacPhail, National League President Warren Giles, and Selig. Several of Aaron's former teammates and opposing player friends were on hand, including Warren Spahn, Johnny Logan, Eddie Mathews, Felix Mantilla, Willie Mays, and Mickey Mantle.

Aaron said after the game that he wanted to provide the fans with a hitting thrill, but admitted his reflexes were gone. "I can't pull the trigger like I used to," he commented. "After a certain age Mother Nature takes over. There's no more there."[65]

Aaron spent the bulk of his time on the bench as the season ended. He didn't play in the season-ending home series against the Detroit Tigers until the final game. Grammas penciled Aaron in to hit fourth and play his customary DH role that day. Yount, Moore, and Lezcano were also in the lineup as a sign of good things to come for the team.

Dave Roberts took the mound for the Tigers and induced Aaron into grounding out to third base and shortstop in his first two at-bats. In the sixth inning, Aaron had another chance to bat after Moore singled and George Scott doubled him to third.

Hammerin' Hank came to the plate next and hit a ball in the hole that bounced off shortstop Jerry Manual's glove for a single. He drove in a run in the process, putting him at 2,297 for his career. It is a record that he holds to this day.

Aaron had no intention of coming out of the game.[66] His hope was to score a run and break a tie with Babe Ruth for second place in career runs scored. They have since dropped to fourth on the all-time list. Not only that, he wanted a chance for another at bat to perhaps get one more hit.[67]

Grammas hadn't talked with Aaron before the game about any of his wishes, and he made the decision to end the storied career with that hit. He sent out Jim Gantner to pinch-run for Aaron. Gantner did not wind up scoring, which gave Grammas an opportunity to defend his decision in hindsight. He said, "He [Aaron] has so many records. Look at it this way: he wouldn't have scored anyway."[68]

As it turned out, Aaron would have gotten another at-bat had he stayed in the game. Gantner remained in the game, batted in his spot in the eighth inning against Roberts, and flied out. The game ended in a 5–2 loss for the Brewers. Aaron's first game had also ended in a loss by a score of 9–8 to the Cincinnati Reds. In that game, he did not get a hit off starter Joe Nuxhall.

As he exited from the game he loved so much, Aaron commented that he was ready to go home, take it easy, spend time with his family, and watch his youngest son play football. "It was a sad occasion," he said. "I thought about the championship teams I played on and the all-star appearances. I just feel very fortunate."[69]

He added, "I've been playing on borrowed time the last couple of years. It has been kind of embarrassing for the kind of career I've had to be finishing with a .229 batting average. There are plenty of things I wanted to do but couldn't."[70]

One thing that Hammerin' Hank could do was mentor young players. In retrospect, we may be able to view Aaron as a bridge to the successful Brewers teams of 1978–1982. But it took one more year of futility to reverse the team's fortunes from bottom feeder to contender.

Ten

Saturday Night Massacre

After seven consecutive losing seasons in Milwaukee, the franchise looked for a huge bounce-back year in 1977, both on the field and at the gate. Changes in baseball economics became a theme that ran in the background as the year began, and Bud Selig often weighed in regarding how his team was impacted by dollar signs.

Selig ushered in the New Year by getting married to Sue Steinman in a private ceremony at the home of the bride's parents. The mid–January wedding was the second for both Selig and Steinman. The team president went right back to work on promoting his team as his group made their annual winter visits around Wisconsin.

Selig would not predict where the Brewers would finish in the standings.[1] He expressed disappointment in how the team finished the previous year, but not a lack of desire to continue building a winning club. Selig promised considerable progress toward that goal by the following winter.

General manager Jim Baumer also expected progress in a winning direction and thought a fourth-place finish could be possible.[2] Manager Alex Grammas refused to put pressure on himself over Baumer's expectation; he planned to go out and do his job, leading the team that had a few key new faces.[3]

The team had signed veteran infielder Sal Bando as a free agent in November. He would become an important veteran team member who fit in alongside Don Money as a utility infielder. Selig saw the signing of Bando as a top priority due to his leadership, but Bando said he wasn't the one who would turn the team around—that job fell to Selig and Baumer.[4]

Bando was a proven winner, having played on several great teams in Oakland. He was a four-time All-Star with five American League division championships and three World Series titles under his belt. It was a shocking move to go from contender to pretender, but Bando explained his relocation. "The people in the Milwaukee organization were the main reason why I signed with them," Bando stated. "I don't believe you can be happy with money alone." After being asked about departing from Oakland, Bando replied rhetorically, "Was it difficult to leave the Titanic?"[5]

Milwaukee also completed a trade in the winter meetings to send pitcher Jim Colborn and catcher Darrell Porter to Kansas City in return for catcher Jamie Quirk, outfielder Jim Wohlford, and pitcher Bob McClure. Porter would come back to haunt the Brewers as a St. Louis Cardinal in the 1982 World Series, but the Brewers got a lot of mileage and good efforts from McClure for seasons to come.

Porter believed his downfall in Milwaukee stemmed from poor communication with Grammas, to which Grammas disagreed.[6] Grammas said he had spent as much or more time with Porter than any other player, and Baumer and Selig also tried to straighten the talented catcher out, to no avail.[7]

Some fans groaned during the winter meetings when Baumer traded their favorite player, George "Boomer" Scott, and Bernie Carbo to the Boston Red Sox in exchange for left-handed first baseman Cecil Cooper. On the surface, it appeared as though the Brewers were merely exchanging experience for youth—and getting similar offensive numbers in the process.

In re-acquiring Scott and Carbo, the Red Sox acknowledged that they were trying to keep pace with their rivals, the New York Yankees.[8] Reggie Jackson and Don Gullet had recently been signed as free agents by the Yankees. Suddenly the American League East had gotten a lot tougher.

Cooper felt disappointment after learning of the trade, but came around after speaking with Selig and Baumer.[9] The GM had a long conversation with Cooper that ended with a contract extension beyond the three-year deal the Brewers inherited from Boston.[10] It also helped that manager Alex Grammas promised to put Cooper in the lineup as the everyday first baseman.

"I like him," Grammas said. "He's a good hitter and I think we've added more speed than we gave up in the deal. Cooper killed us with his bat last year, he's a home run threat, and several years younger than Scott." He added, "You'll need a scorecard to identify our club."[11]

New Brewers Cooper, Bando, Wohlford, and Quirk were celebrated guests at the annual Diamond Dinner of Baseball Writers in Milwaukee. The crowd of 700 welcomed the new teammates with open arms, cheering for them loudly during introductions.

Ten. Saturday Night Massacre

American league president Lee MacPhail spoke at the annual dinner and spoke optimistically about the upcoming baseball season. He expressed happiness over a four-year contract with the players and was glad that baseball didn't have any court cases going on at the moment.[12]

Oakland owner Charles Finley filed a $3.5 million suit against commissioner Bowie Kuhn, and hearings had just ended before the Milwaukee dinner. Finley had sold pitcher Rollie Fingers and outfielder Joe Rudi to Boston for $1 million each the previous June. He also sold pitcher Vida Blue to the New York Yankees for $1.5 million. Kuhn said the sales were not in the best interests of baseball and voided the transactions, leading Finley to file suit.[13]

Finley's side argued that his deals were within the rules and didn't disrupt baseball's competitive balance.[14] Kuhn's defense team stated that the commissioner's powers were absolute, therefore he had the authority to void the sales.[15] The Yankees and Red Sox were dismissed from the trial, leaving the matter between Finley and Kuhn.

On the trial's final day, Kuhn spent time being cross-examined by Finley's chief counsel. Kuhn claimed that no teams had called him to complain about the game's competitive balance.[16] However, there were indications moving toward unfair balance brought up in a conference call the day after the deals. Selig had complained about competition in his division, the American League East.[17]

U.S. District Court Judge Frank J. McGarr handed down his decision during spring training, ruling in favor of Kuhn's authority. Finley claimed after the trail that Kuhn had ulterior motives in keeping his A's intact so a future buyer could move the team to Washington.[18] Whether deeper motives were at work, this was just one of several times a commissioner would invoke the "best interests of baseball" provision in the Major League Baseball Constitution.

Major league baseball owners met in Tampa during spring training, and a group broke off called the "Young Turks." George Steinbrenner of the Yankees called the informal meeting with the youngest owners and club presidents. Selig (then 41 years old) had a chance to speak with a few other executives about the economics of baseball.[19]

The new economic formula in baseball involved some owners handing out large contracts for free agents in an attempt to build a winning team. Ticket prices were on the rise, leading to some fans backing away from the sport, and causing media outlets to comment on the shaky economic state of teams such as the Baltimore Orioles and Chicago White Sox.

Rather than continuing to move into warring faction territory, Selig and the other executives discussed how to build bridges while working on keeping escalating stadium and player costs in check. With no official committee formed and no power, the young group could only hope future discussions could lead to solutions. Selig said, "Off the field we are all partners. I don't think there is anything clandestine about that theory."[20]

Marvin Miller, executive director of the Major League Baseball Players Association, remarked that ticket prices had nothing to do with rising salaries and everything to do with demand.[21] Selig agreed with Miller and estimated that ticket prices would be raised ten times over to match demand. The burden being passed on to fans through increased ticket prices was pure myth, said Selig.[22]

An area of disagreement among owners was the subject of interleague play. The AL came into the meeting more on board with a schedule that could be implemented for the 1978 season. A three-division idea was again floated, with Selig lukewarm over the setup.[23] Geographical realignment would bring cost savings, and a wild card playoff team would add revenue. Yet some rivalries would be on the schedule fewer times.

Selig could not believe interleague play didn't happen in the 1950s and did believe the fans were overwhelmingly in favor of the setup.[24] Other owners believed interleague play could have happened in the mid–1970s, when Kuhn was in favor of the San Francisco Giants moving to Toronto, followed by a NL expansion team added to Washington and an AL expansion team added to Seattle.[25]

When those moves didn't happen, the AL had a hard time coming up with an interleague schedule with unbalanced numbers of teams in each league. If the NL agreed to 13 teams split into three divisions, each team would play 12 games against the other league. Even though some owners believed interleague would be happening soon and was in the best interests of baseball, the idea again took a back seat as the season started.

In Milwaukee, the Brewers jumped out to a great April, then hovered around the .500 mark until early July, when everything fell apart. Along the way, Baumer made two moves on the pitching staff that made a big difference in the long term.

Baumer called up 21-year-old righty Lary Sorensen to make his big-league debut at County Stadium on June 7. Sorensen lasted 6⅓ innings, giving up seven hits and four runs. He didn't figure into the 7–6 win that Milwaukee pulled off in the bottom of the ninth inning over Baltimore. For the season, Sorensen put up a 7–10 record with a 4.36 ERA. He pitched 23 games, 20 of which were starts, and completed nine of those games.

Ten. Saturday Night Massacre

Sorensen logged 142⅓ innings and allowed a little over a hit per inning, but walked just 36 hitters.

On the same day that Sorensen made his debut, the Brewers made a fantastic draft choice in the first round, selecting a future member of the 3,000-hit club and the National Baseball Hall of Fame. His name was Paul Molitor, a Minnesota native who grew up lettering in soccer, basketball, and baseball for his final three years of high school. Molitor had previously been drafted by St. Louis in 1974, but he was picked in the 28th round and offered just a $4,000 signing bonus, which he turned down in favor of attending the University of Minnesota on a scholarship.

Molitor was called Paulie or Molly by his friends. Milwaukee Brewers fans later referred to him by those names and used the nickname "The Ignitor," due to the spark he created at the top of the batting order (although Molitor himself was not fond of that moniker).[26]

The team rolled out the red carpet and brought Molitor to Milwaukee not too long after the draft to tour the stadium and meet the players. Molitor was sitting next to 22-year-old Robin Yount in the dugout when Sal Bando stopped by. He tossed an outfielder's glove to Yount, saying, "Well, I guess this will be your last year at shortstop, kid."[27]

Molitor admitted later to being embarrassed over the comment made by Bando, and said he had no intention of forcing Yount out of the shortstop job.[28] He was sent to the Class A team in Burlington, Iowa, where he hit .346 over 64 games in 1977 with eight home runs and 50 runs batted in.

Baumer added the second notable pitcher to the roster on June 15. He sent minor leaguers Garry Pyka and former first-round draft pick Rick O'Keeffe to Cincinnati in exchange for lefty pitcher Mike Caldwell. The deal looked even on paper—two prospects for a journeyman starter/reliever. But the trade turned out to be one of the most lopsided in franchise history. Pyka and O'Keeffe never made it to the major leagues, while Caldwell went on to eight years and great success with the Brewers.

Not too long after Molitor, Sorensen, and Caldwell became part of the franchise, the Brewers played their first game in Seattle since being the Pilots eight years earlier. The 16,119 fans in attendance on July 1 repeatedly showered the Brewers with boos. The sting of losing the Pilots to Milwaukee and the years without big league baseball left a sour taste in the city—the same way Braves fans felt when their team took off for Atlanta. Succeeding visits to Seattle brought less animosity as the fan base embraced their new Mariners team and let go of the past.

While the Mariners played to low expectations as an expansion team, the Brewers ran off the rails in the second half of 1977. Selig and Baumer were at a loss in figuring out an immediate fix, but witnessed the team lacking spirit and a desire to win. Selig said he would accept any criticism from fans as long as it was constructive criticism.[29]

At the end of the season, the team assessed itself critically rather than constructively. What looked good on paper didn't translate to results on the field. Interviews revealed players sick of losing and depressed by poor team performance. A poor collective attitude appeared to be a chief factor in why the team finished with a 67–95 record. "There's just something lacking," pitcher Jim Slaton said. "It seems like everyone is waiting for something to happen, to go wrong."[30]

The season had been marked by tragedy off the field as well. Veteran reliever Danny Frisella was killed in a tragic dune buggy accident on New Year's Day. He reacted to the buggy-tipping and attempted to jump off, but his foot got stuck and he was crushed by the rollbar. The friend Frisella was riding with escaped without serious injury.

Team officials and teammates expressed shock and sadness upon learning the news. Frisella had brought a much-needed leadership and good sense of humor to the bullpen. He revitalized his career after coming to Milwaukee the previous June via a trade, leading the team with nine saves while posting a 2.74 earned run average.

Another sad story played out on a national level during the season. The Brewers allegedly demoted outfield prospect Dan Thomas due to his religious beliefs, rather than needing to clear a spot on the roster for a pitcher, as claimed. Thomas had a .271 batting average at the time of his demotion in May.

Thomas was a bona-fide prospect when the Brewers selected him with the sixth overall pick in the 1972 draft. He spent the better part of three years kicking around the minors, trying to cut down on strikeouts and find the power he had in high school and college. He regained his hitting stroke in 1975 but punched an umpire in a parking lot after a game over a disputed call. Thomas sat out a two-month suspension and appeared to be headed backward on the depth chart.

Thomas pulled himself together the following season and tore up the AA Eastern League, winning the league's MVP Award and Triple Crown. The Brewers skipped him over AAA and called him up for September, when he hit .276 in 105 at-bats, setting the stage for 1977.

Thomas's mother bounced from one religious faith to another before deciding to follow the World Wide Church of God (WWCG). Thomas joined his mother for a time but stopped during his baseball career—at least until the Brewers sent him to Venezuela to play winter ball. Anxiety

Ten. Saturday Night Massacre

overtook Thomas, and he passed out from taking too many muscle relaxers. The Brewers brought him back to Milwaukee and paid for his stay in a hospital, plus an apartment for his wife and daughter.

As the off-season wore on, Thomas spent time with psychologists, trying to come to terms with his personal problems. He turned back to the WWCG before joining the Brewers for spring training in Arizona. One of the decrees of the WWCG was that members were forbidden from working from sundown Friday to sundown Saturday. Thomas became known as the "Sundown Kid" because of his refusal to play in that time frame, meaning he would miss roughly 40 games in 1977.

Thomas spoke out after being demoted early in the season, claiming it had to do with his refusal to play on the Sabbath.[31] He hit poorly in AAA Spokane and ended his stint there by talking the Brewers into letting him try pitching, so he could skip the Sabbath with less impact. After one appearance, he was sent down another level to AA—a demotion he refused.

The Brewers released Thomas prior to the following season, and he struggled for two seasons to catch the attention of another major league team. He sadly took his own life in jail a few years later after being charged with rape. The 29-year-old Thomas didn't have money for a funeral and was buried in a potter's field. Selig commented, "It's just a tragic story. I know a lot of people are mad at us because of what they think we've done to him ... he's really a nice kid who wants to do the right thing."[32]

The top choice in the draft a year after Thomas had a decision looming about whether to continue with a losing ball club. Robin Yount had been a bargain for the Brewers at $80,000 per year over the previous two seasons, and the team was hoping to lock him into a long-term contract before he gained free agency after 1978. Selig spoke privately with Yount, assured him that a better team would be built for the coming season, and said that he should stick around.[33]

Still, Yount voiced his frustrations to the press. He said, "I can't say I've enjoyed baseball that much. It's not as much fun as it should be."[34] Yount also claimed that his run in Milwaukee hadn't been very rewarding, and he hadn't gotten anything out of it.

Selig assessed the team as he always did after a season ended. This time, he seemed to be a bit more cautious when he commented about the state of the team. He agreed with the players that attitude was a top concern, but he refused to comment on the status of Alex Grammas as manager or on whether the Brewers would try to sign big-name free agents in the off-season.[35]

Some of Selig's reluctance to discuss Grammas' job security stemmed from worry about how his remarks would be taken. Giving Grammas a vote of confidence might appear to be a smoke screen before removing him from the position. Selig would tell reporters only that there was no reason to discuss the matter when Grammas had one year remaining on a three-year contract.[36]

Grammas continued moving forward with a business-as-usual attitude. He planned to visit the Arizona instructional league to look at young Brewers prospects and would attend the winter meetings in Honolulu. Grammas included himself in the long list of those connected with the organization who needed to do some self-analysis about how to improve for the next season. He expected to spend a good portion of the off-season devising ways to get better production from his coaching staff and players.

The business end of the franchise remained Selig's priority, and he noted that his opinion of field operations might not be valued much higher than that of a fan.[37] From a business standpoint, Selig saw loyal fans supporting a franchise that was one of six to operate in the black in 1976. All his ownership group's original goals had been met except for fielding a winning club.

Kansas City had gone light-years beyond Milwaukee in terms of building a successful team. The Royals had their first winning season in 1971 (85–76) and finished 102–60 in 1977. Selig was sick of comparisons between the two teams and said no one wanted to talk about other expansion teams that never won. Despite coming into the league at the same time, Selig felt that Kansas City had a four- or five-year head start due to Seattle's sorry financial state and weak farm system.[38]

At every turn, the Brewers front office met with opinions about how the team could turn the corner into respectability. Sportswriters speculated that Grammas would be removed and replaced by any number of candidates.[39] Cecil Cooper said the team needed more power and two good relievers.[40] Don Money opined that pitching, defense, and hitting were lacking and should be obtained via trades.[41]

Many of the players who could turn the Brewers' fortunes around were already on the big league roster or were in the minors, like Paul Molitor. Yount, Cooper, Bando, Money, and Sixto Lezcano all had good seasons, but the lineup still had holes. Cooper had the first .300 batting average for a starting player since George Scott and Dave May did it in 1973, while Money led the team with 25 homers and 83 runs batted in.

It started to become apparent that Baumer might not be the general manager shaping the roster for the following season. One of the last mentions of Baumer before his firing came on November 6.[42] The baseball free agent re-entry draft had just happened, allowing 14 teams (13 new teams and the free agent's former team) to go through open bidding for the player.

Baumer and Selig listed 14 players in the draft, with their top selections being slugging Minnesota outfielder Larry Hisle and his teammate, Lyman Bostock. The two expressed a desire to sign together with a team, but Bostock preferred the West Coast, while Hisle leaned toward Milwaukee and later signed a six-year contract worth $3 million.

Hisle spurned a reportedly similar offer from Texas and said his decision came down to the way he was courted by the Brewers—including Selig himself. Bando and Cooper gave Hisle a tour of the city, and he found Milwaukee to be a place where he felt he'd fit in well, not being a big city type.[43]

Selig mentioned that being able to sign higher-tier free agents was contagious, although he admitted that after landing Hisle, the team would not also be able to pursue Bostock due to economic constraints.[44] The Brewers were also out of the running after drafting outfielders Oscar Gamble and Richie Zisk, plus top relievers Rich "Goose" Gossage and Rawly Eastwick. Veteran catcher Ray Fosse came at a more affordable price and signed with the Brewers on New Year's Eve.

As the Brewers took huge leaps forward with their roster, Selig found himself amid an ownership debate in Boston. Longtime Red Sox owner Tom Yawkey had passed away in the summer of 1976, leaving the ownership of the team in question. Initially the team went into a trust, but then a deal came about to sell the franchise to executive Haywood Sullivan and former team trainer Buddy LeRoux for just a $200,000 down payment.

Jean Yawkey, the widow of the late Boston owner, worked out a way for her friend Sullivan and LeRoux to get 52 percent of the franchise. They came in third in bidding for the team behind Ohio-based A-T-O Inc. and Boston businessmen Marty Stone and Jack Satter. The executors of Yawkey's will (his widow and his two lawyers) named Sullivan and LeRoux winners of the bidding war.[45]

The executors fired GM Dick O'Connell, assistant GM John Claiborne, and Vice President Gene Kirby as a means to clear the way for Sullivan and LeRoux. Things got sticky from there. House Speaker Tip O'Neill was a friend of O'Connell and reportedly asked Commissioner Bowie Kuhn to take a closer look at the deal.

The financial state of LeRoux came into question when the *Boston Globe*'s Spotlight team began to look into his assets, which LeRoux had claimed were worth $4.7 million. American League owners were unhappy over the handling of the firing of O'Connell and appeared unanimous in voting down the transfer of ownership, if it did in fact come to a vote.[46]

Selig chaired the league finance committee and said some owners asked if the potential ownership team understood how unstable the baseball business could be and how much operating cash they needed to be effective. There were many other stronger ownership groups that could better handle running the team, according to Selig.[47]

"This isn't Cleveland, it's Boston," Selig said. "This is the most important franchise in the American League, and we can't afford to let it be underfinanced or second rate. This situation is a mess. It seems inconceivable that what Tom Yawkey built could come to this."[48]

The ownership debacle continued until being resolved the following May. Jean Yawkey was named as a general partner with LeRoux and Sullivan. Yawkey also held a limited partner share with eight other investors. She served as team president, while Sullivan stayed on as general manager and LeRoux handled VP duties. Yawkey formed a trust and ran it as president and sole stockholder until her death in 1992.

Selig put himself back into the thick of things in Milwaukee by mid-November. He was forced to act on a planned front office house-cleaning two days earlier than he wanted, due to a story leak to Hank Stoddard, sports director of WTMJ-TV. Stoddard held his story until after Selig concluded his mass purge.[49]

The exits began on Friday, November 18, when Selig fired Baumer. He then terminated Grammas and Director of Player Development Al Widmar. Also dismissed were coaches Jimmy Bragan and Hal Smith, leaving only Frank Howard, Cal McLish, and Harvey Kuenn as holdovers from Grammas' staff.

Selig's extreme house-cleaning wound up being dubbed the "Saturday Night Massacre."[50] He emphasized that many of the things that had gone on for eight years would not go on in the future. "We are grieved by the whole situation, but we concluded after months of long and agonizing thought that it simply was time for a change," Selig said.[51]

Grammas said that Selig informed him by phone of the termination. The two had spoken earlier in the week about plans for 1978 and progress in negotiating with players they drafted in the November re-entry draft. Grammas found the firing to be a surprise and thought it would have come earlier in the off-season. Injuries to key players such as Sixto Lezcano and Bill Travers were cited by Grammas as reasons why the Brewers failed in 1977.[52]

Ten. Saturday Night Massacre

Insiders saw it differently—Grammas and Baumer didn't agree on how to motivate players. Baumer didn't think Grammas spent enough time working with younger players and had a hard time relating to the entire team.[53] Grammas may have sealed his fate mid-season when he left the team to go to his office late in the second game of a losing doubleheader. Players lost respect for Grammas over that move and started quietly questioning his desire to win, or to at least care about the outcome of games.[54]

Grammas didn't believe the Brewers would improve just because he was fired. Grammas commented, "You can't improve but one step at a time. This year we had some young pitchers who were getting better. I don't believe they feel in their hearts that a managerial change will do any good. What they do feel is this is an important year for them, as far as ticket sales go. They had to do something."[55]

Selig wasn't done doing "something." His next move turned out to be the best front-office hiring in the history of the seven-year-old franchise. Selig wasted no time after the "Saturday Night Massacre" in announcing his next move—hiring Harry Dalton as the general manager of the Milwaukee Brewers.[56] Dalton had quite an amazing background in baseball alone—but beyond the game had earned a Bronze Star serving with the United States Air Force during the Korean War.

Dalton was the main man in creating a Baltimore Orioles dynasty that started in the mid–1960s and lasted long after he departed in 1971. Some of the players Harry Dalton had a hand in acquiring were still with the O's when Selig hired him to take control in Milwaukee. Dalton's first big move in Baltimore came in 1965, when he was Director of Player Personnel. He wrapped up a trade that brought star outfielder Frank Robinson to Baltimore from Cincinnati. It was a key move that helped Baltimore to World Series titles in 1966 and 1970. The Orioles also captured pennants in 1969 and 1971.

It was Harry Dalton who hired Earl Weaver as manager, and Weaver would run the team until 1982, then came back for 1985–1986. Weaver finished with a .583 winning percentage as a major league manager. Dalton was also credited for acquiring Mike Cuellar and Pat Dobson to strengthen the O's rotation, if not make them virtually unstoppable.

California called on Dalton after the 1971 season to right a sinking ship, but he didn't have the same success with the Angels that he had with Baltimore. Dalton's biggest move was to trade with the New York Mets for future Hall of Fame pitcher Nolan Ryan, yet he was never able to construct a roster to play even .500 ball. Still, his past work with Baltimore gave Brewers fans a reason to get excited.

Dalton laid out three projects he wanted to tackle upon his hiring with Milwaukee. First, he recognized a need to continue upgrading the farm system by signing more players and potentially adding another farm club. He also wanted to sign free agents for the big league team. Finally, he planned to seek out trades that would fill any remaining gaps. Hiring a manager wasn't high on his to-do list.[57]

Dalton said, "Unlike some of you, I don't think there's a great urgency to name a manager. I have no self-imposed deadlines. I'd rather wait 45 or 60 days and find the right man."[58]

It would be over two months before Dalton named his field manager. Until then, he kept busy acquiring players. His first move was to acquire catcher Ned Yost from the New York Mets in the Rule 5 draft. Yost would make it to the majors with the Brew Crew in 1980 and played primarily as a backup—but he did have some memorable moments with the 1982 World Series team. Milwaukee fans would become a lot more familiar with Yost a couple of decades later when he returned to manage the team.

Beginning in 1978, Harry Dalton led the Brewers into an era of contending baseball for the first time in franchise history (National Baseball Hall of Fame Library, Cooperstown, New York).

Dalton made two trades on consecutive days that December to help shape his roster. He acquired veteran catcher Buck Martinez from St. Louis. Martinez was known for his defense more than his bat, and he became an effective platoon partner with Charlie Moore from 1978 through 1980.

Next, Dalton traded pitchers Rich Folkers and Jim Slaton to Detroit for outfielder Ben Oglivie. Dalton made out like a bandit, as Folkers would never throw another big league pitch, while Slaton returned to Milwaukee after the 1978 season and stuck around until 1983. Ben "Spider Man" Oglivie (or "Benji") would provide plenty of thrills for Brewers fans over the next nine years, typically ranking high in many offensive stats.

Ten. Saturday Night Massacre 169

Dalton finally made his choice for Brewers manager on January 20, 1978, when he hired longtime Baltimore pitching coach George Bamberger. Dalton told reporters that he believed Bamberger to be a very independent person with leadership qualities and excellent knowledge not only of pitchers, but in handling players.[59] "Bambi" came highly regarded as the man behind a pitching staff who racked up five American League East Division championships, a World Series win in 1970, and three pennants. Bamberger's roots with the O's staff went back as far as 1964, when he was hired as roving minor league pitching instructor. From there, Bamberger moved up to work under Earl Weaver after Dalton moved him into the Orioles' pitching coach position in late 1967. Weaver lamented that he'd rather lose a 20-game winner than Bamberger to the Brewers.[60]

Dalton commented, "George was our first choice. We asked no one else for permission to talk to anyone else." He continued, "George is a winner. In ten years at Baltimore, we had 18 pitchers who were 20-game winners and four Cy Young award winners, Jim Palmer three times and Mike Cueller once."[61]

Bamberger was 54 years old and had spent much of his adult life in baseball. He was a native New Yorker who joined the United States Army during World War II, serving in the Mediterranean and European theaters. After the war, "Bambi" caught on with the New York Giants and had a great minor league career. He managed to post double-digit wins in four of his first five seasons. However, his major league career consisted of just 14⅓ innings of work.

Bamberger made it to the Giants' big league roster briefly in 1951 and 1952. He spent the rest of the decade in the minors and racked up 213 wins, retiring in 1963. His only other major league stint happened in 1959 with the Orioles, but again was brief. In 1960, he became a player/manager with the Vancouver Mounties and later the Dallas-Fort Worth Rangers.

All the experience and success made Bamberger confident in his new job. He was ready to have his Milwaukee Brewers contend in the tough American League East—even against his former Baltimore club—and saw himself as an educator, motivator, and communicator. He said, "I'm not conceding a thing. I see no reason why this team can't play better than .500 ball this year. I think this ball club in the near future will win the pennant."[62]

One of Harry Dalton's biggest roster moves came less than a month after the hiring of George Bamberger. Dalton purchased Gorman Thomas back from the Texas Rangers after Thomas had been sent over in late

October to complete an August trade for Ed Kirkpatrick. Thomas never appeared in a game for Texas.

When Bamberger assessed the Brewers' roster, he noticed that Thomas was notably absent.[63] Bamberger reportedly asked where the big kid was who loved to catch the ball, prompting Dalton to ask for Thomas back.[64] Thomas had yet to hit more than ten home runs in a season, but Bamberger saw unlimited potential in the slugger. Thomas had a monster Triple-A season in 1977 with a .322 batting average to go with 36 home runs and 114 runs batted in. He appeared ready to break out at the big league level.

Thomas would not have to worry if he sported a mustache or long hair. Selig wrapped up his role in the front office changes by removing the ban on excess hair that Grammas imposed when he became manager of the team. Players such as pitcher Bill Travers rejoiced over the reversal— as Travers had gone around and around with Grammas over his long hair rule.[65]

The hot stove, rather than hair length, kept coming up as an off-season theme with the front office. As team officials made their annual winter tour stops and held court at the annual Diamond Dinner, they spoke of capturing the attention of opposing teams with their free agent signings and what might lie ahead.[66] Much of the remaining hot stove discussion centered on Yount possibly not signing a new contract with the club.

Yount played just ten games in spring training and was placed on the disabled list due to foot issues. Late in March, he asked for a leave of absence from the team.[67] From there, things with the young shortstop tumbled downhill. Selig went so far to hop a plane for Arizona to meet with Yount, but it wasn't enough to get him to rejoin the team immediately.

Rumors swirled about Yount around the time of the season opener, regarding everything from his whereabouts to being traded elsewhere.[68] But the biggest story was that Yount was considering retirement to become a professional golfer.[69] He would refute the rumor later in the year,[70] but would backtrack a bit in 1982 when he told *Sports Illustrated* that he'd mentioned golf, but he didn't mean to be taken seriously.[71]

Another angle to the Yount saga was his personal life. He had dated a former high school classmate who lived with him during the 1977 season. After the season, she decided that she preferred to live in California, leaving Yount split over what he should do. By the next year they would be married, but in early 1978 the relationship weighed heavily on Yount's mind.[72]

Ten. Saturday Night Massacre

Yount returned for Opening Day in Milwaukee but did not suit up, instead spending time with his teammates and in the broadcast booth. Yount's absence opened the door for the 21-year-old Molitor not only to make the team, but also to be inserted as the starting shortstop and leadoff hitter on Opening Day.

He also had an interaction with Molitor that Molitor later described as really awkward. Molitor said, "I mean, my career is hanging on Robin's fingers. If he comes back, I'm gone. I really wanted him right then to tell me what he was going to do, but I was hardly in a position to ask him. It's none of my business."[73]

Yount announced his return to the team in early May and said that he'd be ready for game action within a week.[74] It took just three days before he made a pinch-hit appearance and popped out. It's hard to imagine Robin Yount hearing boos directed at him, but that's exactly what he got from the home crowd at County Stadium. The next day, he again pinch-hit and turned things around with a single.

By the following week, Yount was back at shortstop full-time and Molitor moved over to second base. It was a step toward Yount signing a lucrative five-year contract extension later in the year worth $2.35 million, making it clear that the team had no intentions of letting him walk in free agency.

As the Brewers readied themselves for field action in 1978, the front office also prepared to unveil new uniforms to go with the new look team. A contest had been held the previous fall for a new logo. The consensus among the Brewers leadership was that the uniforms adapted and modified from the Seattle Pilots days had run their course.

When the Milwaukee Brewers organization decided to create new uniforms, the timing also seemed right for replacing the "Barrel Man" logo. While initially the logo made sense as a nod to the old Milwaukee Brewers minor league team, Bud Selig admitted it was rather cartoonish and hard to replicate on promotional items.[75]

By late November 1977, a winner was announced out of 1,931 entries in the contest. Tom Meindel, a graphic art and design major at the University of Wisconsin–Eau Claire, beat out the competition with his unique "ball and glove" logo.

Meindel said he found out about the contest through a TV station and took a crack at designing something during what he called a very boring psychology class.[76] At first, he had the "M" and "B" side-by-side, but then decided to stack them in lower-case lettering. Once Meindel got them into what resembled a baseball glove, he knew he was on to something.

He sent his entry off to the Brewers' marketing department and heard back just a couple of weeks later that he was one of two finalists for the new team logo. Most of the entries came from within the state of Wisconsin, but the Brewers did receive one from a serviceman stationed in Turkey.

The team flew Meindel to Milwaukee for a meeting with Dick Hearn, the Vice President of Marketing. After some modification to his original design, Meindel returned home and found out he had won the contest. The Brewers presented Meindel with a check for $2,000 that he used toward a down payment for a house. Meindel said of his logo, "It can be enlarged to the size of a billboard or reduced to the size of a button, without losing its legibility."[77]

The new logo remained masked in secrecy until Opening Day. Player photos were taken behind closed doors, and promotional materials such as the media guide featured Larry Hisle in a non-descript uniform with the plain "M" cap.

Milwaukee debuted their new pinstripe uniforms to mixed initial reviews from fans and the press. Road uniforms were also new—in powder blue with "Milwaukee" across the front. Selig had vowed to put player names on the home uniforms, but this was impossible because the pinstripes ran through the letters.[78] Selig mentioned that he wanted the pinstripes for the 1970 uniforms, but the move from Seattle to Milwaukee happened too fast for these to be produced.[79]

Milwaukee took the field in their new uniforms on Opening Day at home against rival Baltimore. Bamberger sent out the following lineup, with many players who would become fan favorites in the coming seasons:

> Paul Molitor   SS
> Don Money   3B
> Sal Bando   DH
> Larry Hisle   LF
> Sixto Lezcano   RF
> Cecil Cooper   1B
> Gorman Thomas   CF
> Lenn Sakata   2B
> Andy Etchebarren   C
> Jerry Augustine   P

Fans packed County Stadium to the tune of 47,824 in attendance. The Brewers blew out the O's in all three games of the series by scores of

11–3, 16–3, and 13–5. Milwaukee not only reached the goal of being respectable, but turned the corner into contender with a 97–65 record in 1978.

Times had certainly changed. Selig said, "I remembered that seven years ago we opened against the Detroit Tigers and we drew 8,900 people. You'd think that 8,900 people would cut off the freeway here by accident. We've come a long way."[80]

Epilogue

Economics has been a part of baseball since the early days of the New York Knickerbockers and two decades later when professional baseball arrived in Milwaukee. It took until the American Association Milwaukee Brewers were founded in 1902 for the city to back a team with their pocketbooks, and this carried over when the Braves moved to Milwaukee in 1953.

Bud Selig observed not only those teams on the field, but also the economics and cultural impact of having a professional team in Milwaukee, which led him to take charge of keeping baseball in the city. Selig has stated that had his efforts not ended in the purchase of the Seattle Pilots, he may have moved on from the auto dealership and become a history professor. Instead, Selig became a part of history himself as the commissioner of baseball.[1]

Selig's complicated history and legacy are impossible to deny, as he is viewed by many as one of the most polarizing figures in sports. Beginning with the ouster of then-Commissioner Faye Vincent in 1992 and Selig taking over first in an interim role, then in an official capacity in 1998, Selig's actions have been well-documented and debated.

In his 22-year term, some of the changes Selig helped bring about included realignment of teams, interleague play, playoff wild card teams, expansion and relocation, instant replay, increased diversity, merging of the NL and AL offices under the commissioner, the World Baseball Classic, steroid testing, unprecedented years of labor peace, and a 400 percent increase in MLB revenue, making it a $10 billion industry.

Getting to the end result of many of those alterations and Selig's motivations behind the moves have been debated ad nauseam. Did he sit idly by during baseball's Steroid Era until he had no choice but enact a steroid testing policy? Was he distracted by fallout from the 1994 players' strike and thus failed to act, even though the subject had been on the table during labor talks?

The Brewers were in the thick of many of Selig's changes, for better or worse. Even before he became commissioner, Selig was an early supporter of publicly funded sports complexes.[2] He has stated on numerous occasions that they make the community a better place to live, and the economic impact is immeasurable.[3] Five new ballparks had opened or were in the works before he became acting commissioner, and that was just the beginning. Another 18 stadiums were built during his tenure, with $8 billion of taxpayer money used, according to a study by Judith Grant Long of the University of Michigan.

Ballparks built with public money are just the tip of the argument. Critics say the job and income growth brought about by a new stadium or professional franchise is minimal.[4] They point toward the consumer spending money they would have spent anyway—rather than going to the movies, they attend a baseball game.[5] Unemployment may remain high within a city with a franchise, even when politicians claim the franchise puts the city on the map.

Countless studies on sports economics and financial impact have been conducted and cited by both critics and proponents. Does the sports team have the financial impact of a department store, or do visitors from outside the city spend enough money at restaurants and hotels to stimulate the economy?

An aging stadium, lack of luxury boxes, no revenue from parking, and local economic impact were all reasons Brewers executives brought forth in the early 1990s when proposing a new ballpark.[6] Plans called for replacement of County Stadium with a retractable-roof facility complete with luxury boxes and other amenities.

The initial cost estimate came in at $125 million, with $63 million coming from city, state, and federal authorities. By the time Miller Park opened in 2001, construction costs had more than tripled to $400 million.

Wisconsin governor Tommy Thompson appointed an 11-member commission with the task of looking at ways to finance the proposed stadium. Meanwhile a constitutional amendment had been approved by the Wisconsin Legislature to create a sports lottery to help finance a new Brewers stadium. But before it could be placed on a statewide ballot in 1995, it would have to clear the Legislature again.

By September of 1995, Thompson and a few lobbyists worked to land the votes needed for the new stadium. None were sure the votes would pass the Assembly, especially Speaker David Prosser. "It's like pulling teeth,"[7] he commented.

The Legislature eventually came through and passed a law that created a five-county sales tax to underwrite a new Milwaukee stadium. The 0.1 percent tax began on January 1, 1996, and initially was set to expire in 2010, but now looks to end in late 2019 or early 2020. In actuality, tax is being collected for reserve funds to continue subsidizing Miller Park until 2040. An annual maintenance payment and other capital costs include possible scoreboard or roof engine (bogey) replacement.

Racine County voters showed their opposition of the stadium bill by recalling state Sen. George Petak for casting the deciding vote. He changed his vote in favor of the bill early in the morning of October 6, 1995, after Racine County was added into the final plan for the sales tax plan. Years later, Petak looked back on the historic vote and said he believed the Brewers couldn't survive in County Stadium. "It came down to a question, after hours and weeks of debate, should it pass or should it go down to defeat and see the Brewers leave town."[8]

Petak recalled the loss of the Braves to Atlanta, saying, "It created all kinds of problems in terms of identity of the city."[9] He also said that if he didn't vote yes, the Brewers would have moved to Charlotte. Petak had no regrets even after being recalled from office.

Governor Thompson, however, did have buyer's remorse as Miller Park entered the final stages of construction, after actively campaigning for the new stadium. His speeches were often on an emotional level, asking attendees how they would feel if the team moved and became the Buffalo Brewers.[10]

Thompson claimed the Brewers provided misleading financial information to get the stadium built, then broke promises to use the increased revenue to make the Brewers competitive. He also vowed never to set foot in the park he helped build as long as Selig's family remained owners of the team.[11]

The heartstrings connected to the team that Thompson tugged on could be felt across County Stadium on September 28, 2000, when the old ballpark had a blowout goodbye party. Over 40 former players from the Braves, Brewers, and Green Bay Packers were involved in the post-game celebration.

The final game was played between Milwaukee and Cincinnati in front of 57,354 fans and had a playoff atmosphere from beginning to end. The Reds won in blowout fashion, 8–1, after rocking Jeff D'Amico for six earned runs and ten hits over six innings, ending his bid to win the

Epilogue 177

Fans were able to watch Miller Park rise up beyond County Stadium's bleachers from 1996 to 2000, when this photo was taken. The ballpark would open in April 2001, a little more than a month after County Stadium was demolished (courtesy Bob Busser).

National League ERA title. A special moment happened in the middle of the fifth inning, when Olympic pitching star and Milwaukee prospect Ben Sheets was introduced to the crowd.

Warren Spahn threw out the "last pitch" after the game to Braves catcher Del Crandall. It was a repeat of the battery that opened County Stadium 48 years previously. Before the game, Spahn said, "I'm concerned I won't get it there. I told Crandall to make sure he had a glove that popped because I don't know if I could throw it hard enough for it to pop."[12]

In a throwback to the post–1982 World Series celebration, Robin Yount raced around the field on his Harley-Davidson motorcycle. After all the former players were introduced, they created a line from second base to center field. A flag was sent down from Bernie Brewer's chalet to the chain of players. When the flag reached Yount, he passed it on to then-shortstop Mark Loretta with some words of wisdom.

Yount said, "Each of us has touched this flag, symbolic of how County Stadium has touched us. Don't ever forget where it all started." Loretta replied, "County Stadium has served us well and we will never forget her. But oh, it will be sweet across the street."[13]

Bob Uecker fittingly gave a speech near home plate as the banks of lights went out one set at a time: "It was here that boys became men. And men became champions. And champions became legends. Tonight is the final curtain. It's time to say goodbye. For what was, will always be. So long, old friend."[14]

Miller Park opened on April 6, 2001, with the Cincinnati Reds again opposing the Brewers. Selig and President George W. Bush threw out the first pitches to bring in a new era of Milwaukee baseball. A few County Stadium mainstays were part of the new ballpark, including mascot Bernie Brewer in his new home high above the left field bleachers. Uecker's famous home run call of "Get up, get out of here, Gone!" was placed above Bernie's dugout and slide with Uecker's permission.

The game was a sellout, but a capacity crowd in Miller Park was smaller than in County Stadium. Still, 42,024 were on hand to see the inaugural game—a 5–4 victory for Jeff D'Amico and the Brewers. Nearly three million fans came through the turnstiles to see the 68–94 Brewers by the season's end, even though it was their worst record in 17 seasons.

Selig's family didn't hold on to the team much longer and sold the franchise to Los Angeles investor Mark Attanasio. He purchased the team in September 2004, for a reported $220 million. Insiders thought he spent about $40 million more than the team was worth, but he proved to be ready to spend even more money to build a winning team. "I think the biggest thing we face is the small market perception," Attanasio said. "I have really been on [general manager] Doug [Melvin] and everyone around the organization and city leaders: 'Let's stop saying we're small. Let's not make any excuses.'"[15]

Selig's top concern when his family sold the Brewers was making sure the new ownership kept the team in Milwaukee for years to come, and he felt Attanasio was a perfect choice as team owner. "Now they don't have to go through what people went through in '64 and '65, when the Braves were leaving Milwaukee," Selig explained. "Whatever the controversy was about the ballpark or anything else, the Brewers are there. They're secure, and they're a marvelous asset."[16]

The franchise proved itself as a marvelous asset to Attanasio's ownership group in the following years. After hitting a low attendance mark in 2003 of 1,700,354 fans, Miller Park and the Milwaukee Brewers have welcomed over two million fans each year since then. When the team returned to the playoffs in 2008 they drew over three million fans for the first time, and eclipsed that number again in 2011.

In April 2018, Forbes valued the Brewers at $1 billion, based on operating income, revenue, expenses, and other factors. That number had nearly doubled from the $565 million value in 2014, before the team started a rebuilding phase. The increases are staggering when one considers the $10.8 million Selig's ownership paid for the franchise in 1970.

Forbes has only limited access to franchise information and makes a few guesstimates on valuation, yet the possibility of a $1 billion sale of the Brewers isn't hard to believe. Numbers that can be believed are the Brewers being in the top six for economic growth in 2017 and in the top ten for debt-to-value ratio and operating income. Miller Park saw a 10 percent increase in attendance in 2017, while TV viewership also increased by 35 percent.

Through all the studies of baseball economics and the arguments about whether Bud Selig was the greatest or worst baseball commissioner of all time, one fact remains—without Selig, there most likely would not be a major league team in Milwaukee. His tireless efforts in bringing the Brewers to Milwaukee may never be repeated anywhere in baseball. But Selig doesn't seem too worried about his overall legacy, and instead looks back to one special accomplishment as his favorite moment in a long career. "I always say I'm going to let historians determine my legacy,"[17] Selig says.

Attanasio has often given credit to Selig for his efforts as the person that took the reins in bringing major league baseball back to Milwaukee.[18] With the team came organizational and stadium jobs, not to mention giving countless baseball fans a team to call their own for the last five decades.

Loyalty to the Brewers has been passed down from generation to generation, through highs such as reaching the 1982 World Series, 1987's "Team Streak," playoff berths in 2008 and 2011, and exiting pennant chases in 2017–2019. Fans also shared in the misery of the early years and the post-expansion rebuild, a horrific 56–102 record in 2002, and the aftermath of losing the aforementioned World Series.

Allan Huber "Bud" Selig's time in baseball as commissioner and owner of the Milwaukee Brewers culminated when the 83-year-old was inducted into the National Baseball Hall of Fame on Sunday, July 31, 2017. His career once again was open for debate, starting with Seattle Pilots fans insisting that Selig stole the team in bankruptcy court.[19]

Montreal Expos fans at the ceremony to see Tim Raines' induction chanted "Let's Go Expos!" Several fans wearing Expos jerseys turned their backs for the duration of Selig's speech, to make it clear how they felt about Selig's role in moving their team to Washington.

Selig did have the support of Hall of Famers in ex-Brewers Don Sutton, Rollie Fingers, Robin Yount, and Henry Aaron. Paul Molitor was managing the Minnesota Twins and couldn't attend the ceremony. Selig called Aaron one of the best, most decent and dignified people he had ever known, and he had kind words for Yount, Fingers, and Molitor.

Selig said, "Robin and Rollie and Molly represented the Brewers in so many ways. You three were more than just players to me and the city of Milwaukee and the state of Wisconsin. You are forever etched in the minds of Brewers fans. You are forever etched in the journey of my life."[20]

One now almost forgotten important event not mentioned in Selig's speech happened 52 years prior—almost to the day of his Hall of Fame induction. On July 29, 1965, a group of businessmen including Selig filed incorporation papers with the secretary of state. Their primary aim was to land a baseball franchise to replace the Braves, and Selig talked about that in his speech:

> "I got into baseball 53 years ago for the simplest reason of all: I wanted to bring Major League Baseball back to my hometown. I made it my mission, my quest, and I devoted five long years in a relentless effort.
> We would try and we would fail;
> We would try and we would fail;
> We would try and we would fail,
> but we would never quit.
> And that day when the Brewers arrived—March 31, 1970—will forever be one of the proudest days of my life."[21]

That piece of Selig's journey is commemorated in the final sentence of his Hall of Fame plaque: *Bridge-builder and devoted fan who returned baseball to Milwaukee before serving as second-longest tenured commissioner.*

Current Brewers owner Mark Attanasio stated before the induction ceremony that he wanted to be in Milwaukee to see his team take on the Chicago Cubs, but there was no way he'd miss Selig's induction.[22] Selig gave him a nod during the speech, saying, "And by the way, I love that the Brewers flourish today under the great care of Mark Attanasio. The Brewers and their fans throughout Milwaukee and Wisconsin are in good hands."[23]

Selig also talked about the impact his parents had on him growing up. He said that if Marie and Benjamin Selig were there, they would be proud of his journey. It had taken him full-circle to the ceremony on his 83rd birthday, from the love of baseball passed on to him in childhood by Marie.

Epilogue

Selig ended his speech by saying, "As a kid, I read the newspapers, studied the box scores, and memorized the statistics. I dreamed the dreams that little boys dream. On my last night as Commissioner, I gave a speech at the New York Baseball Writers Dinner.

That night, I said, 'What you have seen here are a little boy's dreams that came true.'"[24]

Chapter Notes

Chapter One

1. Dennis Pajot, "Otto Borchert," SABR Biography Project, accessed May 3, 2018. https://sabr.org/node/33019.
2. "When Baseball First Met Radio In Milwaukee," *Milwaukee Journal*, August 20, 1944, 65.
3. Ibid.
4. J.F. Helfert, "Borchert Is Stricken at Elks' Club," *Neenah News Record*, April 28, 1927, 1.
5. Associated Press, "Otto Borchert Dies During Address," *Wisconsin Rapids Daily Tribune*, April 28, 1927, 1.
6. Pajot, "Otto Borchert."
7. Associated Press, "Woman to Keep Baseball Club," *Escanaba Daily Press*, February 3, 1929, 15.
8. "Florence Killilea Forsakes Diamond for the Kitchen," *Milwaukee Sentinel*, January 7, 1931, 13.
9. "Brewer Players Grieved by Untimely Death of Florence Killilea," *Milwaukee Sentinel*, June 16, 1931, 16.
10. Brian A. Podoll, *The American Association Milwaukee Brewers, 1859–1952* (Jefferson, NC: McFarland, 2003), 338.
11. Bill Veeck and Ed Linn, *Veeck—As in Wreck: The Autobiography of Bill Veeck* (Chicago: University of Chicago Press, 2012), 48.
12. Eldon Ham, *Larceny and Old Leather: The Mischievous Legacy of Major League* (Chicago Review Press, 2005), 68.
13. Veeck and Linn, *Veeck—As in Wreck*, 52.
14. "New Pitcher Steps From Birthday Cake as Veeck's Gift to Grimm," *Milwaukee Journal*, August 29, 1943, 25.
15. Vera Williams, "The Stormy Career of Casey Stengel," *Independent Press-Telegram*, June 25, 1961, 81.
16. Podoll, *American Association Milwaukee Brewers*, 338.
17. Tyler Kepner, "Baseball Lifer Leaves Office, but Not the Game," *New York Times*, January 22, 2015, accessed July 22, 2017, https://www.nytimes.com/2015/01/23/sports/baseball/bud-selig-ends-his-reign-as-commissioner-with-no-regrets.html.
18. Tom Haudricourt, "Bud Selig's Love of Baseball Came from His Mother," December 23 2014, accessed January 19, 2017, http://archive.jsonline.com/sports/brewers/bud-seligs-love-of-baseball-came-from-his-mother-b99413960z1–286744061.html.
19. Phil Rogers, "Wrigley Always Special for Selig," Chicago Cubs Official Website, accessed July 22, 2017, http://chicago.cubs.mlb.com/news/print.jsp?ymd=20140422&content_id=72968276&c_id=chc.
20. Barry M. Bloom, "'Emotional Day' for Selig," MLB.com, accessed July 21, 2017, http://mlb.mlb.com/content/printer_friendly/mlb/y2004/m04/d15/c718150.jsp.
21. Associated Press, "Perini Envisions 12-Team Big Loop," *Pensacola News Journal*, January 17, 1948, 2.

Chapter Two

1. Joe Hand and Jack Reichler, "Bill Veeck Forced Transfer of Braves to Mil-

waukee," *Clarion-Ledger*, March 22, 1953, 38.

2. *Ibid.*
3. *Ibid.*
4. *Ibid.*
5. Alexander Edelman, "Johnny Antonelli," SABR Biography Project, accessed January 25, 2016, https://sabr.org/bioproj/person/e1774181
6. Joe Hand and Jack Reichler, "Bill Veeck Forced Transfer of Braves to Milwaukee," *Clarion-Ledger*, March 22, 1953, 38.
7. Associated Press, "Did Braves Move Set Off Chain Reaction?" *Akron Beacon Journal*, March 19, 1953, 26.
8. *Ibid.*
9. Associated Press. 1953. "60,000 Cheer Braves in Milwaukee Parade," Wausau Daily Herald, April 9, 17.
10. *Ibid.*
11. Chicago Tribune Press Service, "Speeches Mark Milwaukee Debut in National League," *Chicago Tribune*, April 15, 1953, 53.
12. Lloyd Larsen, 1953. "B-Day!" *Milwaukee Sentinel*, April 15, 1.
13. Associated Press, *Chippewa Herald*, accessed July 22, 2017, http://chippewa.com/sports/braves-title-still-remembered/article_afcfd1af-9559-5785-9995-281febf107a6.html.
14. Associated Press, "Stengel Lauds Haney, Burdette," *Janesville Daily Gazette*, October 11, 1957, 12.
15. *Ibid.*
16. *Ibid.*
17. Kathryn Jay, *More Than Just a Game: Sports in American Life Since 1945* (New York: Columbia University Press, 2005), 81.
18. Monte McCormick, "The Cloak of Honest Wooing Was Ripped Off," *Wisconsin State Journal*, October 22, 1964, 59.
19. *Ibid.*
20. Broeg, Bob. "Braves' Doorbell Rings: It's Atlanta," *Sporting News*, August 3, 1963, 7.
21. UPI, "Braves Chairman Denies Club Moving," *Capital Times*, September 13, 1963, 19.
22. McCormick, "The Cloak of Honest Wooing Was Ripped Off," 59.
23. *Ibid.*

24. Monte McCormick, "Veeck Labels Move 'Greedy,'" *Wisconsin State Journal*, October 22, 1964, 59.
25. Tom Briere, "Record Crowd Sees Twins Win," *Star Tribune*, July 25, 1967, 19.

Chapter Three

1. Bob Wolf, "Tepee Makes Whoopee Over Top Ducat Huckster Bragan," *Sporting News*, February 22, 1964, 23.
2. *Ibid.*
3. UPI, "Braves Bit Worried Over Fans' 'Boycott,'" *Clarion-Ledger*, May 2, 1965, 28.
4. Associated Press, "Braves Mishandled Move to Atlanta, Declares Perini," *The Post-Crescent*, January 16, 1965, 5.
5. Chicago Tribune Press Service, "In the Wake of the News," *Chicago Tribune*, February 10, 1966, 101.
6. Associated Press, "Thunderous Ovations Given Mathews, Aaron on Last At-Bat," *Marshfield News-Herald*, September 23, 1965, 15.
7. Robert Lipsyte, "Perspective: The Urban Myth of Baseball as Savior," *New York Times*, accessed July 21, 2017, http://www.nytimes.com/1996/04/28/sports/perspective-the-urban-myth-of-baseball-as-savior.html.
8. "CenterStage Preview: Bud Selig," YESNetwork.com, accessed July 20, 2017, http://web.yesnetwork.com/news/article.jsp?ymd=20120927&content_id=39100554&fext=.jsp&vkey=news_milb.
9. Associated Press, "League Authorizes Braves to Play in Atlanta," *Greenville News*, January 29, 1966, 7.
10. *Ibid.*
11. Red Smith, "Still the Braves No Matter What," *Independent Press-Telegram*, April 3, 1966, 124.
12. *Ibid.*
13. Associated Press, "Views of Sport," *Daily Reporter*, March 17, 1966, 25.
14. Associated Press, "Judge Orders Braves to Play 1966 Campaign In Milwaukee," *Salem News*, January 28, 1966, 11.
15. *Ibid.*
16. Associated Press, "BB's Anti-Trust Trial in 4th Week," *Meriden Morning Record*, March 22, 1966, 5.

17. Ken Hartnett, "Schedule Maker Takes Stand, Defense Howls," *Stevens Point Journal*, April 2, 1966, 6.
18. *Ibid.*
19. Cleon Walfoort, "Braves Salaries $783,815 in '64," *Milwaukee Journal*, March 11, 1966, 21.
20. *Ibid.*
21. *Ibid.*
22. *Ibid.*
23. Associated Press, "Says Attendance Estimate Too High," *Racine Journal Times*, March 30, 1966, 19.
24. Associated Press, "Grobschmidt Testifies as Adverse Baseball Witness," *Post-Crescent*, March 23, 1966, 19.
25. *Ibid.*
26. *Ibid.*
27. *Ibid.*
28. *Ibid.*
29. *Ibid.*
30. Larry Whiteside, "Majors May Boycott After the Trial: Robinson," *Milwaukee Journal*, April 1, 1966, 19.
31. *Ibid.*
32. *Ibid.*
33. *Ibid.*
34. Raymond E. McBride, "Braves Say They Won't Return Despite Judge Roller's Decision," *Milwaukee Journal*, April 14, 1966, 1.
35. *Ibid.*
36. William Povletich, *Milwaukee Braves: Heroes and Heartbreak* (Madison: Wisconsin State Historical Society Press, 2009, 171).
37. Associated Press, "Braves' Return Order Stayed by Judge Roller," *Chicago Tribune*, May 18, 1966, 66.
38. *Ibid.*
39. Bob Wolf, "Some Milwaukeeans Plan to Battle On—Some Toss in Towel," *Sporting News*, December 24, 1966, 30.
40. Ben Reiter, "For Love and Money," *Sports Illustrated*, accessed July 20, 2017, https://www.si.com/vault/2014/10/20/106650435/for-love-and-money.
41. Bill Dwyre, "Selig Is Driven by His Lifelong Love of the Game," *Los Angeles Times*, April 22, 2011, accessed February 8, 2016, https://www.latimes.com/archives/la-xpm-2011-apr-21-la-sp-dwyre-selig-20110422-story.html.
42. Gary Derong, *Milwaukee Brewers: Inside MLB* (Edina, MN: Sportszone, 2015), 13–14.
43. Gary D'Amato, "After Four Decades of Ups and Downs in Milwaukee, Brewers Still Shaping Legacy," *Journal Sentinel*, accessed July 19, 2017, http://archive.jsonline.com/sports/brewers/89477932.html/.
44. Bob Wolf, "We'll Keep Plugging to Land Franchise—Milwaukee Lead," *Sporting News*, December 18, 1965, 20.
45. *Ibid.*
46. *Ibid.*
47. Clifford Kachline, "Expansion Years Away, Majors Insist," *Sporting News*, December 18, 1965, 1.
48. *Ibid.*
49. *Ibid.*
50. Associated Press, "American League Rejects Milwaukee Bid," *Daily Telegram*, December 4, 1965, 14.
51. *Ibid.*
52. *Ibid.*
53. Bob Wolf, "Baseball Indeed Monopoly," *Milwaukee Journal*, January 24, 1966, 15.
54. Lou Chapman, "A's Move Here Possible: Allyn," *Milwaukee Sentinel*, January 24, 1966, 9,10.
55. Tom Haudricourt, "After 5 Year Struggle, Bud Selig Gets His Team," *Milwaukee Journal Sentinel*. December 24, accessed July 19, 2017, http://archive.jsonline.com/sports/brewers/after-5-year-struggle-bud-selig-gets-his-team-b99414784z1-286813521.html.
56. Bud Selig, "Voice of the Fan," *Sporting News*, April 1, 1967, 4.
57. Bob Wolf, "Selig Knocks Foam from Report Milwaukee to Get AAA Franchise," *Sporting News*, August 13, 1966, 5.
58. Bob Wolf, "Ticket Sales Brisk for Milwaukee Tilt," *Sporting News*, May 27, 1967, 5.
59. Lou Chapman, "Milwaukee's Goal—Expansion Club by 1970," *Sporting News*, April 29, 1967, 7.
60. *Ibid.*
61. Lou Chapman, "Czar Eckert, Cronin Here for Sox Tilt," *Milwaukee Sentinel*, June 24, 1967, 13.
62. Tom Briere, "Record Crowd Sees Twins Win," *Star Tribune*, July 25, 1967, 19.
63. *Ibid.*
64. *Ibid.*

65. Associated Press, "Milwaukee Tilt Draws 51,144 Record Crowd," *Racine Journal Times*, July 25, 1967, 15.

Chapter Four

1. Bob Wolf, "Three Pro Cage Games Booked For Milwaukee," *Sporting News*, September 30, 1967, 32.
2. *Ibid.*
3. C.C. Johnson Spink, "Oakland Jumps Back Into Finley Plans," *Sporting News*, July 29, 1967, 15.
4. *Ibid.*
5. *Ibid.*
6. *Ibid.*
7. *Ibid.*
8. *Ibid.*
9. UPI, "McHale For Milwaukee Franchise," *Wisconsin State Journal*, August 3, 1967, 17.
10. Wolf, "Three Pro Cage Games Booked for Milwaukee," 32.
11. *Ibid.*
12. Lou Chapman, "City Must 'Push' for Franchise—Selig," *Milwaukee Sentinel*, September 27, 1967, 1.
13. *Ibid.*
14. *Ibid.*
15. *Ibid.*
16. *Ibid.*
17. UPI, "No Comment From Selig on Expansion," *Green Bay Press-Gazette*, October 19, 1967, 22.
18. Richard Dozier, "Missourians Ransom: New Club by 1971," *Chicago Tribune*, November 11, 1967, 85.
19. Ron Fimrite, "They're Just Mad About Charlie," *Sports Illustrated* (online), accessed January 5, 2018, https://www.si.com/vault/1979/05/21/823638/theyre-just-mad-about-charlie-as-few-as-653-fans-have-seen-the-as-play-but-its-owner-finley-whos-being-sued-for-nonsupport.
20. Richard Dozier, "Missourians Ransom: New Club by 1971," *Chicago Tribune*, November 11, 1967, 85.
21. Dave Eskenazi, "Wayback Machine: Dewey Soriano Story, Part II," SportsPressNW.com, accessed July 10, 2017, http://sportspressnw.com/2149857/2013/wayback-machine-dewey-soriano-story-part-ii.
22. Jerome Holtzman, "White Sox Will Stretch '68 Home Schedule to Milwaukee," *Sporting News*, November 11, 1967, 38.
23. UPI, "No Comment From Selig on Expansion," 22.
24. *Ibid.*
25. Jerome Holtzman, "White Sox Will Stretch '68 Home Schedule to Milwaukee," *Sporting News*, November 11, 1967, 38.
26. "White Sox Owner Says They Won't Be Moving," *Waukesha Daily Freeman*, December 11, 1967, 18.
27. Jerome Holtzman, "N.L. Owners Unload Weapons," *Sporting News*, November 25, 1967, 30.
28. *Ibid.*
29. *Ibid.*
30. Bob Wolf, "Milwaukee Fans Storm Ticket Booth," *Sporting News*, December 23, 1967, 31.
31. Holtzman, "N.L. Owners Unload Weapons," 30.
32. Bob Wolf, "1968 Called Year of Decision for Milwaukee," *Sporting News*, February 3, 1968, 32.
33. Associated Press, "Ed Short Speaks at Diamond Dinner," *Appleton Post-Crescent*, January 22, 1968, 20.
34. *Ibid.*
35. Bob Wolf, "1968 Called Year of Decision for Milwaukee," *Sporting News*, February 3, 1968, 32.
36. *Ibid.*
37. "Group Meets On Expansion," *Baltimore Sun*, March 21, 1968, 34.
38. Bob Wolf, "20,759 Brave a Frigid Wind to See Chisox in Milwaukee," *Sporting News*, April 20, 1968, 33.
39. UPI, "Halfway Home Says Milwaukee's Cannon," *Sheboygan Press*, April 20, 1968, 11.
40. *Ibid.*
41. *Ibid.*
42. Bob Wolf, "Milwaukeeans Laud Selig, City's Big Baseball Booster," *Sporting News*, May 11, 1968, 25.
43. Joe Mooshil, "Baseball Takes International Glow, Adds San Diego, Montreal," *Fond Du Lac Commonwealth*, May 28, 1968, 23.
44. Shirley Povitch, "Milwaukee Will Get Franchise," *Capital Times*, November 16, 1968, 28, 29.

45. Mooshil, "Baseball Takes International Glow," 23.
46. Povitch, "Milwaukee Will Get Franchise," 28, 29.
47. Ibid.
48. Edward Prell, "Don't Be Too Sure N.L. Will Expand," Chicago Tribune, May 21, 1968, 57.
49. Lou Chapman, "Milwaukee Fate on Line Today," Milwaukee Sentinel, May 27, 1968, 9.
50. Dick Kaegel, "Sweating, Waiting...as NL Debated," Sporting News, June 8, 1968, 5, 32.
51. Mooshil, "Baseball Takes International Glow," 23.
52. Ibid.
53. Edward Prell, "N.L. Expands to Montreal, San Diego," Chicago Tribune, May 28, 1968, 52.
54. Ibid.
55. Ibid.
56. Tom Haudricourt, "After 5 Year Struggle, Bud Selig Gets His Team."
57. UPI, "Milwaukee Not Ready To Jump Ship Yet," Oshkosh Northwestern, May 29, 1968, 17.
58. Mooshil, "Baseball Takes International Glow," 23.
59. Bob Wolf, "Kuhn Offers Milwaukee a Ray of Hope," Sporting News, January 31, 1970, 38.
60. Joe Mooshil, "Allyn Repeats That He Won't Move or Sell Chisox," Appleton Post-Crescent, July 21, 1968, 47.
61. Lloyd Larson, "Brewers Still Working for '9' Here," Milwaukee Sentinel, June 11, 1968, 10.
62. Ibid.
63. UPI, "Griffith Urges Sox Increase," Wisconsin State Journal, June 23, 1968, 23.
64. Bob Wolf, "Chisox Struck Oil in 9 Visits to Milwaukee," Sporting News, September 7, 1968, 15.
65. Len Wagner, "Atlanta Foiled Franchise for Milwaukee: Mathews," Green Bay Press-Gazette, March 4, 1969, 16.
66. Jim Hutcheson, "The Clubhouse," Evening Independent, February 3, 1944, 14.
67. Ibid.
68. Associated Press, "Seattle Lists Board, Name," Statesman Journal, March 31, 1968, 19.
69. Bill Mullins, Becoming Big League: Seattle, the Pilots, and Stadium Politics. Seattle: University of Washington Press, 2013.
70. Associated Press, "American League Expansion Clubs Slate Player Draft," Wilmington News-Journal, October 15, 1968, 11.

Chapter Five

1. Kenneth Hogan, The 1969 Seattle Pilots: Major League Baseball's One-Year Team. Jefferson, NC: McFarland, 2006, 92–93.
2. Ibid., 173
3. The Seattle Pilots: Short Flight Into History, directed by Steve Cox and Brad Powers, performed by Jim Bouton, Greg Goossen and Bob Locker (unknown city: Play Ball Films, 2010), DVD, 84 mins.
4. Scooter Chapman, "Spotlight on Sports," Port Angeles Evening News, October 14, 1968, 6.
5. Ibid.
6. Bill Mullins, Becoming Big League, 100–103.
7. Jack Hewins, "Builders Busy Getting Seattle Stadium Ready," The Times, February 9, 1969, 37.
8. Hy Zimmerman, "Pilots Look Toward Mincher," Sporting News, February 1, 1969, 40.
9. Hy Zimmerman, "Pilots Bank On Blue Chip Revelers," Sporting News, February 15, 1969, 43.
10. Ibid.
11. Mullins, Becoming Big League, 113.
12. Richard Dozer, "Sox Start New Era in Seattle Today," Chicago Tribune, April 11, 1969, 67.
13. Bob Wolf, "Novice Pilots Flying High," Milwaukee Journal, June 13, 1969, 18.
14. Associated Press, "Seattle Socked By Sox," Centralia Daily Chronicle, June 17, 1969, 10.
15. Joe Sargis, "Seattle Has Enthusiasm," Wausau Daily Herald, March 18, 1969, 10.
16. Associated Press, "Rent Troubles Plague Pilots," Arizona Republic, September 7, 1969, 131.
17. Associated Press, "Seattle Pilots

Manager May Walk the Plank," *San Francisco Examiner*, August 26, 1969, 47.

18. Jerome Holtzman, "Chisox to Stay, New Boss John Allyn Promises," *Sporting News*, October 11, 1969, 15.

19. *Ibid.*
20. *Ibid.*
21. *Ibid.*
22. *Ibid.*

23. Hy Zimmerman, "Angry Seattle and Pilots Sitting on Powder Keg," *Sporting News*, October 18, 1969, 32.

24. *Ibid.*

25. Associated Press, "Pilot Transfer to Texas," *Baltimore Sun*, August 31, 1969, 31.

26. *Ibid.*

27. UPI, "Soriano Denies He'll Be Replaced," *Honolulu Star-Bulletin*, October 8, 1969, 20.

28. Associated Press, "Plaza, Maglie Fired By Pilots," *Cincinnati Enquirer*, October 17, 1969, 32.

29. Associated Press, "Seattle Tries to Save Pilots," *Berkshire Eagle*, October 20, 1969, 7.

30. *Ibid.*

31. Dan McGuire, "Strange Happenings in Seattle," *Honolulu Star-Bulletin*, October 20, 1969, 56.

32. Associated Press, "Pilots Talk of Franchise Shift," *Baltimore Sun*, October 21, 1969, 29.

33. Associated Press, "Disposed Red Manager to Discuss Pilot Job," *Spokane Daily Chronicle*, November 20, 1969, 31.

34. Associated Press, "Crosetti Says Seattle Fired Him," *Los Angeles Times*, November 21, 1969, 57.

35. *Ibid.*

36. Associated Press, "Disposed Red Manager to Discuss Pilot Job," 31.

37. Associated Press, "Schultz Linked to Twins Post," *Capital Times*, October 20, 1969, 34.

38. UPI, "Seattle Pilots Name Dave Bristol as New Manager," *Nevada State Journal*, November 25, 1969, 4.

39. Associated Press, "Bristol to Manage Seattle," *Belvidere Daily Republican*, November 29, 1969, 7.

40. Don Merry, "Suffering Along With Seattle," *Long Beach Independent*, March 13, 1970, 35.

41. *Ibid.*

42. Associated Press, "Seattle's Danz: All We Need Is the Money," *Los Angeles Times*, November 6, 1969, 48.

43. Associated Press, "Seattle Mayor Uhlman Enters Into Dispute," *Oshkosh Northwestern*, January 6, 1970, 17.

44. Associated Press, "Cronin Tells Seattle to Solve Own Problem," *Racine Journal Times*, January 13, 1970, 15.

45. Associated Press, "Seattle Mayor Uhlman Enters Into Dispute," 17.

46. Associated Press, "Seattle Hopes Fade," *Spokane Daily Chronicle*, January 10, 1970, 8.

47. Bob Wolf, "Kuhn Offers Milwaukee a Ray of Hope," *Sporting News*, January 31, 1970, 38.

48. *Ibid.*
49. *Ibid.*

50. Associated Press, "Daley May Favor Milwaukee," *Racine Journal Times*, January 24, 1970, 15.

51. UPI, "Hunt Optimistic," *El-Paso Herald*, January 26, 1970, 18.

52. Associated Press, "Views of Sport," *Daily Reporter*, March 17, 1966, 25.

53. Associated Press, "Franchise to Remain in Seattle," *Tucson Daily Citizen*, February 11, 1970, 29.

Chapter Six

1. Associated Press, "$8.8 Million Pricetag Set if Seattle Loses Franchise," *Allentown Morning Call*, January 26, 1970, 22.

2. Associated Press, "Courts Will Hear Case for Seattle," *Spokane Daily Chronicle*, January 24, 1970, 9.

3. UPI, "Finley's Got A Plan," *Sheboygan Press*, January 29, 1970, 25.

4. *Ibid.*

5. Associated Press, "Courts Will Hear Case For Seattle," *Spokane Daily Chronicle*, January 24, 1970, 9.

6. *Ibid.*

7. Associated Press, "Seattle Owners Unchanged," *Spokane Daily Chronicle*, February 12, 1970, 20.

8. *Ibid.*

9. Associated Press, "Pilots Get Help," *Wisconsin State Journal*, February 15, 1970, 28.

10. *Ibid.*

11. *Ibid.*
12. UPI, "Spring a Bad Thing for Pilots-Brewers," *Cherry Hill Courier-Post*, March 26, 1970, 27.
13. UPI, "Seattle Group Won't Renew Bid for Franchise," *St. Louis Post-Dispatch*, March 13, 1970, 17.
14. Hy Zimmerman, "Mistakes by All Parties Marked Seattle Fiasco," *Sporting News*, April 18, 1970, 20.
15. UPI, "Surprise! It's Seattle," *San Francisco Examiner*, February 12, 1970, 50.
16. UPI. 1970. "Seattle Will Retain Pilots, Say Owners," *Ogden Standard-Examiner*, February 12, 1970, 21.
17. Bill Dwyre, "Bud Selig's Time as Head of MLB Is Worth Admiring," *Los Angeles Times* (online), accessed July 13, 2017, http://www.latimes.com/sports/la-sp-bud-selig-dwyre-20150108-column.html.
18. Hy Zimmerman, "Nothing So Refreshing as Stein of Cold Milwaukee Brew," *Sporting News*, April 4, 1970, 20.
19. *Ibid.*
20. Associated Press, "Injunction Blocks Shift of Pilots to Milwaukee," *Racine Journal Times*, March 17, 1970, 13.
21. *Ibid.*
22. Bill Mullins, *Becoming Big League*, 275.
23. *Ibid.*
24. *Ibid.*
25. Orval Jackson, "AL Hit With Another Restraining Order," *Sheboygan Press*, March 18, 1970, 45.
26. Associated Press, "Seattle Loses Complex," *Arizona Republic*, March 18, 1970, 28.
27. UPI, "Judge Berates Both Sides in Pilots Case," *Muncie Evening Press*, March 24, 1970, 10.
28. *Ibid.*
29. Associated Press, "Bankruptcy Referee Clears Way for Pilots," *Lubbock Avalanche-Journal*, March 25, 1970, 158.
30. *Ibid.*
31. Associated Press, "Judge May Tell Pilots No Go," *Wisconsin State Journal*, March 31, 1970, 1.
32. Associated Press, "No Team Yet but Milwaukee Store Offers Tickets," *Green Bay Press-Gazette*, March 27, 1970, 13.
33. *Ibid.*
34. Associated Press, "Pitching Is Key to Seattle Penannt Hopes," *La Crosse Tribune*, March 30, 1970, 17.
35. Lew Krausse, response to questionnaire, July 23, 2015.
36. Associated Press, "Judge May Tell Pilots No Go," *Wisconsin State Journal*, March 31, 1970, 1.
37. *Ibid.*
38. *Ibid.*
39. *Ibid.*
40. *Ibid.*
41. *Ibid.*
42. Associated Press, "Pilots Head for Milwaukee," *Carrol Daily Times Herald*, March 25, 1970, 5.
43. Associated Press, "It's Official! Pilots Are on Their Way to Milwaukee," *Salina Journal*, April 1, 1970, 26.
44. *Ibid.*
45. Eric Fisher, "Recalling Selig's Fight to Keep Milwaukee in the Game," *Sports Business Journal*, accessed July 13, 2015, http://www.sportsbusinessdaily.com/Journal/Issues/2015/01/19/In-Depth/Pilots.aspx.
46. Associated Press, "Sigh of Relief by Pilots Players," *Stevens Point Journal*, April 1, 1970, 15.
47. *Ibid.*
48. Dave Baldwin, response to questionnaire, May 1, 2015.
49. UPI, "Spring a Bad Thing for Pilots-Brewers," *Cherry Hill Courier-Post*, March 26, 1970, 27.
50. Associated Press, "Pilots Luncheon 'Irish Wake,'" *Centralia Daily Chronicle*, April 7, 1970, 7.
51. Associated Press, "It's Official! Pilots Are on Their Way to Milwaukee," 26.
52. Murray Chass. "Selig, The Fan, Pulls For Packers," *New York Times*, accessed July 10, 2017, https://nytimes.com/1997/01/26/sports/selig-the-fan-pulls-for-the-packers.html.
53. Gary D'Amato, "Ken Sanders Left His Mark as Brewers Reliever," *Milwaukee Journal Sentinel*, accessed July 14, 2017, http://archive.jsonline.com/sports/brewers/ken-sanders-left-his-mark-as-a-brewers-reliever-b9948031z1-214325381.html/.
54. *Ibid.*

55. *Ibid.*
56. Associated Press, "Sale Becomes Official Today," *Racine Journal Times*, April 2, 1970, 19.
57. Staff, "We're Big League Again!," *Milwaukee Journal*, April 1, 1970, 1, 14.
58. *Ibid.*
59. Associated Press, "Sale Becomes Official Today," 19.
60. *Ibid.*
61. *Ibid.*
62. *Ibid.*
63. Bob Greene, "Moral Obligation to Friend—Kuhn," *Capital Times*, April 2, 1970, 26, 27.
64. Staff, "We're Big League Again!," *Milwaukee Journal*, April 1, 1970, 1, 14.
65. Jerome Holtzman, "Pirates Seek Another Starter," *Sporting News*, August 8, 1970, 12.
66. Jerome Holtzman, "Owners Peeved at Kuhn," *Sporting News*, October 24, 1970, 12.
67. Associated Press, "Pitching Is Key to Seattle Penannt Hopes," *La Crosse Tribune*, March 30, 1970, 17.

Chapter Seven

1. Staff, "Thousands Greet Brewers," *Milwaukee Sentinel*, April 6, 1970, 1, 16.
2. Associated Press, "8,000 Greet Brewers," *Fond du Lac Commonwealth Reporter*, April 6, 1970, 27.
3. UPI, "Milwaukee Jams Airport in Welcome," *Sheboygan Press*, April 6, 1970, 31.
4. *Ibid.*
5. UPI, "General Manager of Brewers Elated by Long Ticket Lines," *Chicago Tribune*, April 4, 1970, 54.
6. Terry Bledsoe, "In This Corner," *Milwaukee Journal*, April 8, 1970, 20.
7. Bob Meyer, response to questionnaire, July 10, 2015.
8. Bledsoe, "In This Corner," 20.
9. *Ibid.*
10. "Brews Like Milwaukee," *Green Bay Press-Gazette*, April 8, 1970, 19, 20.
11. John Morris, response to questionnaire, August 9, 2015.
12. "Brews Like Milwaukee," 19, 20.
13. Bud Selig, "First Person: Selig on Favorite Opening Days," MLB.com, accessed June 1, 2017. http://m.mlb.com/news/article/69708630/commissioner-bud-selig-recalls-memorable-exciting-opening-days/.
14. Associated Press, "Brewers to Retire No. 1 in Honor of Selig," *USA Today* (online), accessed May 9, 2017, https://www.usatoday.com/story/sports/mlb/2014/09/26/brewers-to-retire-no-1-in-honor-of-selig/16294655/.
15. UPI, "Milwaukee 'Witches' Cast Spell for Brews," *Sheboygan Press*, April 22, 1970, 45.
16. Jerome Holtzman, "Flood Opposed One-Day Strike," *Sporting News*, June 13, 1970, 8.
17. UPI, "Aaron Rekindles Old Flames of Love in Milwaukee," *Palm Beach Post*, May 16, 1970, 26.
18. *Ibid.*
19. Associated Press, "Bernie Brewer an Avid Fan," *Manitowoc Herald-Times*, July 6, 1970, 19.
20. Clifford Terry, "Heads-Up Ball Isn't Everything," *Chicago Tribune Magazine*, August 23, 1970, 21.
21. *Ibid.*
22. *Ibid.*
23. *Ibid.*
24. Larry Whiteside, "Bernie Brewer Battles Cancer," *Milwaukee Journal*, March 1, 1972, 20.
25. *Ibid.*
26. Lou Chapman, "Brewers Hope to Be Spoilers," *Milwaukee Sentinel*, September 1, 1970, 8.
27. *Ibid.*
28. Associated Press, "Brews Win Home Finale; Bristol Contract Renewed," *Green Bay Press-Gazette*, September 25, 1970, 13.
29. Bob Woessner, "Bud Selig Takes Milwaukee Back Out to the Ballgame," *Green Bay Press-Gazette*, September 13, 1970, 57.
30. Lou Chapman, "Brewers Launch Drive For 6,000 Season Tickets," *Milwaukee Sentinel*, November 4, 1970, 14.
31. *Ibid.*
32. Staff, "State CC Names Kellett and Selig to Hall of Fame," *Wisconsin State Journal*, November 3, 1970, 19.
33. Associated Press, "Milkes Quits As

Brews' GM," *Ironwood Daily Globe*, December 17, 1970, 15.
34. *Ibid.*
35. *Ibid.*
36. UPI, "Milkes Denies Health Reason," *Honolulu Star-Advertiser*, December 18, 1971, 43.
37. Staff, "Brewer Arrival Was Top Story," *Wisconsin State Journal*, December 30, 1970, 27.
38. Tom Flaherty, "88 Days To Baseball," *Wisconsin State Journal*, January 7, 1971, 21.
39. Associated Press, "Lane Assumes GM Postion; Quinn Hired," *Manitowoc Herald-Times*, January 25, 1971, 20.
40. UPI, "Frank Lane Starts New Job At 74," *Zanesville Times Recorder*, January 26, 1971, 11.

Chapter Eight

1. John Pustian, "Brewers Make No Rash Promises," *Appleton Post-Crescent*, January 13, 1971, 37.
2. UPI, "Brewers Plan Expensive Draft," *Wisconsin State Journal*, May 18, 1971, 36.
3. *Ibid.*
4. Staff, "Bob Uecker Returns to Milwaukee," *Manitowoc Herald-Times*, July 20, 1971, 14.
5. Richard Sandomir, "Bob Uecker Returns to the Booth," *New York Times*, accessed January 11, 2017, http://www.nytimes.com/2010/08/14/sports/baseball/14uecker.html?mcubz=0.
6. *Ibid.*
7. Scott Miller, "Bud Selig: Commissioner's Life in Baseball Leaves an Indelible Mark," CBS Sports.com, accessed January 9, 2017, http://www.cbssports.com/mlb/story/22812383/bud-selig-commissioners-life+&cd=1&hl=en&ct=clnk&gl=us.
8. *Ibid.*
9. Gretchen Brown, "For Milwaukee Baseball Legends, It All Comes Back to the Game," NPR.org, accessed August 11, 2017, https://www.wpr.org/milwaukee-baseball-legends-it-all-comes-back-game.
10. Associated Press, "Brewer VP Advises Early Games in South," *La Crosse Tribune*, August 17, 1971, 15.
11. Associated Press, "$1.3 Million Loss Rumored For Brewers," *Marshfield News-Herald*, September 10, 1971, 12.
12. Associated Press, "White Sox Want to Replace Nationals in East," *Baltimore Sun*, September 24, 1971, 25.
13. *Ibid.*
14. Richard Dozer, "Allyn Denies Sox Snubbed Baseball Fete," *Chicago Tribune*, January 25, 1972, 47.
15. Associated Press, "Brewers Make Shift," *Wisconsin State Journal*, October 10, 1971, 23.
16. *Ibid.*
17. Larry Whiteside, "All That's Left of Original Brewers Is Burp," *Sporting News*, November 6, 1971, 47.
18. Associated Press, "Brewers Let Mattick Go," *Oshkosh Northwestern*, October 25, 1971, 4.
19. Tom Hawley, "Brewers' Pitch is No Curve," *Wisconsin State Journal*, January 25, 1972, 29, 32.
20. Koziol, "Emprise Finger Found In Nearly Every Major U.S. Sports Pie," *Chicago Tribune*, November 15, 1971, 1.
21. *Ibid.*
22. *Ibid.*
23. *Ibid.*
24. Associated Press, "Brewers' Prexy Confirms Loans From Sportservice," *Arizona Republic*, November 16, 1971, 22.
25. Koziol, "Emprise Finger Found in Nearly Every Major U.S. Sports Pie," 1.
26. Dwight Pelkin, "Brewers Exude Optimism About Coming Campaign," *Sheboygan Press*, January 21, 1972, 20.
27. Dozer, "Allyn Denies Sox Snubbed Baseball Fete," 47.
28. *Ibid.*
29. *Ibid.*
30. *Ibid.*
31. *Ibid.*
32. *Ibid.*
33. Associated Press, "Brewers Search for Financial Happiness," *Green Bay Press-Gazette*, January 18, 1972, 13.
34. Associated Press, "Badgers/Brewers Slate Exhibition Game May 7," *La Crosse Tribune*, December 14, 1972, 23.
35. Associated Press, "Give Different

Views on Kuhn's Lack of Action in Strike," *La Crosse Tribune*, April 15, 1972, 9.
36. *Ibid.*
37. *Ibid.*
38. *Ibid.*
39. UPI, "Selig Feels Kuhn's Strike Handling Was Right Path," *Oshkosh Northwestern*, April 15, 1972, 1.
40. Associated Press, "Give Different Views On Kuhn's Lack of Action in Strike," *La Crosse Tribune*, April 15, 1972, 9.
41. Lou Chapman, "Brewers Fire Bristol, Pick Crandall," *Milwaukee Sentinel*, May 29, 1972, 1, 16.
42. Associated Press, "Crandall Debut Set," *Wausau Daily Herald*, May 30, 1972, 19.
43. Chapman, "Brewers Fire Bristol, Pick Crandall," 1, 16.
44. Associated Press, "Crandall Returns to Site of Glory," *La Crosse Tribune*, May 30, 1972, 20.
45. Associated Press, "Says Team Considered Folding Seven Years Ago," *Wisconsin Rapids Daily Tribune*, April 28, 1979, 4.
46. *Ibid.*
47. Larry Whiteside, "Scott Adjusts to His Job As A Brewmaster," *Sporting News*, November 25, 1972, 53.
48. *Ibid.*
49. Wire Services, "Brewers Shuffle Front Office," *Wisconsin State Journal*, October 6, 1972, 13.
50. *Ibid.*
51. *Ibid.*
52. *Ibid.*
53. UPI, "All-Star Tilt in Milwaukee," *Oshkosh Northwestern*, December 1, 1972, 17.
54. *Ibid.*
55. *Ibid.*
56. UPI, "Brewers Make Plans to Enliven Stadium," *Wisconsin State Journal*, February 9, 1973, 22.
57. Lew Cornelius, "Brewers in Sales Pitch to Area Fans," *Capital Times*, February 16, 1973, 25, 26.
58. Larry Whiteside, "Brewers Try New Wrinkle on Winter Tour," *Milwaukee Journal*, February 7, 1973, 15.
59. Tom Hawley, "Brewers Sales Pitch Hits Optimism, Progress," *Milwaukee Journal*, February 16, 1973, 25, 28.
60. Ralph Trower, "Brewers Tell Their Story Here," *Racine Journal Times*, February 10, 1973, 8.
61. Cornelius, "Brewers in Sales Pitch to Area Fans," 25, 26.
62. *Ibid.*
63. *Ibid.*
64. *Ibid.*
65. Lloyd Larson, "Jim Wilson Fits Nicely Into Brewers' Solid Building Plans," *Milwaukee Sentinel*, October 30, 1971, 11, 14.
66. *Ibid.*
67. Cornelius, "Brewers in Sales Pitch To Area Fans," 25, 26.
68. Russell Schneider, "Baseball Facing Civil War," *Sporting News*, January 6, 1973, 28.
69. *Ibid.*
70. *Ibid.*
71. *Ibid.*
72. Matt Pommer, "Area Paralyzed by Spring Blizzard," *Capital Times*, April 9, 1973, 1, 4.
73. Mike O'Brien, "Hockey Growth Lifted by UW's Johnson," *Wausau Daily Herald*, April 20, 1973, 20.
74. *Ibid.*
75. *Ibid.*
76. *Ibid.*
77. Associated Press, "Baseball Owners Meeting," *Baltimore Sun*, August 24, 1973, 24.
78. Lou Chapman, "Kuhn Ducks AL-NL Play," *Milwaukee Sentinel*, August 17, 1973, 12, 15.
79. *Ibid.*
80. Lou Chapman, "Scott Fires Opening Salvo in Bid for $120,000 Pact," *Sporting News*, December 22, 1973, 42.
81. Lou Chapman, "Boomer Joins Century Club," *Milwaukee Sentinel*, December 21, 1973, 11.
82. *Ibid.*
83. Lou Chapman, "Brewers' Mouths Water Over Farm Crop of Future," *Sporting News*, December 8, 1973, 45.
84. *Ibid.*
85. Lou Chapman, "Lane and Selig Disagree on 1973 Brewer Profits," *Sporting News*, May 11, 1974, 23.
86. *Ibid.*
87. *Ibid.*

Chapter Nine

1. Tom Butler, "Brewers' Buds May Blossom," *Wisconsin State Journal*, January 23, 1974, 35.
2. *Ibid.*
3. *Ibid.*
4. Jerome Holtzman, "Bob Fishel a First-Rate Publicist," *Sporting News*, June 1, 1974, 12.
5. Dick Miller, "Angels to Lop 2 Weeks Off 1975 Camp," *Sporting News*, May 11, 1974, 10.
6. Associated Press, "Wilson Leaving Brewers to Head Scouting Bureau," *Racine Journal Times*, August 6, 1974, 13.
7. *Ibid.*
8. *Ibid.*
9. *Ibid.*
10. Larry Whiteside, "Lane Raps Honochick on Ragamuffin Tag," *Sporting News*, July 12, 1971, 49.
11. UPI, "Milwaukeeans Send Congrats," *El Paso-Herald*, April 10, 1974, 25.
12. *Ibid.*
13. Associated Press, "Aaron Plays One Last Game in Milwaukee," *Racine Journal Times*, May 7, 1974, 15.
14. *Ibid.*
15. *Ibid.*
16. Inquirer Wire Services, "Braves Are Sending Aaron 'Home' to Milwaukee," *Philadelphia Inquirer*, November 3, 1974, 66.
17. Associated Press, "Hank's Back as Brewer," *Manitowoc Herald-Times*, November 15, 1974, 12.
18. Free Press Wire Services, "Aaron Traded To Brewers," *Detroit Free Press*, November 3, 1974, 61.
19. Associated Press, "Hank's Back As Brewer," 12.
20. *Ibid.*
21. Milton Richman, "Hank Aaron's Last Time at Bat," *Eureka Times Standard*, March 4, 1975, 8.
22. UPI, "Aaron Looks Back on 1974 Season," *Bonham Daily Favorite*, March 4, 1975, 6.
23. *Ibid.*
24. Lou Chapman, "Brewers Better Than Yanks, Says Selig," *Sporting News*, January 25, 1975, 40.
25. *Ibid.*
26. *Ibid.*
27. Lou Chapman, "Brewers Fans Salute Returning Aaron," *Sporting News*, February 15, 1975, 35.
28. Milt Richman, "For the First Time I Feel Wanted: Aaron," *Indianapolis News*, January 29, 1975, 52.
29. Associated Press, "Grammas New Brewers Pilot," *Abilene Reporter-News*, November 7, 1975, 10.
30. Milt Richman, "For the First Time I Feel Wanted: Aaron," 52.
31. Associated Press, "Hank Aaron—Most Valuable .239 Hitter," *Poughkeepsie Journal*, July 13, 1975, 8B.
32. Tony Walter, "Song, Cameras, Robust Crowd Greet Henry," *Green Bay Press-Gazette*, April 12, 1975, 13.
33. Associated Press, "Brewers Maul Detroit 17–3," *Marshfield News-Herald*, May 2, 1975, 12.
34. *Ibid.*
35. UPI, "Hard Man to Introduce," *Stevens Point Journal*, July 15, 1975, 23.
36. Keith Spore and Kenneth R. Lamke, "51,840 At Ballgame," *Milwaukee Sentinel*, July 16, 1975, 1.
37. Gordon Edes. "Not A Happy Ending for Boomer," *ESPN Online,* accessed June 15, 2017, https://www.espn.com/boston/mlb/story/_/id/9520950/george-boomer-scott-died-feeling-some-resentment.
38. Associated Press, "Grammas New Brewers Pilot," 10.
39. Associated Press, "Brewer Copouts Disgust Grammas," *Los Angeles Times*, July 13, 1977, 43.
40. Associated Press, "Brews Activate Travers, Cort, Place Mike Hegan On Waivers," *Wausau Daily Herald*, July 16, 1977, 13.
41. Associated Press, "Forster Stops Brewers in Rare Starting Role," *Waukesha Daily Freeman*, August 14, 1973, 10–11.
42. Lou Chapman, "Brewers' Outlook Differs in Top Views," *Sporting News*, February 14, 1976, 44.
43. *Ibid.*
44. Staff, "Selig's Wife Given Divorce," *Milwaukee Sentinel*, July 16, 1976, 11.
45. Associated Press, "Peking Reds May Become Serious Foe?" *Manitowoc Herald-Times,* October 23, 1973, 15.

46. Ian McDonald, "Baseball Planning Intelligent Growth," *Montreal Gazette*, January 24, 1975, 23.
47. Associated Press, "Expansion of Teams, Leagues," *Baltimore Sun*, April 1, 1975, 31.
48. Ibid.
49. Ibid.
50. Staff, "Meetings End With Little Done," *Baltimore Sun*, December 12, 1975, 43, 46.
51. Ron Bergman, "A Strutting Finley Hogs the Spotlight," *Sporting News*, August 2, 1975, 19, 26.
52. "Meetings End With Little Done," *Baltimore Sun*, December 12, 1975, 43, 46.
53. Charles Maher, "A Capital Gain," *Los Angeles Times*, December 10, 1976, 50, 55.
54. Ian McDonald, "Giants Still No Closer To Toronto," *Montreal Gazette*, January 8, 1976, 16.
55. Ralph Ray, "A.L. Moves Closer To Seattle Peace Treaty," *Sporting News*, February 14, 1976, 33.
56. Ibid.
57. UPI, "Aaron Ball Cost Job," *Berkshire Eagle*, July 24, 1976, 17.
58. Jerry Crowe, "There Was a Big Catch Holding On to No. 755," *Los Angeles Times*, July 2, 2007, 69.
59. Arnie Stapleton, "Aaron Locked in Tug of War Over Historic Ball," *Indiana Gazette*, August 27, 1996, 12.
60. Ibid.
61. Ibid.
62. Crowe, "There Was a Big Catch Holding On To No. 755," 69.
63. "Brewers Unveil Plaque to Memorialize the Final Home Run of Hank Aaron's Career, #755," Milwaukee Brewers Official Website, accessed November 3, 2016, http://milwaukee.brewers.mlb.com/content/printer_friendly/mil/y2007/m06/d07/c2011816.jsp.
64. Ibid.
65. Associated Press, "Mother Nature Has Finally Caught Aaron," *Oshkosh Northwestern*, September 18, 1976, 17.
66. Associated Press, "Aaron Ends 23-Year Career With Hit Against Tigers," *Stevens Point Journal*, October 5, 1976, 22.
67. Ibid.
68. Associated Press, "Aaron Ends 23-Year Career With Hit Against Tigers," 22.
69. UPI, "Hammerin' Hank's Last RBI," *Ottawa Journal*, October 5, 1976, 18.
70. Associated Press, "Aaron Ends 23-Year Career With Hit Against Tigers," *Stevens Point Journal*, October 5, 1976, 22.

Chapter Ten

1. Lou Chapman, "Brewers Boost Better Balance With New Faces," *Sporting News*, January 8, 1977, 38.
2. Ibid.
3. Ibid.
4. UPI, "Bando Goes to Bat for Ballplayers," *York Daily Record*, April 13, 1977, 18.
5. Ibid.
6. Associated Press, "Grammas Raps Porter's Play," *Appleton Post-Crescent*, January 21, 1977, 20.
7. Ibid.
8. Bob Ryan, "A Real Break for Cooper," *Boston Globe*, December 7, 1976, 35.
9. Lou Chapman, "New Brewer Cooper Knows How To Say We," *Sporting News*, February 5, 1977, 45.
10. Ibid.
11. Associated Press, "Brewers Will Show Lot of New Faces," *Wilmington News Journal*, December 7, 1976, 16.
12. Ray Doherty, "Brews Still Seeking Deals," *Capital Times*, January 17, 1977, 9.
13. Associated Press, "Verdict Is A Long Way Off," *Santa Cruz Sentinel*, January 14, 1977, 22.
14. Ibid.
15. Ibid.
16. Ibid.
17. Ibid.
18. Associated Press, "Finley Claims Kuhn Voided Sales With D.C. Move in Mind," *Baltimore Sun*, March 15, 1977, 35.
19. Michael Janofsky, "Baseball Future Concerns 'Young Turks,'" *Baltimore Evening Sun*, April 15, 1977, 27.
20. Ibid.
21. Ron Rapoport, "Fear of Unknown Puts Baseball in Hot Box," *Sporting News*, January 8, 1977, 33, 46.
22. Ibid.
23. Associated Press, "Baseball: Interleague Play Is Getting Closer," *Baltimore Sun*, March 20, 1977, 47.

24. *Ibid.*
25. *Ibid.*
26. Richard Hoffer, "Career Move," *Sports Illustrated* (online), accessed October 20, 2016, https://www.si.com/vault/1993/03/29/128285/career-move-after-15-notable-if-unnoticed-years-in-milwaukee-paul-molitor-steps-up-to-the-large-market-advantages-of-toronto#.
27. *Ibid.*
28. *Ibid.*
29. UPI, "Brewer President Sad," *Santa Rosa Press Democrat*, September 9, 1977, 22.
30. Associated Press, "Slaton Depressed, Tired of Losing," *La Crosse Tribune*, September 1, 1977, 15.
31. Mike O'Brien, "'Sundown Kid' Fades on Baseball Horizon," *Wisconsin State Journal*, August 16, 1977, 37.
32. *Ibid.*
33. Roger Pitt, "Another Long Season for Brewers' Bud Selig," *Racine Journal Times*, September 25, 1977, 49.
34. Associated Press, "Brewers Fall, Yount Talks," *Green Bay Press-Gazette*, September 8, 1977, 26.
35. Lou Chapman, "Brewers Hope for Respectability—Next Year," *Sporting News*, January 8, 1977, 38.
36. *Ibid.*
37. Pitt, "Another Long Season For Brewers' Bud Selig," 49.
38. *Ibid.*
39. Chapman, "Brewers Hope For Respectability-Next Year," 38.
40. *Ibid.*
41. *Ibid.*
42. Roger Pitt, "Time for Fantasies and Bankrolls," *Appleton Post-Crescent*, November 6, 1977, 55.
43. Lou Chapman, "Hisle A Brewer for Almost $3 Million," *Milwaukee Sentinel*, November 19, 1977, 7.
44. *Ibid.*
45. Peter Gammons, "There's a Rub in the Hub," *Sports Illustrated* (online), accessed September 7, 2018, https://www.si.com/vault/1977/11/14/627004/theres-a-rub-in-the-hub.
46. *Ibid.*
47. *Ibid.*
48. *Ibid.*
49. Lou Chapman, "Brewer Purge Puts Dalton in Charge," *Sporting News*, December 3, 1977, 58.
50. *Ibid.*
51. Associated Press, "Brewers Fire Grammas," *Ithica Journal*, November 21, 1977, 29.
52. *Ibid.*
53. *Ibid.*
54. *Ibid.*
55. Associated Press, "Brewers Improved, Grammas Insists," *Stevens Point Journal*, December 13, 1977, 14.
56. *Ibid.*
57. Associated Press, "Dalton Ponders Priorities," *Manitowoc Herald-Times*, November 22, 1977, 6.
58. *Ibid.*
59. Associated Press, "Oriole Pitching Coach to Manage Brewers," *Great Falls Tribune*, January 21, 1978, 15.
60. Staff, "Star-Studded Dinner Draws Sellout of 1100," *Boston Globe*, January 27, 1977, 18.
61. Associated Press, "Oriole Pitching Coach to Manage Brewers," 15.
62. Mike O'Brien, "Bamberger Accepts Challenge," *Fond Du Lac Commonwealth Reporter*, January 21, 1978, 12.
63. Daniel Okrent, *Nine Innings* (Boston: Mariner Books, 2000), 46.
64. *Ibid.*
65. Associated Press, "Travers Holds Grudge Against Ex-Manager," *Oshkosh Northwestern*, January 9, 1978, 19.
66. Tom Butler, "Brewers Make Mid-Winter Pitch," *Wisconsin State Journal*, January 11, 1978, 17.
67. Robert W. Creamer. "This Robin Is a Rare Bird," *Sports Illustrated Vault*, accessed October 12, 2016, https://www.si.com/vault/1982/09/27/625002/this-robin-is-a-rare-bird.
68. *Ibid.*
69. *Ibid.*
70. *Ibid.*
71. *Ibid.*
72. *Ibid.*
73. Associated Press, "Molitor's Chance Comes Right Now," *Springfield News-Leader*, April 7, 1978, 38.
74. *Ibid.*
75. Associated Press, "Brewers Running New Logo Contest," *Stevens Point Journal*, October 6, 1977, 14.

76. Associated Press, "Brewers Get New Logo," *La Crosse Tribune*, November 29, 1977, 13.
77. *Ibid.*
78. Matthew Prigge. "The New-Look Crew: The Birth of the Brewers Most Classic Uniform Set," *Shepherd Express*, accessed April 17, 2017, https://shepherdexpress.com/sports/brew-crew-confidential/new-look-crew-birth-brewers-classic-uniform-set/.
79. *Ibid.*
80. Jim Hawkins, "How Brewers Shot Past Tigers in Just One Year," *Detroit Free Press*, April 19, 1979, 72.

Epilogue

1. Mark Tauscher and Michael Popke, "Full Circle," *Madison Isthmus*, accessed May 13, 2017, https://isthmus.com/arts/sports/bud-selig-returns-to-alma-mater-uw-madison-to-teach/.
2. Steve Fainaru, "Selig Plays Hard Ball on Stadium Deals," *Washington Post*, accessed June 20, 2018, https://www.washingtonpost.com/archive/politics/2004/06/27/selig-plays-hardball-on-stadium-deals/0878ddc9-66c2-43ca-baba-e9c97540e347/?noredirect=on.
3. *Ibid.*
4. Scott A. Wolla, "The Economics of Subsidizing Sports Stadiums," Federal Reserve Bank Of St. Louis, accessed June 22, 2018, https://research.stlouisfed.org/publications/page1-econ/2017-05-01/the-economics-of-subsidizing-sports-stadiums/.
5. *Ibid.*
6. Larry Whiteside, "Milwaukee Squeezed by Small Market, Escalating Costs," *Chicago Tribune*, accessed June 29, 2018, http://www.chicagotribune.com/news/ct-xpm-1991-04-07-9102010143-story.html.
7. "Brewers Stadium Vote Goes Down to Wire," *Chicago Tribune* (online), accessed May 1, 2018, http://www.chicagotribune.com/news/ct-xpm-1995-09-27-9509270125-story.html.
8. "Miller Park, Ten Years Later: Stadium Changed the Brewers' Fortunes," On Milwaukee.com, accessed April 17, 2017, https://onmilwaukee.com/sports/articles/millerpark10intro.html.
9. Stephanie Jones, "Recalled Sen. Petak's Advice to Recall Candidates: 'Take Nothing for Granted,'" *Racine Journal Times* (online), accessed April 17, 2017, http://journaltimes.com/news/local/recalled-sen-petak-s-advice-to-recall-candidates-take-nothing/article_8a8fd668-c211-11e0-b8e6-001cc4c03286.html.
10. Murray Chass, "Selig's Job Could Change Because of Brewers' Problems," *New York Times*, accessed July 1, 2018, https://www.nytimes.com/1995/09/03/sports/baseball-notebook-selig-s-job-title-could-change-because-of-brewers-problems.html.
11. Phillip Torsrud, *America Unraveled: 2008–2012: The Political, Cultural and Economic Collapse* (Bloomington, IN: iUniverse Publishing, 2012, 272–273).
12. Susan Shemanske, "Say Goodbye," *Racine Journal Times* (online), accessed April 23, 2017, http://journaltimes.com/sports/say-goodbye/article_3a33c32e-4e15-5f6e-8a02-4a611dbaae6c.html.
13. Arnie Stapleton, "Milwaukee Says Goodbye," *Northwest Herald*, September 29, 2000, 26.
14. Associated Press, "Past Greats Bid Farewell to 'Old Friend,'" ESPN.com, accessed April 25, 2017, http://a.espncdn.com/mlb/news/2000/0928/786751.html.
15. Mike Bernadino, "Brewers' Owner Is Thinking Big," *South Florida Sun Sentinel*, March 14, 2005, 36.
16. Associated Press, "Selig Family Sells to Attanasio," ESPN.com, accessed May 7, 2017. http://www.espn.com/mlb/news/story?id=1966198.
17. Mark Tauscher and Michael Popke, "Full Circle," *Madison Isthmus*, accessed May 13, 2017, https://isthmus.com/arts/sports/bud-selig-returns-to-alma-mater-uw-madison-to-teach/.
18. Tom Haudricourt. "When Bud Selig Goes in Baseball Hall of Fame, Entire Organization Goes With Him," *Milwaukee Journal*, accessed July 30, 2017, https://www.jsonline.com/story/sports/mlb/brewers/2017/07/29/when-bud-selig-goes-hall-fame-brewers-organization-joins-him/514079001/
19. *The Seattle Pilots: Short Flight Into*

History, directed by Steve Cox and Brad Powers, performed by Jim Bouton, Greg Goossen and Bob Locker (unknown city: Play Ball Films, 2010), DVD, 84 mins.

20. "Media Info," National Baseball Hall of Fame website, accessed July 31, 2017, http://baseballhall.org/media-info.

21. *Ibid.*

22. Tom Haudricourt. "Brewers' Attanasio Would Love to Be at Cubs Series but Wouldn't Miss Selig's HOF Induction," *Milwaukee Journal*, accessed July 30, 2017, https://www.jsonline.com/story/sports/mlb/brewers/2017/07/28/attanasio-would-love-cubs-series-but-chose-seligs-induction/519092001/

23. "Media Info," National Baseball Hall of Fame website.

24. *Ibid.*

Bibliography

Newspapers

Abilene (TX) Reporter-News
Akron Beacon Journal
Alexandria (LA) Town Talk
Allentown (PA) Morning Call
Anniston (AL) Star
Appleton (WI) Post-Crescent
Arizona Republic
Asheville (NC) Citizen-Times
Baltimore Sun
Belvidere (IL) Daily Republican
Berkshire Eagle (Pittsfield, MA)
Bloomington (IL) Pantagraph
Bonham (TX) Daily Favorite
Boston Globe
Bridgewater (PA) Allegheny Times
Burlington (VT) Free Press
Carbondale Southern Illinoisan
Carroll (IA) Daily Times Herald
Cedar City (UT) Daily Spectrum
Central New Jersey Home News
Centralia (WA) Daily Chronicle
Cherry Hill (NJ) Courier-Post
Chicago Tribune
Chippewa Herald (Chippewa Falls, WI)
Cincinnati Enquirer
Crystal Lake (IL) Northwest Herald
Daily Sitka (AK) Sentinel
Decatur (IL) Herald
Des Moines (IA) Register
Detroit Free Press
Eau Claire (WI) Daily Telegram
El Paso (TX) Herald
Escanaba (MI) Daily Press
Eureka (CA) Times Standard
Fond Du Lac (WI) Commonwealth
Fort Lauderdale (FL) News

Great Falls (MT) Tribune
Green Bay (WI) Press-Gazette
Greenville (SC) News
Hartford Courant
Honolulu Star-Bulletin
Imlay (MI) Tri-City Times
Indiana Gazette
Ironwood (MI) Daily Globe
Ithaca (NY) Journal
Jackson (MS) Clarion-Ledger
Jackson (TN) Sun
Janesville (WI) Daily Gazette
Kenai (AK) Peninsula Clarion
Kokomo (IN) Tribune
La Crosse (WI) Tribune
Lawrence (KS) Journal-World
Lincoln (NE) Star
Logansport (IN) Pharos-Tribune
Long Beach Independent
Los Angeles Times
Lubbock (TX) Avalanche-Journal
Madison (WI) Capital Times
Madison (WI) Isthmus
Manitowoc (WI) Herald-Times
Marion (OH) Star
Marshfield (WI) News-Herald
Meriden (CT) Morning Record
Miami News
Milwaukee Daily Reporter
Milwaukee Journal Sentinel
Minneapolis Star-Tribune
Montreal Gazette
Muncie (IN) Evening Press
Nevada State Journal (Reno, NV)
New York Times
Ogden (UT) Standard-Examiner

Orange County (CA) Register
Oshkosh (WI) Northwestern
Ottawa (ONT) Journal
Palm Beach (FL) Post
Paris (TX) News
Pensacola (FL) News Journal
Philadelphia Daily News
Philadelphia Inquirer
Pittsburgh Post-Gazette
Port Angeles (WA) Evening News
Poughkeepsie (NY) Journal
Racine (WI) Journal Times
Salem (OH) News
Salina (KS) Journal
San Francisco Examiner
Sandusky (OH) Register
Santa Cruz (CA) Sentinel
Santa Rosa (CA) Press Democrat
Seattle Post-Intelligencer
Sheboygan (WI) Press

Shreveport (LA) Times
South Florida Sun-Sentinel (Broward County)
Spokane (WA) Daily Chronicle
Springfield (MO) News-Leader
St. Cloud (MN) Times
St. Louis Post-Dispatch
Statesman (OR) Journal
Stevens Point (WI) Jounal
Tallahassee (FL) Democrat
Tucson Daily Citizen
Tyrone (PA) Daily Herald
USA Today
Waukesha (WI) Daily Freeman
Wausau (WI) Daily Herald
Wilmington (OH) News Journal
Wisconsin Rapids Daily Tribune
Wisconsin State Journal
York (PA) Daily Record
Zanesville (OH) Times Recorder

Articles

"Alex Grammas: The Second Time Around." *Milwaukee Brewers Official Program*, 1977.
Associated Press. "BB's Anti-Trust Trial in 4th Week." *Morning Record*, March 22, 1966.
_____. "Brewers Offered to Buy Senators." *Journal Times*, November 27, 1968.
_____. "Combine Efforts for More Expansion, Ruess Urges 'Left Out' Cities." *Post-Crescent*, May 29, 1968.
_____. "County Board Offers Increase in Revenue." *Stevens Point Journal*, September 24, 1964.
_____. "Did Braves Move Set Off Chain Reaction?" *Akron Beacon Journal*, March 19, 1953.
_____. "Fans Can See Frank Howard in Milwaukee." *Journal Times*, August 4, 1969.
_____. "Otto Borchert Dies During Address." *Wisconsin Rapids Daily Tribune*, April 28, 1927.
_____. "Seattle Effort May Set Pace." *Spokane Daily Chronicle*, February 9, 1976.
_____. "Seattle to Press Stadium Suit Despite Stadium Site Turn-Down." *Daily Chronicle*, May 21, 1970.
_____. "Short, Ex-Laker Owner, Buys Nats." *Independent*, December 4, 1968.
_____. "Stengel Lauds Haney, Burdette." *Janesville Daily Gazette*, October 11, 1957.
_____. "The Chippewa Herald." October 10, 2007. http://chippewa.com/sports/braves-title-still-remembered/article_afcfd1af-9559-5785-9995-281febf107a6.html (accessed July 22, 2017).
_____. "Veeck Forsakes Baseball for Horse Racing Post." *Decatur Herald*, November 21, 1968.
_____. "Wisconsin Continues Push On Baseball Anti-Trust Laws." *Lawrence Journal-World*, March 9, 1966.
_____. "Woman To Keep Baseball Club." *Escanaba Daily Press*, February 3, 1929.
Axisa, Mike. "CBS Sports—The Complicated Legacy of Hall of Fame Commissioner Bud Selig." July 30, 2017. https://www.cbssports.com/mlb/news/the-complicated-legacy-of-hall-of-fame-baseball-commissioner-bud-selig/ (accessed August 3, 2017).
Baldassaro, Larry. "Planting Seeds for the Future." *Milwaukee Brewers Official Yearbook*, 2003.
"Ballparks of Baseball, 2001–2018." https://www.ballparksofbaseball.com/baseball-ballpark-attendance/ (accessed December 15, 2017).

Bibliography

"Baseball Lifer Leaves Office, but Not the Game." *New York Times,* January 22, 2015. https://www.nytimes.com/2015/01/23/sports/baseball/bud-selig-ends-his-reign-as-commissioner-with-no-regrets.html (accessed July 22, 2017).

"Ben Oglivie: He Has a Sweet Craving for Baseball." *Milwaukee Brewers Official Program,* 1978.

Bisher, Furman. "Another Injunction—This Time Atlanta Fires at Milwaukee." *The Sporting News,* January 1, 1966.

Bledsoe, Tery. "It's 'Bottoms Up' To Brewers In Milwaukee." *The Sporting News,* April 18, 1970.

Bliss, Mary. "Brewers Toast 80's With World's Most Advanced Scoreboard System." *Milwaukee Brewers Official Program,* 1980.

Bloom, Barry M. "*Emotional day" for Selig.* April 15, 2004. http://mlb.mlb.com/content/printer_friendly/mlb/y2004/m04/d15/c718150.jsp (accessed July 21, 2017).

"Bob Uecker: More Than a Baseball Icon." *Between The Lines,* July 2005.

"Brewers Boast Top Fireman in Ken Sanders." *Milwaukee Brewers Scorebook,* 1972.

Broeg, Bob. "Braves' Doorbell Rings: It's Atlanta." *The Sporting News,* August 3, 1963.

Burke, Liz. "The Scoreboard: Anatomy of an Animation." *Official ALCS Program,* October 8, 1982.

"Caught on the Fly—Milwaukee Sales Brisk." *The Sporting News,* February 1, 1969.

"Cecil Cooper: There's Gold in That Thar Glove!" *Milwaukee Brewers Official Program,* 1980.

Chanin, Abe. "Caught on the Fly." *The Sporting News,* March 2, 1968.

Chapman, Lou. "Del Crandall Returns to County Stadium." *Milwaukee Brewers Scorebook,* 1972.

_____. "Hank Aaron: Now a Brewer, Always a Champion." *Milwaukee Brewers Official Scorebook,* 1975.

_____. "Milwaukee's Goal—Expansion Club by 1970." *The Sporting News,* April 29, 1967.

_____. "Then and Now." *Milwaukee Brewers Scorebook,* 1974.

"City Gets Ready to Welcome Team." *The Milwaukee Sentinel,* April 2, 1970.

Cleghorn, Renee. "Braves' Owners Fail to Ask Permission to Move to Atlanta." *Milwaukee Journal,* October 22, 1964.

Coenen, Greg. "Baseball in Milwaukee: It's Older Than It Looks." *Milwaukee Brewers Official Scorebook,* 1975.

Corbett, Warren. "Bill Veeck." https://sabr.org/bioproj/person/7b0b5f10 (accessed March 21, 2018).

"County Will Offer Braves More Money to Stay Here." *Milwaukee Journal,* September 24, 1964.

"'Dallas Will Step Up Bid For A.L. Team' — Hunt." *The Sporting News,* February 28, 1970.

"Dave Bristol, Young But Experienced Guides Team." *Milwaukee Brewers Scorebook,* 1971.

"Dave May Does it All." *Milwaukee Brewers Scorebook,* 1972.

Davidson, Don. "Braves Seek to Repeat 1957 Victory." *Official World Series Program,* October 1958.

DeGrace, Dave. "Buck Rodgers: Winner as a Rookie." *Milwaukee Brewers Official Program,* 1982.

_____. "Charlie Moore: The Defense Rests." *Official ALCS Program,* October 8, 1982.

"Determination Shapes New Brewers Manager." *Milwaukee Brewers Official Yearbook,* 2000.

Durso, Joseph. "A.L. Juggle Seattle—A Hot Potato." *The Sporting News,* March 21, 1970.

"Everything Go For Brewers Debut." *The Milwaukee Sentinel,* April 7, 1970.

"Expansion Pitch to Take Milwaukee Group to W.S." *The Sporting News,* October 9, 1965.

Fallstrom, Bob. "Once Over Lightly—A Change for the Better." *Decatur Herald,* November 20, 1968.

Flaherty, Tom. "Colborn Leads the Way." *Milwaukee Brewers Scorebook,* 1974.

Flynn, Gary. "Brewery Gems—Emil Sick." 2004. http://www.brewerygems.com/emil.htm (accessed July 31, 2017).

Bibliography

"A Foundation for the Future." *Milwaukee Brewers Official Program*, 1976.
"George Bamberger: He's Pitching to Win." *Milwaukee Brewers Official Program*, 1978.
"A Glimpse of the Past for Milwaukee Fans." *The Sporting News*, April 22, 1967.
Grosshandler, Stan. "The American League's Opening Season—1901." *Milwaukee Brewers Official Program*, 1976.
———. "The Hegans: A Record Breaking Family." *Milwaukee Brewers Official Program*, 1976.
Hand, Jack, and Joe Reichler. "Bill Veeck Forced Transfer of Braves to Milwaukee." *Clarion-Ledger*, March 22, 1953.
"Hank Aaron: The Last Hurrah." *Milwaukee Brewers Official Program*, 1976.
"Harry Dalton: A Successful Track Record." *Milwaukee Brewers Official Program*, 1978.
"Harvey Kuenn: Having Fun at the Top." *Milwaukee Brewers Official Program*, 1983.
Harwell, Ernie, and Denny Matthews. *1982 American League Championship Series (Games 1–5)*. Comp. CBS Radio. 1982.
"History of the Milwaukee Brewers." *Milwaukee Brewers Official Program*, 1980.
Hoffmann, Gregg. "It's All Here, Under One Roof." *Milwaukee Brewers Official Yearbook*, 2001.
Holtzman, Jerome. "Chisox to Stay, New Boss John Allyn Promises." *The Sporting News*, October 11, 1969.
———. "White Sox Will Stretch '68 Home Schedule to Milwaukee." *The Sporting News*, November 11, 1967.
Hylton, J. Gordon. "Marquette University Law School Faculty Blog—Why Milwaukee Lost The Braves." January 1, 2012. https://law.marquette.edu/facultyblog/2012/01/01/why-milwaukee-lost-the-braves-perspectives-on-law-and-culture-from-a-half-century-later/ (accessed March 30, 2018).
Jenkins, Lee. "Strange Brew (But It's Working)." *Sports Illustrated*, August 29, 2011.
"Jim Baumer: Fukuoka to Milwaukee." *Milwaukee Brewers Official Scorebook*, 1975.
Kaegel, Dick. "Sweating, Waiting...as NL Debated." *The Sporting News*, June 8, 1968.
"Lach Catches on With Brewer Fans." *Milwaukee Brewers Official Program*, 1984.
"Larry Hisle: Not Your Average Superstar." *Milwaukee Brewers Official Program*, 1978.
Larson, Lloyd. "City Told How to Get Club Back." *Milwaukee Sentinel*, January 23, 1967.
———. "National League's Choice of Montreal the Real Surprise." *Milwaukee Sentinel*, May 29, 1968.
"Late-Inning Rallies Gave Brewer Fans Thrills Galore in '70." *Milwaukee Brewers Scorebook*, 1971.
LeMoine, Bob. "SABR—Boston Braves Team Ownership History." 2018. https://sabr.org/research/boston-braves-team-ownership-history (accessed June 1, 2018).
Lindholm, Scott. "SB Nation—Major League Attendance Trends Past, Present, and Future." February 10, 2014. https://www.beyondtheboxscore.com/2014/2/10/5390172/major-league-attendance-trends-1950–2013 (accessed March 30, 2018).
Lucas, Mike. "Given the Chance, Thomas Produces." *Wisconsin—The Capital Times*, July 21, 1979.
McBride, Raymond E. "Baseball Fans Back in Swing." *Milwaukee Journal*, April 8, 1970.
Michaels, Chance. "Borchert Field—This Week in 1913: After the Flood, Before the Storm." April 8, 2013. http://www.borchertfield.com/2013/04/this-week-in-1913-after-flood-before.html (accessed May 2, 2018).
"Milwaukee Brewers, Miller Park to Host 2002 All-Star Game." *Milwaukee Brewers Official Yearbook*, 2000.
"Milwaukee's Return to Big Leagues a Second 'Miracle.'" *Milwaukee Brewers Scorebook*, 1971.
Munzel, Edgar. "Allyn Spikes Rumors of a Chisox Move." *The Sporting News*, September 22, 1968.
"National Baseball Hall of Fame—Bowie Kuhn." https://baseballhall.org/hall-of-famers/kuhn-bowie (accessed April 15, 2018).

Bibliography

"New League Brings New Challenges." *1998 Brewers Yearbook Magazine (Leadoff)*, 1998.
Nitz, Jim. "SABR—Happy Felsch." https://sabr.org/bioproj/person/cd61b579 (accessed March 29, 2018).
O'Hara, Dave. "National League Learning $ Lesson." *Tri-City Times Daily*, May 9, 1965.
Pajot, Dennis. "SABR—Otto Borchert." https://sabr.org/node/33019 (accessed May 3, 2018).
Parry, Jason. "A Force at First." *Milwaukee Brewers Official Yearbook*, 2001.
"Playing on His Home Grounds Suits Augustine Just Fine." *Milwaukee Brewers Official Program*, 1977.
Polk, James R. "Washington Sale Hinted." *Asheville Citizen-Times*, November 6, 1968.
Prell, Edward. "Atlanta Gets Vote of 12–6 As New Home." *Chicago Tribune*, October 22, 1964.
"Radio Announcers." *1998 Brewers Yearbook Magazine (Leadoff)*, 1998.
Rogers, Phil. http://chicago.cubs.mlb.com. April 22, 2014. http://chicago.cubs.mlb.com/news/print.jsp?ymd=20140422&content_id=72968276&c_id=chc (accessed July 22, 2017).
Sell, Dennis. "That Championship Season." *Milwaukee Brewers Official Yearbook*, 1983.
"Showing the Way—Del and His Coaches." *Milwaukee Brewers Scorebook*, 1973.
Sorgi, Jay. "Forbes: Brewers Value Exceeds 1 Billion for First Time." WTMJ-TV website. Accessed June 13, 2018. https://www.tmj4.com/sports/baseball/milwaukee-brewers/forbes-brewers-value-exceeds-1-billion-for-first-time.
_____. "Today's TMJ 4." April 12, 2018. https://www.tmj4.com/sports/baseball/milwaukee-brewers/forbes-brewers-value-exceeds-1-billion-for-first-time (accessed June 13, 2018).
"Speed + Power = MVP Votes for Tommy Harper." *Milwaukee Brewers Scorebook*, 1971.
Spink, C. C. Johnson. "Oakland Jumps Back into Finley Plans." *The Sporting News*, July 29, 1967.
"The Brass Guiding the Brewers." *Milwaukee Brewers Scorebook*, 1973.
"This Great Game—1953 Brave New World." 2018. http://www.thisgreatgame.com/1953-baseball-history.html (accessed June 15, 2018).
"Thousands Greet Brewers." *Milwaukee Sentinel*, April 6, 1970.
"Time Was ... 1978." *1998 Brewers Yearbook Magazine (Leadoff)*, 1998.
"Time Was ... 1988." *1998 Brewers Yearbook Magazine (Leadoff)*, 1998.
UPI. "Braves Ask Transfer To Atlanta." *Wisconsin State Journal*, October 22, 1964.
_____. "Milwaukee Should Get New Team Next Year: Bob Short." *Sheboygan Press*, August 7, 1969.
_____. "Milwaukee Wins Round 1 In Braves Court Fight." *Chicago Tribune*, October 22, 1964.
Voiss, Dale. "SABR—Harry Dalton." https://sabr.org/bioproj/person/0e17944e (accessed February 10, 2017).
"Vote Deal is Denied." *Tampa Times*, March 5, 1969.
Walfoort, Cleon. "Fan Poll Backs Expansion Club for Milwaukee." *The Sporting News*, April 30, 1966.
_____. "Milwaukeeans Will Find Bristol an Intense, Hard Working Man." *Milwaukee Journal*, April 3, 1970.
_____. "Milwaukee's Faithful Flock to Empty Park." *The Sporting News*, April 13, 1968.
_____. "Player Value Cited in Milwaukee Case." *The Sporting News*, April 9, 1966.
"We're Taking This Thing National Press Conference." *1998 Brewers Yearbook Magazine (Leadoff)*, 1998.
Whiteside, Larry. "A Great Year for Bristol and Brewers." *The Sporting News*, October 10, 1970.
_____. "Brewers Beaming Over Better Slate." *The Sporting News*, November 28, 1970.
_____. "Will the Real Frank lane Please Stand Up." *Milwaukee Brewers Scorebook*, 1972.

Bibliography

Wikipedia—"1950 Green Bay Packers Season." April 18, 2018. https://en.wikipedia.org/wiki/1950_Green_Bay_Packers_season (accessed June 14, 2018).
Wikipedia—"Commissioner of Baseball." 2018. https://en.wikipedia.org/wiki/Commissioner_of_Baseball (accessed April 1, 2018).
Wikipedia—"List of Recessions in the United States." 2018. https://en.wikipedia.org/wiki/List_of_recessions_in_the_United_States (accessed May 15, 2018).
Williams, Vera. "The Stormy Career of Casey Stengel." *Independent Press-Telegram*, June 25 1961, 1961.
Wisnia, Saul. "SABR—Lou Perini." https://sabr.org/node/27103 (accessed June 30, 2018).
Wolf, Bob. "1968 Called Year of Decision for Milwaukee." *The Sporting News*, February 3, 1968.
____. "20,759 Brave a Frigid Wind to See Chisox in Milwaukee." *The Sporting News*, April 20, 1968.
____. "Braves' Gate Purchased by Civic Group." *The Sporting News*, April 3, 1965.
____. "Braves Ruined Fan Group's Idea, Fitzgerald Charges." *The Sporting News*, March 27, 1965.
____. "Braves Said Pact Suited Them in '64, County Exec Testifies." *The Sporting News*, March 5, 1966.
____. "Braves Tomahawk Hush-Hush Swap Huddle in Capital." *The Sporting News*, August 7, 1965.
____. "Eckert, Cronin to See Game in Milwaukee." *The Sporting News*, July 8, 1967.
____. "Milwaukee Fans Eager Buyers of Chisox Ducats." *The Sporting News*, February 10, 1968.
____. "Milwaukee Park Spic and Span Just in Case of Brave Retreat." *The Sporting News*, April 16, 1966.
____. "Milwaukee Rated Solid TV Market." *The Sporting News*, October 14, 1967.
____. "Milwaukee Will Seek Team in A.L." *The Sporting News*, June 15, 1968.
____. "Milwaukee's Video Market Better than Atlanta's—Air Exec." *The Sporting News*, March 5, 1966.
____. "N.L. Fires Volley at Veeck's Expansion View." *The Sporting News*, January 1966, 1966.
____. "New Bid from Milwaukee: $1.1 Million Radio-TV Pact." *The Sporting News*, November 18, 1967.
____. "Selig Kknocks Foam from Report Milwaukee to Get AAA Franchise." *The Sporting News*, August 13, 1966.
____. "Some Milwaukeeans Plan to Battle On—Some Toss in Towel." *The Sporting News*, December 24, 1966.
____. "Tepee Makes Whoopee Over Top Ducat Huckster Bragan." *The Sporting News*, February 22, 1964.
____. "Three Pro Cage Games Booked for Milwaukee." *The Sporting News*, September 30, 1967.
____. "We'll Keep Plugging to Land Franchise—Milwaukee Lead." *The Sporting News*, December 18, 1965.
____. "Wisconsin Fans on Brave Fadeaway." *The Sporting News*, August 13, 1966.
Worzalla, Ross. "Making The Right Moves Has Been Harry Dalton's Trademark." *Official ALCS Program*, October 8, 1982.
Ziino, Mario. "Bob Uecker: More Than a Baseball Icon Part 2." *Between The Lines*, September 2005.
____. "Manager Ned Yost: Having the Right Attitude." *Between The Lines*, July 2005.
____. "Special 'K'—Don Sutton Gets a Call from the Hall." *1998 Brewers Yearbook Magazine (Leadoff)*, 1998.
Zimmerman, Hy. "Storm-Tossed Pilots Struck By New Crisis." *The Sporting News*, January 17, 1970.

Bibliography

Books

Baldwin, Dave. *Snake Jazz*. Xlibris, 2008.
Bouton, Jim. *Ball Four: The Final Pitch*. North Egremont, MA: Bulldog, 2001.
Derong, Gary. *Milwaukee Brewers: Inside MLB*. Edina, MN: Sportszone, 2015.
Ham, Eldon. *Larceny and Old Leather: The Mischievous Legacy of Major League*. Chicago: Chicago Review Press, 2005.
Hamann, Rex, and Bob Koehler. *The American Association Milwaukee Brewers*. Charleston, SC: Arcadia, 2004.
Haudricourt, Tom. *100 Things Brewers Fans Should Know & Do Before They Die*. Chicago: Triumph, 2013.
Hoffman, Gregg. *Down in the Valley: The History of Milwaukee County Stadium*. Holt, MI: Partners, 2000.
Jay, Kathryn. *More Than Just a Game: Sports in American Life Since 1945*. New York: Columbia University Press, 2005.
Lockwood, Kathleen. *Major League Bride: An Inside Look at Life Outside the Ballpark*. Jefferson, NC: McFarland, 2010.
Mishler, Todd. *Baseball in Beertown: America's Pastime in Milwaukee*. Denver: Trails Books, 2005.
Mullins, Bill. *Becoming Big League: Seattle, the Pilots, and Stadium Politics*. Seattle: University of Washington Press, 2013.
Okrent, Daniel. *Nine Innings*. Boston: Mariner Books, 2000.
Povletich, William. *Milwaukee Braves: Heroes and Heartbreak*. Madison: Wisconsin Historical Society Press, 2009.
Selig, Bud, and Phil Rogers. *For the Good of the Game: The Inside Story of the Surprising and Dramatic Transformation of Major League Baseball*. New York, NY: William Morrow, 2019.
Torsrud, Phillip. *America Unraveled: 2008–2012: The Political, Cultural and Economic Collapse*. Bloomington, IN: iUniverse Publishing, 2012.
Van Lindt, Carson. *The Seattle Pilots Story*. New York: Marabou Pub, 1993.
Veeck, Bill, and Ed Linn. *Veeck—As in Wreck: The Autobiography of Bill Veeck*. Chicago: University of Chicago Press, 2012. First published 1962 by G.P. Putnam's Sons.

Websites

baseball-almanac.com/.
baseball-reference.com/.
mlb.com/brewers.
mlb.com/.
sabr.org/.
wikipedia.org/.

Media

1982 American League Championship Series. ABC Television. Keith Jackson, Jim Palmer, and Earl Weaver.
1982 World Series. CBS Radio. Vin Scully and Sparky Anderson.
1982 World Series. NBC Television. Joe Garagiola, Dick Enberg, and Tony Kubek.
Baseball Classics: 1957 World Series. Directed by Rare Sportsfilms. Warren Spahn and Lew Burdette. 2006.
Harvey's Wallbangers: The 1982 Milwaukee Brewers. Directed by Virgil Films. Bob Uecker, Bud Selig, and Robin Yount. 2007.
The Seattle Pilots: Short Flight Into History. Directed by Steve Cox and Brad Powers. Jim Bouton, Greg Goossen, and Bob Locker. 2010.

Interviews and Questionnaires

Dave Baldwin, questionnaire, May 1, 2015
Dave Bristol, questionnaire, June 17, 2015
Bruce Brubaker, questionnaire, August 3, 2015
Bob Humphreys, questionnaire, August 3, 2015
Lew Krausse, questionnaire, July 23, 2015
Jim Ksicinski, phone interview, September 10, 2015
Ted Kubiak, questionnaire, March 12, 2016
Pat McBride, phone interview, May 12, 2015.
Bob Meyer, questionnaire, July 10, 2015
John Morris, questionnaire, August 9, 2015
Rick Napholz, phone interview, April 20, 2015.
Phil Roof, questionnaire, June 22, 2015
Ken Sanders, questionnaire, September 2, 2015
Wes Stock, questionnaire, February 19, 2016

Brewers Annual Reference Guides

Official Program, 1976–1978, 1980, 1983–1984
Official Yearbook, 1971–1998, 2000–2001
Official Scorebook, 1971–1973, 1975

Index

Aaron, Hank 7, 32–33, 36, 41–44, 48, 55, 88, 113–114, 135, 139, 143–148, 152, 156, 180
Acosta, Julio 20
Alexander, Roger 144
All-American Girls Professional Baseball League 21
All-Star Game 37, 57, 116, 132, 141–143, 145, 147–149, 151, 153, 155–157
Allen, Ivan, Jr. 37
Allyn, Arthur 52, 58, 61–62, 68, 82–83, 113, 130
Allyn, John 82, 90, 93, 127, 129–130
Alou, Filipe 44
Alston, Walter 147
American Association 11–13, 16–17, 19, 21, 23–24, 28, 20, 68, 70–71, 104, 174
American Indoor Professional Soccer Association 57
Anderson, Bill 54, 97
Anderson, Lenny 75
Anderson, Sparky 149
Antonelli, Johnny 27
Appleton Foxes 53
Arndt, Richard 152–154
Asinof, Eliot 14
Associated Press 32, 122, 137
Astrodome 45
Athletic Park 11, 13–15, 17
Atlanta Stadium (Atlanta Fulton County Stadium) 37, 43–44, 47, 52
Attanasio, Mark 178–180
Augustine, Jerry 144, 152, 172
Auld Lang Syne (song) 24, 43

Ball, Phil 17–18
Ball Four (Book) 75, 80

Baltimore Orioles 12, 122, 128, 159, 167, 169
Bamberger, George 7, 169–170, 172
Bando, Sal 157–158, 161, 164–165, 172
Barber, Steve 72
Barkin, Ben 38–39, 42–43, 49
Barrel Kid 21
Barrel Man 20–21, 68
Bartholomay, William 37, 43–47, 52–53, 114, 124, 144
Baumer, Jim 142, 149, 157–158, 160–161, 164–167
Bavasi, Peter 50, 151
Bench, Johnny 92, 148
Blatz 5
Blue, Vida 148
Boeing, William 61, 69
Boggs, Wade 153
Borchert, Idabel 17, 24
Borchert, Otto 14–17, 19–20, 36
Borchert Field 5, 9, 11, 16–19, 21–25, 29, 32, 43, 76, 128
Bostock, Lyman 165
Boston Braves 24–29, 31
Boston Celtics 59
Boston Globe 165
Boston Patriots 88
Boston Red Sox 23, 27–29, 60, 63, 71, 126–127, 137, 139, 148, 158–159, 165
Bowman, Duane 39–40, 43, 50
Bozmoski, Donna 133
Bragan, Johnny 41, 43–44, 48
Braves Field 27
Brewer, Bernie 7, 115–119, 133, 177–178
Briggs, Johnny 147
Broeg, Bob 37
Brooklyn Dodgers 23, 28, 31, 33, 47, 62, 67, 71

207

Index

Brown, Joe 142
Bruton, Billy 30, 88
Bruton, James, Jr. 93–94
Buffalo Bisons 19
Bunker, Wally 72
Burdette, Lew 31, 33–34, 88
Burke, Mike 136
Busby, Steve 148
Bush, George W. 178
Bushville 34

Cairnes, Joe 35
Caldwell, Mike 161
California Angels 45–46, 64–65, 71–72, 77, 80, 100, 108–109, 117, 120, 152, 167
Campbell, Glen 147
Cannon, Robert 39–40, 55, 65, 67, 84, 95, 113, 125–126
Carbo, Bernie 158
Carew, Rod 147
Carey, Harry 75
Carey, Max 22
Carpenter, Bob 66
Carson, Johnny 92
Carty, Rico 44
Castro, Bill 143, 152
Charles, Frank 133
Chicago Bulls 59
Chicago Cubs 19, 21, 23, 43, 45, 63–64, 66, 69, 85, 180
Chicago Tribune 128
Chicago White Sox 6, 13–14, 22, 35, 52–55, 57–59, 61–65, 68–69, 78–79, 82–84, 90, 93, 104–105, 113, 116, 126–130, 150–151, 159
Chicago White Stockings 10
Cincinnati Reds 11, 29, 35–36, 79, 85, 105, 132, 138, 148–149, 156, 176, 178
Civic Stadium 69
Claiborne, John 165
Clark, Harry 14
Clark, Ron 86
Cleveland Indians 21, 36–37, 61, 67, 69, 72, 92, 105–106, 119, 123, 125–126, 131
Cleveland Stadium 36
Cloninger, Tony 47
Cobb, Ty 13, 16
Colavito, Rocky 123
Colborn, Jim 139, 158
Collins, Tom 110, 125
Coluccio, Bob 79, 133
Comiskey, Charles 11–12, 14
Comiskey Park 24, 62, 68–69, 82

Conlan, Jocko 30
Cooper, Cecil 158, 164–165, 172
Crandall, Del 41, 131–132, 135, 138, 145, 147–149, 177
Cream City 4–5, 11, 103
Cream City Athletic Club 14
Cronin, Joe 50–51, 54–56, 58, 60, 68, 82, 84–85, 87–89, 91, 93, 102, 109
Cuellar, Mike 167
Cunningham, Howard 49

Dale, Frank 136
Daley, William (Bill) 72, 83–85, 87, 89–91, 93, 104, 111
Dallas-Fort Worth Rangers 169
D'Amico, Jeff 176, 178
Dark, Alvin 147
Deadball Era 13
Dean, Dizzy 16
Detroit Tigers 128, 146, 155, 173
DiMaggio, Joe 22, 75
Dobson, Pat 167
Doucette, Eddie 110
Doyne, John 58, 109
Drago, Dick 152
Dreschler, Ronold A. 43
Dugdale Field 69–70
Duren, Ryne 71

East Stadium 15
Eastwick, Rawley 165
Eau Claire Bears 32
Eckert, William 51, 54–56, 58, 61–63
Eclipse Park 10
Eight Men Out (film) 14
Ertl, Robert 120
Etchebarren, Andy 172
Evinrude, Ralph 39

Feeney, Chub 138, 149
Felsch, Oscar "Happy" 13–14
Feltzer, John 141
Fenway Park 23–24
Ferguson, Tommy 122
Fidrych, Mark "The Bird" 152
Fingers, Rollie 159, 180
Finley, Charles (Charlie) 55, 58, 60, 63, 90, 151, 159
Fishman, Marvin 59
Fitzgerald, Edmund 38
Flood, Curt 127
Folkers, Rich 168
Fosse, Ray 165
Frick, Ford 26, 30, 49–50, 125

Frisella, Danny 152, 162
Fritchey, Alan 87

Galasso, Bob 125
Gamble, Oscar 165
Garagiola, Joe 148
Garcia, Pedro 135
Gearin, Denny "Dinty" 18
Giles, Warren 30, 43, 50–51, 61–63, 66–67, 155
Gillespie, Earl 30, 109, 114, 155
The Godfather (film) 133
Golden West Broadcasting 98
Gossage, Goose 148, 165
Gowdy, Curt 75
Grammas, Alex 148–149, 152, 155–158, 163–167, 170
Grant, Donald 149
Grant Long, Judith 175
Great Depression 31
Green Bay Packers 15, 28, 33, 36, 62, 97, 101–102, 119–120, 133, 176
Griffith, Calvin 55, 61, 68–69, 86, 127
Grimm, Charlie 19–21, 30, 33
Grobschmidt, Eugene 46, 67, 102, 109
Gross, Milton 54
Gullet, Don 158

Haas, Moose 144
Hackett, Dick 134
Haney, Fred 33–34, 109
Haney, Larry 80
Happy Days (TV show) 49
Harmon, Merle 110, 125
Harper, Tommy 72, 77, 79, 100, 105, 108, 116, 127, 140
Harrison, Roric 80
Hearn, Dick 172
Hedges, Robert Lee 12
Hemus, Solly 30
Hickey, T.J. 16
Hirsch, Elroy 130
Hisle, Larry 165, 172
Hitchcock, Billy 48
Hofheinz, Roy 66
Holcomb, Stu 130
Hornsby, Rogers 71
Howard, Frank 166
Howsam, Bob 138
Hunt, Lamar 67, 82–83, 89
Hunter, Catfish 145, 148
Hutchinson, Fred 71

Inserra, Bob 53

Jackson, Reggie 148, 158
Jackson, "Shoeless" Joe 13
Jacobs, Jeremy 129
Jinkinson, Earl 45, 48
Johnson, Ban 11–12
Johnson, Walter 110
Jones, Randy 148
Juneau, Solomon 4
Junior World Series 19

Kaat, Jim 148
Kansas City Athletics 55, 58, 60, 63
Kansas City Royals 60, 72, 78–79, 83, 86, 90, 107, 121, 128, 149
Kaye, Danny 151
Keefe, Art 134–135
Kenosha Comets 22
Kilbourn, Byron 4
Killilea, Florence 17–18
Killilea, Henry 11
Killilea, Matthew 11–12, 17
Kirby, Gene 165
Kirkpatrick, Ed 170
Kissinger, Henry 147
Knowles, Warren 109, 134
Kohl, Herb 23, 30, 39–40, 59
Kohler, Walter 30
Koufax, Sandy 42
Kubek, Tony 148
Kuenn, Harvey 64, 123, 134, 148, 166
Kuhn, Bowie 45, 47, 68, 82, 87–88, 92, 109, 120–130, 132, 136, 139, 142, 146, 150–151

Labatt Brewing 151
Lake Front Stadium 22
Lane, Frank 121–125, 127, 131–132, 140–141
Larson, Lloyd 68, 99, 129
Laxton, Bill 152
A League of Their Own (film) 22
Leary, Frank 45–46
Lelivelt, Jack 16, 70
Levy, Sam 15, 52
Lezcano, Sixto 143, 152, 155, 164, 166, 172
Lightfoot, Gordon 39
Lloyd Street Grounds 11, 13
Lombardi, Vince 36, 101, 119, 122
Loretta, Mark 177
Los Angeles Dodgers 32, 35–36, 42, 47–48, 65–67, 71, 111, 130, 148
Lurie, Bob 151

Index

Mack, Connie (McGillicuddy, Cornelius) 12, 16
MacPhail, Lee 144, 149, 151, 155, 159
Madison Blues 40
Madison Sports Hall of Fame 40
Maier, Henry 38, 109
Maier, Irwin 39
Mantle, Mickey 154–155
Marquette University 15
Marshall, Mike 72, 86
Martin, Hershel 22
Martinez, Buck 168
Mathews, Eddie 31–32, 36, 42, 44, 55, 84, 155
Matlack, Jon 148
Mattick, Bobby 122, 127–128
May, Dave 144, 164
Maye, Lee 41
Mayer, Oscar 39
Mays, Willie 147, 165
McClure, Bob 158
McCormick, Monte 38
McGarr, Frank J. 159
McHale, John 31, 41, 46, 58, 124, 128, 149
McLish, Cal 166
McNally, Dave 128
McMahon, Don 55
Meindel, Tom 171–172
Melvin, Doug 178
Menke, Denny 41
Mercer, Tommy 67
Midwest League 53, 108
Mifflin, Hugh 95
Milkes, Marvin 73–75, 77–78, 80–81, 84–87, 91, 101, 105, 107–108, 112–113, 115, 117, 119–122
Miller, Floyd 84–85
Miller, Marvin 160
Miller Beer 5, 29
Miller Park 153–154, 175–179
Milwaukee Admirals 57
Milwaukee Arena 29, 59
Milwaukee Badgers 15
Milwaukee Bears 14
Milwaukee Braves 2, 4–7, 13, 24–38, 40–50, 52–55, 58, 60, 63, 65–67, 84, 88, 97, 103–105, 109–114, 116, 120, 124–125, 128, 131–135, 139, 144, 146, 149, 154–155, 161, 174, 176–178, 180
Milwaukee Bucks 23, 59, 110
Milwaukee Chicks 5, 21–22
Milwaukee Hawks 28
Milwaukee Wave 57

Mincher, Don 72, 77, 79, 86
Minneapolis Millerettes 21
Minnesota Twins 36, 53–55, 57, 61, 68, 80, 85–86
Molitor, Paul 161, 164, 171–172, 180
Moll, Charles F. 13
Money, Don 132, 135, 145, 147, 152, 157, 164, 172
Montreal Expos 85–86, 128–129, 149, 179
Moore, Charlie 124, 143, 155, 168
Moore, Jackie 85, 111
Moscone, George 151
Moss, Dick 130
Murtaugh, Danny 147
Musial, Stan 147

Nahin, Louis 17
National Association of Professional Base Ball Players 27
National Baseball Hall of Fame 21–22, 46, 55, 71, 109–110, 121, 123, 153, 161, 167, 179–180
National Basketball Assocation (NBA) 25, 59, 72
NBC 36, 50, 61, 75, 148
Negro League 5, 14
New York Giants (MLB) 23, 35, 169
New York Knickerbockers 5, 10, 174
New York Nine 10
New York Post 54
Northwestern League 69
Northwestern Mutual Life Insurance Company 104
Nuxhall, Joe 156

Oakland Athletics (A's) 60, 80, 90, 120, 131, 150–151
O'Connell, Richard H. (Dick) 63, 165–166
Oglivie, Ben 168
O'Keeffe, Rick 161
O'Malley, Walter 28, 47, 65–66, 130
O'Neill, Tip 165

Pabst Beer 5
Pacific Coast League 69–71, 74, 108
Pacific Northwest Sports, Inc. 61, 87, 91, 93, 95–96, 98
Pagliaroni, Jim 47
Paige, Satchel 16
Palmer, Jim 128, 169
Parsons, Bill 127
Pattin, Marty 72, 101, 104–105, 127, 139

Index

Paul, Gabe 131
Pavalon, Wesley 59
Perini, Charles 27
Perini, Joseph 27
Perini, Lou 24–31, 35–37, 42
Petak, George 176
Philadelphia As (Athletics) 12, 16
Philadelphia Phillies 35–36, 66, 84, 132
Phillips, Sam 44
Piniella, Lou 72, 75, 86
Pittsburgh Pirates 22, 35, 47, 52, 60, 75
players strike 130–131, 174
Porter, Darrell 124, 127–128, 135, 143, 147, 158
Prince, Bob 52
Prosser, David 176
Pyka, Garry 161

Quin, Harry 11, 13
Quinn, John 32, 35, 88
Quirk, Jamie 158

Raines, Tim 179
Rainier Brewing Company 69
Reichler, Joe 129
Reynolds, Thomas 52
Richman, Milton 145
Roberts, Dave 155–156
Robinson, Brooks 75
Robinson, Frank 127
Robinson, Jackie 23, 46–47
Rodriguez, Ed 152
Rogers, Will 87
Roller, Elmer 44–45, 47–48
Roth, Alan 148
Rudi, Joe 159
Ruess, Henry 61
Ruess, Jerry 148
Ruth, Babe 16, 143, 145–146, 153, 156
Ryan, Nolan 167

St. Louis Browns 12, 26, 28
St. Louis Cardinals 26, 29–30, 33, 36, 74–75, 133
Sakata, Lenn 172
San Diego Padres 84, 139, 150
San Francisco Giants 36, 41, 66, 127, 150–151, 160
Satter, Jack 165
Saunders, Richard 112
Schaffer, Rudy 20, 55
Schlitz Beer 5, 37, 39, 51, 58, 65–66, 117–118
Schoenbachler, Robert 113

Schoendienst, Red 147
Scott, George "Boomer" 7, 127, 131, 139, 147–148, 152, 155, 158, 164
Seattle Angels 71–72, 74
Seattle Mariners 72, 161
Seattle Pilots 1–2, 4, 6–7, 38, 69, 71–81, 83–102, 104–105, 108, 110–111, 115–116, 135, 143, 150, 161, 171, 174, 179
The Seattle Pilots: Short Flight into History (film) 1
Seattle Rainiers 69–72
Seattle Supersonics 72
Seaver, Tom 148
Selig, Benjamin 9, 180
Selig, Jerry 9
Selig, Marie 9, 19, 22–23, 180
Sheets, Ben 177
Shibe Park 132
Short, Ed 55
Sick, Emil 69, 71
Sicks' Stadium 61, 70–72, 76–78, 80, 94, 96, 100
Siekert, Fred 120
Simmons, Al 16
Simon, William 142
Slaughter, Enos 30
Smith, C. Arnholt 65
Smith, E.B. 95
Smith, Everitt 113
Smith, Hal 166
Smith, Lester 151
Smith, Red 24
Sorensen, Lary 160–161
Soriano, Dewey 61, 72, 74, 76, 80, 82, 84, 87, 90–91, 93–96
Soriano, Max 61, 72, 80, 87, 90, 93–96, 99
South Pacific (musical) 22
Southworth, Billy 27
Spahn, Warren 30–31, 36, 55, 139, 155, 177
Speaker, Tris 13
Spink, C.C. Johnson 53
The Sporting News 19, 52–53, 57–58, 74
Sportsman's Park 26, 132
Sportservice 94–95, 104, 112, 128–129
The Star-Spangled Banner (song) 30
Stargell, Willie 47
Staub, Rusty 127
Stearns, Roswell 113
Steinbrenner, George 159
Stengel, Casey 21, 34
Stone, Marty 165
Sukront, Max 29

Sullivan, Bill 88
Sullivan, Haywood 165–166
Sullivan, Tim 153
Sutton, Don 148, 180
Symington, Stuart 60

Tanner, Chuck 129
Taps (song) 30
Teams, Inc. 38, 40–42, 49
Tebbetts, Birdie 35
Teich, Larry 15
Thomas, Dan 162–163
Thomas, Gorman 79, 114, 135, 143, 169–170, 172
Thompson, Tommy 175–176
Toledo Mud Hens 28
Toronto Blue Jays 151
Torre, Frank 44, 88
Torre, Joe 44, 47
Travers, Bill 160, 170
Turner, Ted 151

Uecker, Bob 9, 14, 19, 32, 52, 124–125
Uecker, Gus 9
Uihlein, Bob, Jr. 39, 50
United Press International 122, 145
United Soccer Association 57
University of Minnesota 161
University of Wisconsin–Eau Claire 171
University of Wisconsin–Madison 30, 39, 130
University of Wisconsin–Milwaukee 33

Vancouver Mounties 169
Veeck, Bill 19–23, 26, 38, 44, 47, 49, 151
Veeck, William, Sr. 19
Vincent, Faye 174

Walker, George 4
Warneke, Lon 30
West End Grounds 10
West Ends 10
Western League 11–12
WHAD 15
Widmar, Al 166
Wilson, Jim 128, 132, 134, 138, 140–142, 149
Winter, Jack 39–40
Wisconsin-Illinois League 13
Wisconsin State Fair Park 15, 24
Woessner, Bob 120
Wohlford, Jim 158
Womack, Dooley 80, 86
World Series 5, 13, 16, 19, 22, 31–36, 57, 61, 75, 81, 84, 102, 111, 123, 126–127, 131, 157–158, 167–169, 177, 179
The Wreck of the Edmund Fitzgerald (song) 39
Wright Street Grounds 10–11
Wrigley, Phillip K. 21, 45, 66, 69
Wrigley, William, Jr. 19
WTMJ-TV 166

Yankee Stadium 22, 24, 33
Yawkey, Jean 165–166
Yawkey, Tom 165–166
Yost, Ned 168
Yount, Robin 138, 143–147, 155, 161, 163–164, 170–171, 177, 180

Zeidler, Frank 24, 30
Zisk, Ritchie 165